Verses For Zion

Devotional Bible Teachings about The
Land, People, and God of Israel

THE
ISRAEL
BIBLE

ISRAEL365

Verses For Zion

First Edition 2023

Verses For Zion was produced by Israel365 in cooperation with Teach for Israel and is used with permission from Teach for Israel.

All rights reserved.

Cover design: Yehudit Weingarten

ISBN 978-1-957109-51-0 softcover

Verses For Zion is a holy book that contains the name of God and should be treated with respect

A note on Hebrew and transliterations in this book:

Hebrew words appear in lower-case italics throughout the book, except where a Hebrew root is mentioned. English translations of Hebrew words under discussion are almost always between quotation marks.

In Hebrew, almost all words are derived from roots. Hebrew roots are almost always 3 letters. To highlight the 3 letters of the root where essential to the teaching, roots are presented as 3 upper-case letters. At times roots will contain lower-case letters when a second English letter is needed to express the consonant sound made by one of the Hebrew letters. Here are two illustrative examples:

Hebrew | English translation | Hebrew root

yilmod | "will learn" | LMD

tzachak | "laughed" | TzChK

Table of Contents

Rabbi Pesach Wolicki is there cohost of the Shoulder to Shoulder podcast and Director of Israel365action.com.

Preface

Rabbi Elie Mischel

As this book goes to print, the State of Israel is fighting an existential war. On October 7, 2023, Hamas terrorists from the Gaza Strip overran Israel's southern border and committed barbaric atrocities against the Jewish people, massacring over 1,200 innocent people, wounding over 7,000, and taking 242 hostages, including babies and Holocaust survivors. Hamas terrorists and ordinary Palestinians barbarically tortured, raped and executed defenseless women and children. Israel has declared war on Hamas, vowing to destroy the evil terrorists who seek Israel's destruction.

Immediately after the Hamas massacre, mass demonstrations erupted around the world in *support* of the terrorists. Hundreds of thousands marched through the streets of Washington, DC, London, Paris and Berlin shouting "From the River to the Sea," calling for the genocide of Israel and Jews all over the world. In cities throughout America and the West, heartless pro-Palestinians are ripping down posters with photos of Israeli hostages, often laughing as they do so.

Israel is at war, but the west is experiencing a moral crisis. The United States, founded upon Judeo-Christian biblical values, has lost its mooring. Millions of young Americans who support Hamas believe in false narratives instead of eternal truths, blurring the lines between good and evil and truth and falsehood. As the sages wrote over 1,600 years ago: "In the generation in which the son of David comes… truth will be absent, as it states 'And truth will be absent and he who turns away from evil will be considered mad.' (Isaiah 59:15)."

During this time of moral confusion, Christians and Jews must stand up and speak God's truth. We must unabashedly tell the world about God's plan for Israel and for all of mankind, as laid out in the Bible.

Rabbi Pesach Wolicki's masterful work, *Verses from Zion*, is the book of biblical truth that our generation so desperately needs. Readers will understand why it is critical for all Bible believers, both Jews and Christians, to actively stand with Israel during these difficult days before the final redemption.

"And many peoples shall go, and they shall say, 'Come, let us go up to the Lord's mount, to the house of the God of Jacob, and let Him teach us of His ways, and we will go in His paths,' for out of Zion shall the Torah come forth, and the word of the Lord from Jerusalem. And He shall judge between the nations and reprove many peoples, and they shall beat their swords into plowshares and their spears into pruning hooks; nation shall not lift the sword against nation, neither shall they learn war anymore" (Isaiah 2:3-4).

May we soon see the day when Israel's enemies are destroyed, and all nations join together in Jerusalem, in peace and joy, to serve God together as one.

Rabbi Elie Mischel
Director of Education, Israel365

Genesis 12:1 – Go to Yourself

The Lord said to Abram, 'Go forth from your land, from your birth-place, and from your father's house to the land that I will show you.'

The Bible is the word of God. Because it is His word, no word in the Bible is extra or insignificant. In fact, when we pay close attention to words that seem insignificant or extraneous, we usually find that it is precisely in these words where the deepest lessons lie hidden, waiting for us to find them.

What's Lost in Translation

A great example of this is the opening verse of Genesis 12, the very first words spoken by God to Abram. This verse begins the journey of faith of the father of faith. Here are 3 common English translations of this verse:

The Lord had said to Abram, "Go from your country, your people and your father's household to the land I will show you." (NIV)

Now the Lord had said to Abram: "Get out of your country, from your family, and from your father's house, to a land that I will show you." (NKJV)

Now the Lord said to Abram, "Go from your country and your kindred and your father's house to the land that I will show you." (ESV)

Now here is the literal word-by-word translation from the Hebrew.

The Lord said to Abram, "Go forth <u>for yourself</u> from your country, <u>and from</u> your birthplace, <u>and from</u> your father's house to the land that I will show you."

The underlined words are left out of some or all the English translations that I cited. You may notice that the differences between the literal Hebrew and the English translations appear to be insignificant. They seem to serve no real purpose. To illustrate the point, here is the same translation without any of the underlined words:

The Lord said to Abram, "Go forth from your country, your birthplace, and your father's house to the land that I will show you."

It seems that none of the content of the verse is missing at all even though I deleted the underlined words. The Bible did not need to repeat the words "and from" before "your birthplace" and "your father's house." The list would be grammatically correct in Hebrew without that repetition, just as it is in English. So why did the Bible repeat "and from"?

Go, for yourself

We will answer this question by exploring the first underlined word – *for yourself*; a word that does not appear in any of the translations that we cited above.

The first two Hebrew words in this verse are *lech lecha. Lech* means "go forth" or "travel". The best translation of *lecha* is "for yourself" or "to you". The opening words that God spoke to Abram, then, were "Go forth *for yourself.*"

To sum up, the first two Hebrew words in the verse are:

Lech	*Go forth* or *travel*
lecha	*for yourself* or *to yourself*

What does the word *lecha* – "for yourself" - add to what God told Abram?

By adding this seemingly extra word, *lecha*, God sets the tone for the journey of faith of Abram and all who would follow in his footsteps. The message is simple and powerful. Obedience to the word of God is not for God's benefit but for ours. "Go forth *for yourself.*" God does not need us. We need Him. It is we, not God, who benefit from our obedience to Him.

At the same time, the journey of faith leads us to our true identities; obedience to the word of God allows us to discover who we truly are. "Go forth *to yourself*"; this journey would lead Abram to discover his own true self.

A curious order of details

Now we can return to our earlier question. Why does the verse repeat the words "and from" before each of the three places that Abraham must leave; his *country*, his *birthplace*, and his *father's house*?

To answer this question, we will ask another question.

Notice the order in the verse:

1. Your country / land
2. Your birthplace
3. Your father's house

It would make more sense if they were in reverse order. Abram could leave his father's house and still be in his birthplace; he could still be in his country. But it is obvious that once Abram left his country it would impossible for him to still be in his birthplace or in his father's house. Why didn't God simply tell Abram to leave *his country* "to the land that I will show you"?

— *Abram's Journey to Himself*

God's words to Abram were not merely instructions about his physical destination. God was telling Abram that to find His true identity as a servant of God, he would need to leave much of his past behind. Abram was raised in the culture of polytheistic pagan Mesopotamia. He was now being called to a universal mission to bring faith to all the families of the earth. God told Abram that he must sever his ties with the culture and influences of his upbringing. This is a difficult process for anyone, even for someone like Abram.

In Abram's journey to find his true identity, the easiest influence to leave behind was the general culture of his country. Disconnecting from the tribal influences of his birthplace was more difficult. But hardest of all would be the departure from his own family and their idolatrous ways.

These influences are not equal. Think about our own lives. We are influenced by the general culture of the wider society. We are influenced by the city or area where we were raised. Finally, and most profoundly, we are influenced by our home, our family environment. As someone raised in a Godless and immoral pagan society, Abram had to leave all of these behind him. Severing ties with each of these influences is a separate challenge unto itself.

By repeating the words "and from" before each of these three circles of influence in Abram's life, God was telling him, and us, that these three challenges are different from each other. Each requires special attention and must be handled in its own way. They are not accomplished all at once.

In any life of faith there are challenges that we face. Sometimes those challenges are from wider society; sometimes they are closer to home. God's first words to Abram are the first words to all who embark on the journey of faith in Him.

Go forth to your true self. You will find yourself when you strip away all of the negative influences that surround you; some closer to home than others. Then you will arrive at the destination – "the land that I will show you."

Genesis 12:2 – The Call to Be a Blessing

I will make you a great nation and I will bless you and I will make your name great and you shall be a blessing.

After commanding Abram to leave his homeland and his family, God began to describe the mission that Abram will carry through to his descendants after him.

There are four statements in this verse.

1. I will make you a great nation
2. I will bless you
3. I will make your name great
4. you shall be a blessing

The first three statements are quite simple to understand. God promised Abram that He will make him into a great nation, that He will bless him, and that He will make Abram's greatness – his "name" - known in the world. The fourth statement is somewhat unclear. When God said, *you shall be a blessing*, what exactly was he telling Abram?

─── *What does "blessing" mean?*

The Hebrew word *berachah* – "blessing"– in the Bible refers to *abundance*. For example, the very first time the word "blessing" appears in all of Scripture is in reference to the fish during the story of creation:

And God <u>blessed</u> them, saying, "Be fruitful and multiply and fill the waters in the seas, and let birds multiply on the earth." - Gen. 1:22 (see also Deut. 28:3-6)

When God told Abram, "you shall be a blessing", what was God telling him? Was He saying that Abraham would bring abundance to others? Abundance of what? The simple answer may be found in the next verse:

I will bless those who bless you, and he who curses you I will curse; and all the families of the earth shall be blessed through you. – Gen. 12:3

Perhaps the meaning of "you shall be a blessing," is that Abram will be a source of blessings and abundance for other people.

"You SHALL be": Command or Statement?

This leads to a fascinating translation issue that is almost impossible to notice in the English. Consider the following three common translations:

and you will be a blessing – NIV

so that you will be a blessing – ESV

And you shall be a blessing. – NKJV

The Hebrew here is made up of two words:

Ve'heyeh	*you shall be; you will be*
berachah	*a blessing*

There are two different words used in the Bible for "you will be". The word used here, *ve'heyeh*, is quite rare, appearing only 6 times in the entire Bible. The more common word is *ve'hayita*, appearing 30 times. For example, when God spoke to Abram at the covenant of circumcision, He said:

As for Me, My covenant is hereby established with you, and you shall be [ve'hayita] the father of a multitude of nations – Gen. 17:4

Or when Isaac blessed his son Jacob:

May God Almighty bless you, And make you fruitful and multiply you, That you may be [ve'hayita] an assembly of peoples; - Genesis 28:3

Both examples cited here are quite similar to our verse, Genesis 12:2. In all three verses, a blessing is being bestowed, either by God or by Isaac.

So, if both *ve'heyeh* and *ve'hayita* are translated as *"you shall be"* or *"you will be"*, what is the difference between them?

I mentioned that *ve'heyeh* appears only 6 times in the entire Bible. One of them is here in Genesis 12:2. In all other 5 times, *ve'heyeh* is a *command* or *instruction*. Here are two examples:

When Abram was ninety-nine years old the Lord appeared to Abram and said to him, "I am God Almighty; walk before me, <u>and be</u> – ve'heyeh - blameless, - Genesis 17:1

And the Lord said unto Moses, Come up to me into the mount, <u>and remain</u> – ve'heyeh - there: and I will give thee tables of stone, and a law, and commandments which I have written; that thou mayest teach them. – Exodus 24:12

In other words, *ve'heyeh* – "you shall be" – does not mean "you will be" as a prediction or the bestowing of blessing; it is not a statement about what will be in the future. Ve'heyeh is an *instruction* or *command*. For example, if a parent is telling a child to behave in school and they say, "you shall behave", the parent is stating an instruction, not making a prediction about what will be in the future.

The call to be a blessing

When God said to Abram, *ve'heyeh berachah* – "you shall be a blessing," God was not telling Abraham what will be in the future. *God was giving Abraham an instruction and a command. He was giving Abram his mission.*

To sum up, the correct meaning of verse 2 is this: "I will make you into a great nation. I will bless you with abundance, giving you the tools to impact and influence the world. I will make your name known so that people pay attention to you. *Ve'heyeh berachah - It is your job and mission to be a blessing*; to use all the gifts that I have bestowed upon you to bring blessing to others."

The mission of Abram is the mission of all who share the faith of Abram. So too, we must use the blessings and tools of influence that God has given us in order to bring increase and blessing to others. We must strive to be a blessing.

Genesis 12:3 – The Consequences of Cursing Israel

I will bless those who bless you and he who curses you I shall curse; and all the families of the earth shall be blessed through you.

Upon careful reading of this verse, we notice a striking change from the first clause to the second. Namely, the phrase *those who bless you* is written in the plural form whereas *he who curses you* is singular. Are we to assume that those who curse Abraham and his descendants always do so only as individuals while those who bless Israel do so as a collective?

Two Hebrew words for "curse"

To answer this question, we will take notice of another transition in the syntax of this verse. While it is undetectable in most English translations, in the phrase *he who curses you I shall curse* two different Hebrew words are used for the word *curse*. Here is a literal translation:

u'mekalelcha	*and he who curses you*
a'or	*I shall curse*

Just by reading the transliteration of the Hebrew it is easy to see that these two words bear no resemblance to each other. They do not have the same root. In other words, they are not conjugations of the same verb. There are some English translations that translate these two words differently. For example:

I will bless those who bless you, and him who dishonors you I will curse, and in you all the families of the earth shall be blessed. – ESV

The Hebrew root of the first "curse" is KLL. Take note of these 3 root letters in the word. This root means "to ridicule" or "to make light." The second "curse" is a form of the word *aror* It is related to the word *me'erah*, meaning "plague" or "illness." This is the word that is used every time God curses something or someone in the Bible. For example:

So, the Lord God said to the serpent, "Because you have done this, cursed – [aror] - are you above all livestock and all wild animals! You will crawl on your belly and you will eat dust all the days of your life." - Genesis 3:14

The Bible never describes God cursing anyone with the word root KLL. This root refers only to situations where humans are doing the cursing. Why? What is the difference between these two words for "curse"?

God's curse always has an effect

As I mentioned above, the root KLL derives from the Hebrew word for "light," the opposite of heavy. It means "to make light of" or, as translated above by the ESV, "to dishonor." This word refers to a "curse" only in the sense that a curse expresses an idea in words. The disparaging and dishonoring statement – the *curse* – was expressed. Nothing more is implied by this word. On the other hand, *aror-* or *a'or* in our verse - refers to actual damage done by the curse. *Aror* means that there is a tangible result of the curse. This is the reason that God's curses always use some form of the word *aror*. God's words always have an impact. That is how they are known.

In other words, what God said to Abraham was this: I will bless those who bless you; and anyone who even speaks a curse against you, I will curse in such a way that there will be a tangible real-life impact to my curse.

The Power of Negative Words

Now let us return to our first question. Why is "those who bless you" in the plural while "he who curses you" is singular. Obviously, God did not mean that there would be only one person who would curse Abram. Clearly, God's intention was that any and all people who would ever curse Abram and his descendants would be cursed by God. So why the singular?

We explained above that the Hebrew word for "he who curses you" – *mekalelcha* – refers to a curse that expressed as words only. It does not imply action beyond words. It is an unfortunate feature of human nature that ridicule and negative criticism are more powerful in their impact than positive praise. Think about our current media culture. When something negative or damaging is said about Israel in the media it is immediately broadcast loudly and widely. On the other hand, when Israel is praised, there is hardly any impact.

God is the Father Who defends His people

The individual who curses Israel, who publicly shames and dishonors the children of Abraham, may think that he did not really cause any damage because he did nothing more than express an opinion. After all, what is so damaging about words? And words spoken by only one person, no less! To such a person God responds, by saying: If you curse Israel, even if all you do is express your curse in words and think that you should not be held responsible, know that the lasting impact that evil words can have in this world is sufficient for God to punish you for disparaging and dishonoring His chosen people.

To put it another way, both the change in verb root as well as the switch from plural to singular express the extent of God's love and protection of Abram and his descendants. Even if the curse is only words; even if those words are spoken by a single person, God will punish the one who curses His chosen people.

The enemies of Israel never prosper. It is those who bless and praise Israel who share in God's love for Abram and his descendants who are the beneficiaries of blessings. Like the loving father that He is, God jealously defends His beloved from any and all who speak ill against him.

Isaiah 2:2 – The Streaming of the Nations

It shall be at the end of days that the mountain of the house of the Lord will be established at the top of the mountains and will be elevated above the hills; and all the nations will stream to it. This prophecy of the end times describes the multitudes among the nations who will visit Jerusalem and worship God there. Take note of the verb used at the end of the verse to describe this gathering of the nations in Jerusalem; *and all the nations will <u>stream</u> to it.*

The Hebrew verb used here is *naharu*. The *u* at the end of the word is the conjugative third person plural, "they." The word *nahar* means *stream*. This is the same word as the noun *nahar*, meaning "stream" or "river" throughout the Bible. For example:

A river – nahar - emerged from Eden to water the garden; and from there it would part and would become four headwaters. – Genesis 2:10

To sum up this point: the Hebrew word *nahar* means "stream" both as a verb – "to stream," "streaming" – and as a noun.

Nahar is always people streaming

This verse in Isaiah 2 is one of only four verses in the Bible where *nahar* is a verb meaning to *stream* or *flow*. The others are Jeremiah 31:11, Jeremiah 51:44, and Micah 4:1. The last of these is an almost word for word quote of our verse. In all four verses, the verb "to stream" is used metaphorically to describe people *streaming* towards a certain location. It is interesting that *nahar* is never used as a verb to describe literal streaming or flowing of a liquid. This verb is used only to describe human activity, metaphorically likening it to the flowing water of a river.

Of course, there are much simpler and more conventional ways to describe large numbers of people gathering in a certain place. The examples of mass traveling and congregating in the Bible are too numerous to mention. Therefore, we must ask what exactly is being implied by this verb "to stream" to describe the multitudes among the nations who will make pilgrimages to Jerusalem to worship the God of Israel at the end of days?

Streaming = Natural and Perpetual

Water flows naturally. Unlike the movement of people or animals, there is no will or choice whatsoever that causes water to flow. It is drawn by a unseen natural forces. It is beyond instinct. It is simply the nature of water to flow. Furthermore, the force that causes rivers to flow does not ever stop. Unlike the wind or the tides, rivers neither pause nor change direction.

Now we can understand Isaiah's choice of this verb to describe the millions among the nations who will *stream* to Jerusalem at the time of the restoration and rebuilding of Israel. Isaiah is saying that these pilgrims will feel *naturally drawn* to Jerusalem by an instinctive force, rather than by rational free will. They will not be merely deciding to travel to Jerusalem; they will *flow* there naturally, as water flows downstream. And like the waters of a great river that never stop, the flow of people from the nations will not cease. Once it begins, it will be endless.

Another meaning of nahar

Interestingly, the Hebrew verb root *nahar* has another meaning in the Bible. In addition to the four verses mentioned above, there are two more verses where this verb appears, but with a different meaning.

Then you shall see and <u>be radiant</u> – nahar -; your heart shall thrill and exult, because the abundance of the sea shall be turned to you, the wealth of the nations shall come to you. – Isaiah 60:5 (ESV)

Those who look to him are <u>radiant</u> – naharu -, and their faces shall never be ashamed. – Psalm 34:6(5) *(ESV)*

In these two verses, the verb *nahar* is translated as "to be radiant." Just as we saw with the use of *nahar* as a verb meaning "to stream," *nahar* – "to be radiant" - refers only to people who are described as radiant and not to objects that radiate light or energy.

It is highly unusual for a verb root in Hebrew to have two completely different meanings without any change in the vowels. The assumption of linguists of Biblical Hebrew is that there must be an underlying relationship between the variant meanings of a single root. In fact, for one of these verses, the translations in English disagree regarding the correct meaning. To illustrate, here are the original King James version and the New King James version of Isaiah 60:5.

Then thou shalt see, and flow together – nahar -, and thine heart shall fear, and be enlarged; because the abundance of the sea shall be converted unto thee, the forces of the Gentiles shall come unto thee. – (KJV)

Then you shall see and become radiant – nahar -; And your heart shall swell with joy; Because the abundance of the sea shall be turned to you; The wealth of the Gentiles shall come to you. – (NKJV)

I would like to suggest a relationship between these two meanings of *nahar*. Something that is radiant does not choose to be radiant. It simply radiates because of what it is. Radiance is not a choice. It is the natural effect of a certain state of being. Furthermore, radiance is a *flow* of light that emerges from an object that is radiating.

The Radiance of Pilgrims to Jerusalem

To sum up, the verb form of the Hebrew word *nahar*, the word for "river", means to flow *naturally* regardless of the conscious decision of that which is flowing. This word is used in the Bible to describe the flow of people or of spiritual light from people who are described as radiant.

Based on this dual meaning of the verb *nahar*, I would like to suggest that this play on words may have been part of what Isaiah was describing in our verse.

By describing the nations as *streaming* to Jerusalem, Isaiah was saying that in the end times, the millions among the nations who come to Jerusalem to worship God will do so *instinctively. They will feel drawn to Jerusalem naturally.* This is a powerful image. People have a natural draw to their own homeland, to the place they were born or raised, or where they have some historical connection through family or ethnicity. What would make multitudes among the nations feel instinctively drawn to Jerusalem; a place they have never been and to which they have no ancestral connection? The answer is simple: faith in God.

It is faith in the Bible and the God of Israel that produces an instinctive draw to come to Jerusalem and connect to God in His holy city. At the same time, alluded to by the alternate translation of *nahar*, this faith causes those pilgrims to be radiant, illuminated by their journey to the mountain of the house of the Lord in Jerusalem.

The millions from among the Nations who visit Jerusalem each year in our times is a fulfilment of this verse. These pilgrims are drawn to Jerusalem by an instinctive force rooted in their faith in the God of Israel.

Isaiah 2:3 – The Nations and the God of Jacob

Many peoples will go and say: Let us go and ascend to the mountain of the Lord, to the house of the God of Jacob, and He will instruct us of His ways and we will walk in His paths. For from Zion will come forth Torah, and the word of the Lord from Jerusalem.

In this prophecy, Isaiah foretells that in the future, when Israel is restored to the Land of Israel and to Jerusalem, there will be a mass movement among the nations to come to Jerusalem to worship the God of Israel at the site of the Holy Temple. This prophecy has clearly begun to be fulfilled in our days. Each year, millions of Christians, believers in the Bible and in the God of Israel, stream to Jerusalem to draw close to the God of the Bible.

Christian Tourism as Biblical Prophecy Fulfilled

It is all too easy to lose sight of just how miraculous this is. Isaiah lived many centuries before the advent of Christianity. Although this verse, obviously does not refer to any such thing as Christianity, the fact that Isaiah lived so long before Christianity is critical to understanding just how wondrous this prophecy is. Simply put, when Isaiah wrote these words there were no people in the world who worshipped the God of Israel other than the Nation of Israel. When Isaiah described multitudes from the nations of the world streaming to Jerusalem to worship the God of Israel, those who heard this prophecy at the time must have wondered about the unrealistic nature of what Isaiah was saying. After all, why would the nations come to Jerusalem to worship the God of Israel if they are not part of the nation of Israel? Nobody outside of Israel even knew about the God of Israel at that time. How and why would this happen?

Of course, we now know exactly how it happened. The founding of Christianity, while leading to centuries of suffering of the Jewish people at the hands of those who professed its belief, also led directly to the spread of the Bible and the God of Israel to much of the earth's population. This is the irony of the historical relationship between Christianity and Judaism. On one hand, centuries of Christian leaders preached anti-Semitic theological ideas that had devastating consequences. On the other hand, it is only through Christianity that the world has learned about God and the Bible. Without Christianity, it is impossible to imagine the millions of pilgrims who fill the streets of Jerusalem every year; pilgrims who know and love the Bible and the people and land of Israel.

Why the God of Jacob?

It is interesting that God is identified in this verse as the *God of Jacob*. This is an unusual description of God in the Bible. It is used almost exclusively in the book of Psalms. What is intended by this description? Why doesn't the verse refer to *the house of the God of Israel*?

The name *Jacob* is used collectively for the people of Israel on many occasions. To understand our verse, we will need to know more about the specific meaning of this name, and what *Jacob* implies when referring to the entire nation.

The meaning of Jacob's name is explained twice in Genesis. First, when Jacob was born his name is explained as referring to his grasping the heel of his brother Esau (Gen. 25:26). The Hebrew word for "heel" is *akev*. The word for "follow" is *akav* from the same root. Jacob – *Ya'akov* – *followed* his brother out of the womb grasping his *heel*.

Later, after Jacob and his mother Rebekah deceived his father Isaac so that Jacob would receive his father's blessings, Esau unjustly accused Jacob of cheating him, despite the fact that Jacob had earlier purchased the birthright from Esau. In Esau's cry upon discovering what Jacob had done, gave a new meaning of Jacob's name.

Esau said, "Is he not rightly named Jacob? For he has cheated me (alt. deceived / supplanted / tripped) these two times. He took away my birthright, and behold, now he has taken away my blessing." - Genesis 27:36

Esau's play on words is based on the fact that a Hebrew word for "cheated" is *akav* - the same root as Jacob's name. *Akav* – "cheated" - implies lying in wait, ambushing, or acting with deception.

Jacob – Israel's Name in the Exile

Simply put, the name *Jacob* does not have positive connotations. It variously implies *following, being on the heel, deception,* and *trickery*. In fact, if we look at Jacob's own life, we see that he often was compelled to live by his wits and outsmart others - whether it was Laban, Esau, or even his own father.

Not so as *Israel*. Jacob's second loftier name was given to him when he wrestled with and defeated the angel who attacked him. (Gen. 32:29) That was a battle he won without deception but with might. For this victory he was told that he was now capable of truly triumphing.

And yet he retained both names. Sometimes he would need to be *Jacob*, living by his cunning and careful tactics in a hostile and anti-Semitic environment. At other times he would be able to behave as *Israel* – triumphant, dominant, and strong.

What is true of Jacob as an individual is true of his offspring – the People of Israel. Thus, they are sometimes referred to as *Jacob*. The People of Israel, like their forefather and namesake are sometimes forced to live in exile as subordinates and second-class citizens – the *follower*, the *heel* - in a hostile anti-Semitic environment. Like Jacob their father, Jews have repeatedly been forced to flee after being unjustly accused and targeted. When scripture refers to the People of Israel as *Jacob*, it is this weakened, exile identity that is being described.

"For the Lord will deliver Jacob and redeem them from the hand of those stronger than they." - Jeremiah 31:11

God of Jacob = God who protects Israel in Exile

In light of this deeper understanding of the name, we can say that the "God of Jacob" refers to God as He cares for, *protects*, and *redeems* His exiled and subjugated chosen people from the hands of hostile enemies more physically dominant and powerful than themselves.

In fact, when we look at the other verses where God of Jacob is used, we see exactly that. For example,

"May the Lord answer you in the day of trouble! May the name of the God of Jacob protect you!" - Psalm 20:2

Or

"The nations rage, the kingdoms totter; he utters his voice, the earth melts. The Lord of hosts is with us; the God of Jacob is our fortress." - Psalm 46:6-7

Day of trouble? Rage? He is the fortress; the protection. This is the *God of Jacob.* (See also Psalms 76:7, 84:9, 94:7, 75:10, 81:2,5)

To sum up, God is called *God of Jacob* when the Bible describes how He protects his chosen people when they are in exile. Why, then, would this term be used when describing the nations flocking to Jerusalem to worship Him at the end of days?

I would like to suggest that this is exactly the point of the use of this term for God. Isaiah is not telling us only that multitudes from the nations will come to Jerusalem to worship the God of Israel. Isaiah is adding that these nations will acknowledge the unique relationship that God has had with the Jewish people throughout the centuries of their exile. They will learn to respect the miraculous nature of God's protection over His people while they were dispersed and persecuted for two thousand years. They will appreciate the God of Jewish history; a history that culminates in the return to Zion at the end of days.

All who have faith in the Bible and in the God of Israel must ultimately also come to acknowledge the unique bond that God has had with His chosen people throughout their history.

Micah 6:8 – What God Demands from Humanity

He told you, man, what is good, and what the Lord demands from you: only to execute justice, and to love kindness, and to walk humbly with your God.

In this verse, Micah teaches us the basic requirements of the good life that God demands from each and every one of us; justice, kindness, and humility. If we read carefully, we can see a number of interesting word choices in this verse which contain important lessons about these preeminent Biblical values.

Why does the verse say "Man"?

The most glaring anomaly here is the word "man." It seems that this word does not add much to whatever the prophet is teaching us. To illustrate the point, here is the verse again without the word "man."

He told you what is good, and what the Lord demands from you: only to execute justice, and to love kindness, and to walk humbly with your God.

Any time that a word can be deleted from the Bible without changing the meaning of the verse, we must realize that our original understanding of the verse was incorrect. After all, every single word in the Bible is critical. If a word had no purpose, it would not be there. So, what is the purpose of the word *man* in our verse? What does it add to the lesson that Micah is teaching us?

Human vs. man

There are two words in Biblical Hebrew that translate as "man." *Adam* and *ish*. The word used in this verse in Micah is *adam*. *Adam* is, of course, also the name of the first human being in the Bible. The word *adam* describes a person as a *human being*, rather than the more specific *ish* meaning an adult male.

The seemingly superfluous addition of word *adam* in this verse contains an important lesson. Micah is addressing us as *human beings*. Human beings are not animals. Animals do not have a concept of justice. They do not feel love in the human sense and do not understand the concept of kindness. They certainly do not experience humility. All the traits in this verse are unique to the human species. Micah is teaching us that God demands that we live with concern for others, for society, and for God because we are human. We are not animals who live merely by our instincts, seeking comfort, sustenance, and self-preservation. It is as though Micah was saying, "You are a human being. Unlike the animals, you are created in the image of God. As a human being, you are expected to live by higher, more selfless values. You must live a life of justice, kindness, and humility with the Lord."

Why must I LOVE Kindness?

It is interesting to note that the verse does not say that we should *act kindly* or *be kind*; rather, it states that we must *love kindness*. This is a powerful point. It is certainly important that we act with kindness. But this verse teaches us that we must *love* kindness. In other words, kindness must become something that we pursue instinctively because it is a value that we hold dear.

Everyone prioritizes what they love. The people and activities that we love have our attention not only when they happen to present themselves to us. We pursue them. We think about them. We look for opportunities to engage them. This must be our relationship with *kindness*.

Being humble with God

Finally, I would like to draw our attention to the final phrase of the verse, *and to walk humbly with your God*. Why does the verse need to say *with your God*? The verse is addressed to people who have faith in God. This is obvious from the fact that the verse says that these are values and behaviors that the Lord demands from you. It then lists the values of justice, kindness, and humility. The verse could have said,

He told you, man, what is good, and what the Lord demands from you: only to execute justice, and to love kindness, and to walk humbly.

Once again, had the verse left out the words *with your God*, it is difficult to see what would have been missing from the lesson Micah is teaching us.

I believe that this last phrase in the verse not telling us simply that we must be humble. It is telling us that we must be humble *in our walk with God*. It is an unfortunate that many people of faith develop feelings of arrogance because of living according to the will of God. People who perform acts of kindness, who do good works, and who live moral lives according to God's will often feel quite proud of their accomplishments. This "holier than thou" pride easily leads people of strong faith to look down on people who they perceive as less righteous than themselves. This arrogance of the faithful is a tragic byproduct that all too often results directly from the good choices that people make. Such arrogance is the opposite of a proper relationship to God.

Anyone haughty of heart is an abomination to the Lord. – Proverbs 16:5

Our verse does not simply say, *walk humbly*. The verse says *walk humbly with your God*. In other words, walk humbly *in your life of faith*. Your relationship to God and your obedience to His word must never lead to arrogance and "holier than thou" feelings towards others.

God demands of us that we live up to our status as human beings created in His image. We must do good works of justice, love, and kindness. At the same time, we must guard against the creeping arrogance that often leads directly from excess pride in the good works that we are doing. We must walk humbly with God.

Psalm 125:2 - Jerusalem, Israel, and the Battle against Evil

Jerusalem, mountains surround it; And the Lord surrounds His people from now until eternity.

Jerusalem is presented as a metaphor for the people of Israel, and the mountains that surround Jerusalem are a metaphor for God who protects His people. The previous verse in Psalm 125 uses similar imagery with reference to those who put their trust in God.

Those who trust in the Lord are like Mount Zion, which will never topple and will forever endure. – Psalm 125:1

It is important to note that the subject of this psalm is neither Jerusalem nor Mount Zion. Rather, in these two verses the psalmist describes how God protects the righteous who put their trust in Him. Jerusalem and Mount Zion are brought as metaphors to describe this relationship. In fact, after these opening verses, Jerusalem is not mentioned again in the psalm.

Why Mount Zion?

The metaphors of Mount Zion and Jerusalem for "those who trust in the Lord" and "His people" respectively are worth looking at more closely. Verse 1 stated that "those who trust in the Lord" will never fall, just as Mount Zion "will never topple." What exactly does this mean? Is it not the case that most mountains on earth are never going to topple? Couldn't the verse simply have stated that those who trust in the Lord are *like a mountain which will never topple*? Why is Mount Zion singled out as the metaphor, if the point of the verse is that those who trust in the Lord will endure like mountains?

What is this Psalm about?

To understand the true meaning of these verses, let's take a close look at the full text of Psalm 125.

A Song of Ascents

Those who trust in the Lord are like Mount Zion,
*   which will never topple, and will forever endure.*
² Jerusalem, mountains surround it;
*   And the Lord surrounds his people,*
*   from now until eternity.*
³ Indeed, the rod of wickedness will not rest
*   upon the lot of the righteous,*
lest the righteous set
*   their hands to wrongdoing.*
⁴ Be good, Lord, to those who are good,
*   and to the upright in their hearts!*
⁵ As for those who twist their crooked ways,
*   May the Lord lead them away with the evildoers!*
Peace be upon Israel!

As I mentioned above, Mount Zion and Jerusalem are not the primary subject of the psalm. Most of the psalm discusses the struggle between good and evil; asking God to prevent the wicked from getting the upper hand as He protects the righteous from their power and influence. The psalm concludes with the prayerful declaration, *Peace be upon Israel!*

If the subject of Psalm 125 is the struggle of good over the forces of wickedness, why is Jerusalem chosen as the metaphor? And why does it conclude by praying only for Israel? It should be noted that there are several psalms that discuss the battle between good and evil. Psalm 92 is one good example. Unlike our psalm, Psalm 92 makes no mention of Jerusalem, Mount Zion, or Israel. After all, the struggle between good and evil is not limited to a specific place or nation. It is universal.

To sum up our question, the subject of Psalm 125 is how God protects those who trust in Him from the power and influence of corrupt evildoers. The psalm opens with the metaphorical comparison of the "those who trust in Him" and "His people" to Mount Zion and Jerusalem. It then concludes with the words *Peace be upon Israel.* Why is the struggle with the forces of evil framed in this way? Is the psalm about Jerusalem and Israel, or is it about the universal struggle against evil?

Jerusalem and the defeat of Evil

In its long history, the city of Jerusalem has been conquered forty-four different times. It was destroyed twice, besieged twenty-three times, and famously divided by the nations of the world for 19 years. Considering Jerusalem's tumultuous history, it is surprising that this psalm refers to God protecting His people as the mountains protect Jerusalem.

But what exactly is God protecting the righteous *from* in this psalm? Look back at verse 3:

Indeed, the rod of wickedness will not rest upon the lot of the righteous, lest the righteous set their hands to wrongdoing.

The psalmist is concerned not for the *safety* of the righteous, but for their *righteousness*. His concern is "lest the righteous set their hands to wrongdoing." He is worried about the righteous becoming corrupt *as a result of the influence of the wicked.*

The goal of Israel, and of all who have faith in the God if Israel is the kingdom of God; that *knowledge of God should cover the earth like water covers the sea.* (Isaiah 11:9) A critical component of this vision of the perfect world is the restoration of the people of Israel to their land and the rebuilding of Jerusalem. The nation of Israel is called to be a beacon of God's teachings and values to the world. As expressed by Isaiah's end times vision, *from Zion shall go forth Torah and the word of the Lord from Jerusalem.* (Isaiah 2:3) The many verses that elaborate upon this vision of the future are far too numerous to mention here. Many of them are quoted elsewhere in this book.

Zion and Jerusalem represent the kingdom of God; the perfect world that we are striving for. There is no triumph over the wicked without the success of Israel. There can be no defeat of evil without the rebuilding of Zion and Jerusalem. The particularistic declaration that ends Psalm 125 *Peace be upon Israel!* is not separate from the prayerful request for God to protect the righteous and lead the evildoers away. They are one and the same. The success of Israel and the struggle against evil are two sides of the same coin.

Consider the past century. During this period, the greatest forces of evil on earth have been Nazism, Soviet communism, and Islamic fundamentalism. Regardless of the significant differences between these ideologies, they have all shared one central feature. All these evil movements have made the Jewish people their primary enemy. Still today, ask yourself who the greatest forces of evil are in the world, and you will find that they hate Israel. This is exactly as it ought to be.

Israel has always been the focal point of the struggle between good and evil. This is the subject of Psalm 125. God protects those who trust in Him. God holds back the influence of the wicked. He grants victory to the righteous. This victory is ultimately expressed in the success of Israel.

Psalm 137:5 – The power of remembering Jerusalem

If I forget you O Jerusalem, let my right hand forget its skill.

Psalm 137 is a lament over the destruction of Jerusalem and the exile of Israel. The author responds to the sarcastic taunting of his captors who ask the exiled Jews to "sing a song of Zion." (v.3) After stating in the previous verse that he cannot bring himself to sing songs of Zion while heading into exile, the psalmist declares,

If I forget you O Jerusalem, let my right hand forget its skill.

In context, this verse is a commitment to never forget Jerusalem, even though the joyous songs of Zion will not be sung while mourning in exile. More precisely, the psalmist commits himself never to forget how to play these songs on his harp, referred to in verse 2 of this psalm. Harp strings were traditionally played with the right hand. According to this contextual reading, the *skill* mentioned at the end of the verse is the skill of playing the harp.

What will be forgotten?

According to all English translations, the second half of this verse, *let my right hand forget its skill,* is phrased as a wish. In other words, the psalmist is saying that if he forgets Jerusalem, *let it be* that his right hand should forget its skill. This is a rhetorical way of saying *I will never forget Jerusalem.*

Almost every English translation ends the verse with the words *its skill,* or *its power.* While this makes sense in context, if we examine the word-for-word translation of the Hebrew, we find something different.

In Hebrew, the verse is composed of 5 words.

Im	If
eshkachech	I forget you
Yerushalayim	Jerusalem,

tishkach	will forget
yemini	my right hand

In Hebrew, a subject in a sentence can appear before the verb, as in English, or after the verb. So, the final two words *tishkach yemini* are, "my right hand will forget." In other words, the actual exact translation is,

If I forget you Jerusalem, my right hand will forget.

Notice that the verse does not say *what* will be forgotten. The Hebrew does not say *its skill, its power,* or anything else. The psalmist says, simply, that his right hand *will forget.*

A wish or a consequence?

Furthermore, we should note that the exact translation of the Hebrew does not necessarily imply that this forgetting is a wish he is making, in the event he forgets Jerusalem. Rather, the simplest reading of the verse may be that the psalmist is describing cause and effect. Let me explain.

Consider the difference between these two translations:

If I forget you Jerusalem, let my right hand forget

If I forget you Jerusalem, my right hand will forget

In the first, the psalmist is wishing or praying for his right hand to forget should he forget Jerusalem. In the second translation, his right hand forgetting is a consequence of forgetting Jerusalem, not a wish.

A Jew is one who remembers Jerusalem

In the year 1771 the first edition of the Encyclopedia Britannica was published in Edinburgh, Scotland. Below is the complete text of the entry for the word "Jews." It appears on page 833 of volume 2. (The entire encyclopedia consisted of three volumes.)

Jews: Those who profess obedience to the laws and religion of Moses. When a modern Jew builds an (sic) house he must leave part of it unfinished in remembrance that the Temple and Jerusalem now lie desolate. They lay great stress upon frequent washings. They abstain from meat prohibited by Levitical Law; for which reason whatever they eat must be dressed by Jews and after a manner peculiar to themselves. Every Jew is obliged to marry, and a man who lives to twenty unmarried, is accounted as actually living in sin.

The Jews, it is said, were formerly at the disposal of the Chief Lord where they lived and likewise all their goods. A Jew may be a witness by our law being sworn on the Old Testament and taking oaths to the government.

The last two sentences deal with the status of Jews in British law at that time.

The first sentence is a general statement of what Jews are, followed by four examples of Jewish practice. The list includes *Kashruth* – the kosher laws –, "frequent washings" which may be reference to the laws of family purity and the presence of a *mikvah* – ritual bath house – in every Jewish community. Alternatively, it may refer to the requirements to wash hands before eating and praying. The reference to marriage displays the importance of family building in Judaism.

Each of these practices is a custom of Jewish life that would be visible to anyone who is the least bit familiar with Jews.

The first item in the list is the most striking.

When a modern Jew builds an house he must leave part of it unfinished in remembrance that the Temple and Jerusalem now lie desolate.

This practice is one of thousands of codified Jewish laws. After stating that Jews adhere to the Torah, the first detail of Jewish life that the British scholars and academics who wrote this encyclopedia in the 18th century saw fit to mention was the fact that Jews are mourners for the Temple and Jerusalem. Their homes remain unfinished because their "home" is not built. 1700 years after the burning of the Temple and Jerusalem, a non-Jew who interacted with Jews recognized this fact as a primary component of Jewish identity.

Who is a Jew? A Jew is one who adheres to the Torah. A Jew is one who mourns the loss and yearns for the rebuilding of the Temple and Jerusalem. If this was so clear to the writers of the Encyclopedia Britannica in 1771, it must have been prominent among the Jews of 1771.

The power of memory

Today, the Jewish people have returned home. There is no doubt that this would not have happened if not for the power of Jewish memory. Throughout the Bible, the right hand symbolizes strength. This is the meaning of our verse.

If I forget you Jerusalem, my right hand will forget.

If I forget Jerusalem, *I have lost my strength.* It is the memory of Jerusalem that gave the Jewish people the strength to make it through the long and dark exile. To remember Jerusalem is to live in a constant state of yearning for return to Jerusalem. Without this memory there would have been no return.

Remembering Jerusalem, a central component of Jewish identity throughout 2000 years of exile, gave the Jewish people the strength to survive. The ingathering of the exiles of Israel in our times is the expression of the right hand – the strength of Jewish faith that never faltered.

Psalm 137:6 – Taking history personally

Let my tongue cleave to my palate if I do not recall you; if I do not set Jerusalem above my foremost joy. – Psalm 137:6

In the previous verse, the psalmist declared that he would lose his strength should he ever forget Jerusalem. Now he says that he will have lose the ability to express himself as well. In fulfilment of the sentiment of this verse, there are numerous Jewish customs and practices that ensure that Jerusalem will never be forgotten. For example, in the comments on the previous verse we discussed the practice of leaving a portion of one's house unfinished as a reminder of Jerusalem.

Remembering Jerusalem all day, every day

When Jews pray three times each day, morning, afternoon, and evening, the liturgy includes this paragraph:

May You return to Jerusalem with mercy and may You rest within it, as you have spoken. May You rebuild it soon in our days as an eternal edifice, and may You soon establish the throne of David within it. Blessed are You Lord, builder of Jerusalem.

After every meal, the grace after meals includes this line:

Rebuild Jerusalem, the holy city, soon in our days. Blessed are You Lord, builder of Jerusalem.

The life of a Jew is filled with reminders of Jerusalem throughout the day, every day. This has been the case for thousands of years. Simply put, to live a Jewish life is to never forget Jerusalem.

Remembering Jerusalem at every wedding

Among the many Jewish customs that remind us of Jerusalem, there is one that is based directly on our verse. The Talmud, the encyclopedic compendium of rabbinic legal teachings compiled more than 1500 years ago, records it as follows:

What is the meaning of: "Above my foremost joy" (Ps. 137:6)? Rabbi Isaac says: This refers to the burnt ashes that are customarily placed on the head of bridegrooms at the time of their wedding celebrations, to remember the destruction of the Temple. – Babylonian Talmud Bava Batra, 60b

To this day, a small amount of ash is placed on the head of a Jewish groom just prior to the wedding ceremony. Then during the ceremony, the future rebuilding of Jerusalem is explicitly mentioned in two separate blessings. The ceremony ends with the breaking of a glass by the groom symbolizing the destroyed state of Jerusalem so long as it is not fully rebuilt.

To outsiders, these customs may seem excessive and unfair to the bride and groom. After all, it is their wedding day. Why must we cloud their happiness with such dramatic reminders of the destruction of the Temple and Jerusalem? Aren't the constant reminders in the daily prayers enough?

From plural to singular

To answer this question, let us return to the text of Psalm 137. Here is the full text of the Psalm with verses 5 and 6 in bold.

By the rivers of Babylon,
There we sat and also wept
When we remembered Zion.
² On the willows in the midst of it. We hung our harps
³ For there our captors asked us for songs,
And our tormenters, mirth,
Saying, "Sing to us of the songs of Zion!"

⁴ How can we sing the song of the Lord
on foreign soil?
*⁵ **If I forget you, Jerusalem,***
Let my right hand forget its skill!
*⁶ **Let my tongue cleave to my palate — If I do not remember***
you,
If I do not set Jerusalem
Above my foremost joy.

⁷ Remember, O Lord, the day of Jerusalem.
for the sons of Edom,
Who said, "Tear it down! Tear it down

To its very foundation!"
⁸ Thieving daughter of Babylon,
Happy is He who pays you back for what you did to us!
⁹ Happy is He who will seize and dash
Your infants against the rock!

Notice that through the first four verses, the psalm is written in the first-person plural. *There we sat… We hung our harps… our captors… How can we sing…* Then, in verse 5, the psalm switches to the singular. *If I forget you… Let my tongue cleave…* The final verses then revert to the plural (see v.8).

Switching from singular to plural or vice versa occurs throughout the book of Psalms. Psalms will frequently switch between singular and plural, between referring to God in the third person and addressing Him directly, and between tenses. These transitions are always important. They are always worthy of study. What is the meaning of this transition?

Personal and collective identities

Psalm 137 is a lament over the destruction of Jerusalem and the exile to Babylon. The plural language of the opening verses makes sense. The destruction and exile were national events that befell the Jewish people as a collective.

Every person has multiple identities. I am Pesach Wolicki. I am a Jew. I am a husband. I am a father. I am an Israeli citizen. Some components of our identities are personal and private. Others are collective, such as citizenship. It is human nature to be primarily concerned with one's private personal identity over one's collective identity as a member of a nation or group. Every person's highest priority is their own well-being and the well-being of their family. Personal happiness or sorrow tend to override collective reasons to rejoice or mourn.

To illustrate the point, imagine someone who was married on the same day as a national tragedy took place. Understandably, such a person would be rejoicing. It would be difficult, perhaps impossible, for such a person to restrain their happiness. At the same time, their happiness might be tainted by the national tragedy. Or it might not.

The degree to which their happiness is affected by the national tragedy is determined by two factors.

1. How great is the tragedy?
2. How much does this person identify with the collective?

If the tragedy is not great enough to override the joy of getting married, or the bride and groom do not identify strongly with their national identity, the happiness of the wedding will be unaffected.

Psalm 137 describes the tragedy of the destruction of Jerusalem and the exile to Babylon. These are grave national tragedies for the Jewish people. By switching from the first-person plural to the singular, the psalmist teaches us a powerful lesson. The destruction of Jerusalem is powerful enough to affect even our most personal joyous occasions. This is due both to the severity the tragedy and the fact that we personally identify with our history. Had the psalm remained in the plural throughout, this message would have been lost.

By commemorating and remembering the destruction of Jerusalem at every wedding the way we do, the Jewish people continually remind ourselves that our identity is national, historical, and collective. While every married couple is happy on their wedding day, they are reminded that they also share in the collective national hopes and dreams of Israel throughout history. Every marriage is a building block for the future of God's kingdom on earth. Without Jerusalem and the Temple fully rebuilt, that kingdom is incomplete.

To fully participate in the building of God's kingdom, we must take historical events personally. By personalizing historical events, we deepen our concern for the world and become more committed to doing our part to carry out God's plan.

Numbers 6:24 – The Priestly Blessing Part I

The Lord will bless you and keep you

The three verses known as the priestly blessing are, in fact, three separate blessings. In Jewish tradition and practice, the priestly blessing is recited as part of the daily morning prayer service in the synagogue. Members of the congregation from priestly families descended from Aaron the high priest ascend the dais at the front of the congregation. They raise their hands, and they recite the blessing over the congregation. The congregation responds "Amen" after each of the three verses.

—— *The Two Blessings of this Verse*

Each of the three verses comprising the Priestly Blessing contains two verbs, describing what God will do to those who are being blessed. The first of the three verses states that God will do two things; He will *bless* you and He will *keep* you. Let us look at the Hebrew to gain a precise understanding of this blessing.

The verse is made up of three words:

Yivarechecha	will bless you
YHVH (ADONAI)	the Lord
Ve'yishmerecha	and keep you

As we have pointed out earlier in this book, as opposed to English, Hebrew grammar allows for subjects to either precede or follow their verbs. The first two words of this verse are correctly translated *the Lord will bless you*, even though they appear in reverse order.

What exactly is God promising to do in this verse? What is the precise meaning of *blessing*? The second verb root, "keep" - *SHMR* is the same as the word for *guard* or *protect*. In other words, whereas *keep* has the connotation of holding on to something as a possession, the Hebrew verb used here does not indicate ownership at all. Rather, it implies protection from harm.

Blessing = Abundance and Increase

The Hebrew word for blessing is *beracha*. That is the root used here in the first word of our verse. The first time that this word - or its root - appears in the Bible is on the fifth day of creation.

He <u>blessed</u> them [the fish] saying, 'Be fruitful and multiply and fill the water in the seas.' - Genesis 1:22

God told the fish that there would be many of them. *Beracha* – "blessing" – implies *abundance*. God blessed the fish by saying, "May there be a lot of you." More broadly, *blessing* is the actualization of hidden potential for good. For example, two fish, or two people, may have the *potential* to reproduce. This is not a blessing. The *blessing* is the realization of this potential when a child is produced.

Throughout the Bible, *blessing* implies abundance or multiplication of something good. For example, when Isaac blessed his sons, Jacob and Esau, he bestowed gifts upon them both in terms of material wealth as well as spiritual gifts. In this context the word *blessing* indicates material wealth, spiritual gifts, or loftiness of status and power. Another example is: *And He will bless your bread and your water* (Exodus 23:25) which also refers to the bestowing of plenty and prosperity by God.

Now that we understand the precise meaning of the two verbs in our verse, *bless* and *keep*, we can more accurately understand what exactly this blessing promises.

Increase and Protection

"The Lord will bless you" means that God will provide plenty, fertility, and abundant resources. He will give us all that we need to be effective as servants of God in the world. At the same time, "He will keep you" – God will guard us and protect us from harm; from the enemies who would seek to undermine the fulfillment of our sacred mission.

This may seem like a simple idea, but it is not. Many people of faith pray to God for blessings of health and prosperity as ends in and of themselves. They ask God to bless them and correctly see God's hand in the blessings that they receive. They praise and thank God for these blessings. But all too often, they do not ask the next question, "Why is God blessing me? What am I meant to do with these blessings?"

So here in this first verse of the Priestly Blessing we say that God will bless us with great gifts and great potential. At the same time, He will protect us so that we can put that potential to good use. It is up to us to make ourselves worthy of God's blessings.

── *Help and Shield*

Psalm 115:9 echoes the message of our verse.

O Israel, trust in the Lord; He is their helper and their shield.

Help and *shield* describe two ways that God guarantees that His people's *mission is accomplished* in the long term. There are times when God's people are able to do God's work. They are in a position of influence. He has blessed them with strength and ability. At those times we trust that God is with us as a *helper*, assisting us in our mission.

At other times, when the forces that oppose us are riding high; when the attacks on God's people prevent them from doing God's work; when all they can do is fight for survival; God is a *shield*. He protects His people from destruction.

◊ *Helper* in carrying out their mission

◊ *Shield* against those attacks that would hold them back

We have all been blessed by God. We have gifts and potential that can be used to build His kingdom. We must use those gifts. When we do, we are often called upon to take risks. We must trust in Him. He blessed us with strength. He will be there to guard us and protect us when we take to the field of battle.

Numbers 6:25 – The Priestly Blessing Part II

The Lord shall shine His face towards you, and He shall be gracious to you.

The second verse of the priestly blessing, just like the previous one, is made up of two statements. Like the first verse, here too we see two blessings that God will bestow on the blessed.

1. He will *shine His face towards* them
2. He will *be gracious to* them

What exactly does this blessing mean?

The previous verse described God *blessing* and *protecting* those who are blessed. The word "bless" in that verse referred to *abundance*, as we explained. The blessings of that verse, *abundance* and *protection*, are easily understandable. In this verse, by contrast, God promises to "shine His face towards you," and "be gracious to you."

What does it mean for God to *shine His face towards* someone? Does that give them wisdom? Happiness? Success? Strength? Prophetic power? As beautiful as these words are, their precise meaning is unclear. The immediate context of the verse does not provide any clarity on the matter.

Grace or Favor

The second blessing of this verse, *He shall be gracious to you*, is equally unclear, but for a different reason. The Hebrew word used here can be interpreted grammatically in several ways. The Hebrew word for "and He shall be gracious to you" is *vi'chuneka*. The first syllable, *vi*, is the Hebrew prefix meaning "and." The final syllable, *ka*, means "you." The middle of the word, the root, is CHN. This root has several possible meanings. To illustrate, here are two examples among many in the Bible, which use the same root as our word here.

As the eyes of a maid to the hand of her mistress,
So our eyes look to the Lord our God,
Until He has mercy on us. – Psalm 123:2

And Esther obtained favor in the sight of all who saw her. – Esther 2:15

In the quote from Psalm 123, the root CHN means *mercy* or *compassion*. In the verse from Esther, the meaning of CHN is *favor*, meaning that Esther was admired and liked by other people. There are numerous examples in scripture of both meanings of this root. Without getting into the technicalities of Hebrew conjugation, suffice it to say that it is unclear which meaning is the correct one for our verse.

To sum up this point: the root of the word *vi'chuneka* – "and He shall be gracious to you" – is either the *grace* or the *favor*. Our verse is promising either that God will have *mercy* on those who are blessed or that He will grant them *favor* in the eyes of others. This question leads to another question. How would either of these options relate to the first blessing of the verse, *the Lord shall shine His countenance towards you?* Perhaps we can determine which translation is correct by answering this second fquestion.

God "shining His face" in the Bible

Besides ours, there are seven verses in the Bible that speak of God *shining His face*. In five of the seven, the context is God's redemption of Israel from exile and oppression at the hand of other nations. Three of these five are a repeated phrase, all in the same chapter, Psalm 80. The phrase "Cause Your face to shine, and we shall be saved!" appears three times in this one psalm. (Ps. 80:3,7,19) The other verses that refer to the redemption of Israel are Daniel 9:17 and Psalm 67:1.

The remaining two verses that refer to God *shining His face* describe a personal, private redemption from enemies.

Deliver me from the hand of my enemies; And from those who persecute me. Make Your face shine upon Your servant; Save me for Your mercies' sake. – Psalm 31:15-16

Redeem me from the oppression of man, That I may keep Your precepts. Make Your face shine upon Your servant; And teach me Your statutes. – Psalm 119:134-135

To sum up, when the Bible describes God *shining His face*, it means that God is saving Israel or an individual from exile or oppression. That said, if we look more closely at these verses, there is another important implication. The redemption of Israel is not a final goal in and of itself. The redemption of Israel is in order to bring about the kingdom of God on earth.

We see this in Daniel, where we find Daniel praying not only for the end of the exile but for the rebuilding of the Temple in Jerusalem. On the personal level, the verse in Psalm 119 quoted above describes redemption from enemies in order to be free to serve God by keeping the commandments. In other words, when someone in the Bible prays to God to *shine His face*, the meaning of the prayer is that God should redeem the supplicant so that he can accomplish a higher goal in the service of God.

The universal purpose of the redemption of Israel

This implication, that God "shining His face" means that God saves someone so that they can serve a higher purpose, is most evident in Psalm 67:1:

God be merciful to us and bless us,
<u>cause His face to shine upon us</u>, Selah
That Your way may be known on earth,
Your salvation among all nations.

Let the peoples praise You, O God;
Let all the peoples praise You. – Psalm 67:1-3

Here, the stated purpose of the redemption of Israel is the universal goal of all nations and all peoples praising and worshipping the God of Israel.

So what does our verse mean?

Keeping in mind that Israel's mission is to bring all humanity to faith in God, we can now return to our verse in Numbers 6.

I would like to suggest that the meaning of this verse is as follows.

The Lord shall shine His face towards you, - God will redeem you from exile and oppression *and He shall be gracious to you.* - and He will grant you <u>favor in the eyes of others</u> so that you will be able to influence them to have faith in the God of Israel.

Seen this way, the second half of the verse should be translated, *and He shall grant you favor.* In fact, a number of the traditional Jewish commentaries understand the verse exactly this way.

This is an important lesson for all people of faith. Even as we pray to God to bless us and redeem us from trouble and enemies, we must remember the purpose of the redemption for which we pray. When God grants us freedom and elevates us to a position of autonomy and influence, we must use those gifts to build His kingdom.

God's blessing in this verse is that He will redeem us from that which oppresses us. He will then give us favor in the eyes of others so that we can influence them and bring them to faith in the God of Israel.

Numbers 6:26 – The Priestly Blessing Part III

The Lord shall lift up his face to you, and grant you peace.

The first half of this final verse of the priestly blessing describes God *lifting up His face* to Israel, the recipient of the blessing. What exactly does this mean?

Turn or Lift?

The Hebrew for the first phrase of the verse is made up of four words.

Yisa	He will lift up	
ADONAI in Hebrew)	The Lord	(subjects commonly appear after verbs
panav	His face	
elecha	to you	

We should note that there are numerous English translations (e.g NIV, DRA, ISV) that translate this as *The Lord shall <u>turn</u> His face to you.* This translation is imprecise as the Hebrew verb here clearly means *to raise* or *to lift up.* This verb simply does not mean *turn* or *change direction* anywhere in the Bible. Apparently, these translators were uncomfortable with a description of God raising His face to human beings, as though He is below, and we are above. This is an example of translators choosing not to translate directly because the text of the Bible doesn't make sense to them. The problem, of course, is that the Bible is not poorly written. If the word "lift up" is used here, we must seek an understanding of the verse that accounts for this word.

Look favorably?

Another translation that is common is *The Lord will look on you with favor* (e.g. CSB, EHV, GNT). These translations are based on the way the metaphor of "lifting" the "face," is used elsewhere in the Bible. In 20 of

25 times this expression appears, it refers to someone treating or viewing someone favorably or with partiality. Here are a few examples:

You shall not perform injustice in judgement. <u>You shall not favor the impoverished,</u> [lit. "do not lift up the face of the impoverished"] you shall not defer to the great; With righteousness you shall judge your counterpart. – Leviticus 19:15

It is not good <u>to be partial to</u> [lit. lift the face of] the wicked and so deprive the innocent of justice. – Proverbs 18:5

How long will you defend the unjust and <u>show partiality to the wicked?</u> [lit. "lift up the face of the wicked"] – Psalm 82:2

Lifting His own face vs. looking favorably on others

The problem with translating our verse according to this meaning is that here it is God's own face that He is *lifting up*. As we see from the examples cited here, where "lifting the face" refers to treating someone favorably, the face that is being "lifted" is the face of the one who is being treated favorably, not the face of the one who is treating them favorably, the one doing the "lifting."

Confused? Let's simplify this point. If our verse means *The Lord will look on you with favor,* the Hebrew should have said, *The Lord will lift up <u>your</u> face,* not <u>His</u> face.

There are only five verses in the Bible that describe someone lifting their own face. Two of these verses describe someone lifting their face up, either literally, as in 2 Kings, or figuratively, Job 11, without indicating to whom the face is being lifted.

He <u>looked up</u> [lit. lifted his face] at the window and called out, "Who is on my side? – 2 Kings 9:32

If you put away the sin that is in your hand and allow no evil to dwell in your tent, then, free of fault, you will <u>lift up your face</u>; you will stand firm and without fear. – Job 11:14-15

Lifting the face "to" someone

There are only three verses that describe someone lifting their own face <u>to someone</u>. In all cases the "lifting" is figurative, not literal. One is our verse here in the priestly blessing. The other two are:

Surely then you will find delight in the Almighty and will <u>lift up your face</u> to God. You will pray to him, and he will hear you, and you will fulfill your vows. – Job 22:26

And Abner said again to Asahel, "Turn aside from following me. Why should I strike you to the ground? How then could I <u>lift up my face</u> to your brother Joab?" – 2 Samuel 2:22

Both verses describe someone subordinate looking to the other in expectation or supplication. Abner was concerned that he would not be able to justify himself to Joab if he harmed Asahel. Job is obviously in a subordinate position vis a vis God. In both examples the one lifting his own face is in need of help or approval from the one he is lifting his face to. Now our verse is even more puzzling. What does it mean that God will *lift His face* in the priestly blessing?

God depends on us

In the comments on the two previous verses of the priestly blessing I explained that the point of each of these blessings is that God blesses us in order to give us the tools that we need to fulfill our mission to build His kingdom. With this in mind, I would like to suggest that our verse makes a very powerful theological statement.

The three verses of the priestly blessing describe the way God blesses us and gives us the strengths and ability to carry out His will on this earth. In the opening verse, He will bless us with abundance and protect us (Num. 6:24) so that we have resources that can be used in this mission. Then, He will redeem us from exile and hardship and give us the favor in the eyes of the world (Num. 6:25) so that we can influence humanity towards faith in God. Finally, in the third verse we are told that God depends on us for the realization of the ultimate goal of building His kingdom, leading to eternal peace, *Shalom*, the culmination of all things.

The Lord will lift up His face to you means that God will look expectantly and hopefully to us. He waits for us to do our part on His behalf. It is us, people of faith in the God of Israel, who are responsible to build His kingdom. He will bless us with all that we need for the task. He will protect us and redeem us from oppressive forces that stand in our way. He will give us all the talents and resources necessary for the mission.

But in the end, it is God who looks up to us, so to speak, awaiting us to complete the job.

And grant you peace. Peace, Shalom, the ultimate expression of the Kingdom of God on earth is in our hands. He has granted it to us as a task and mission. God raises His face to us, turning to us to use all His blessings for His sake.

The greatest blessing that God bestows on us is the partnership in the building of His perfect world. He empowers us and protects us so that we have the privilege and responsibility of being actively involved in repairing the world and building His kingdom.

Psalm 122:1 - Rejoicing in a future we will not live to see

A song of ascents. Of David. I rejoiced with those who said to me, "Let us go to the house of the Lord." Our feet were standing in your gates, Jerusalem.

Why is David mentioned?

Psalm 122 is the third in a series of fifteen psalms that begin with the words, *A song of ascents*. Of these fifteen chapters, only four name David as the author. One chapter names David's son Solomon (Ps. 127). The remaining ten chapters in this series do not name an author at all. This is not unusual. Many psalms do not name the author in the opening verse.

Since ten of fifteen psalms in this series do not name the author, it is worth studying those psalms that do mention David. Had Psalm 122 been written without the words "Of David" at the beginning, would that change the meaning of the psalm? Since most psalms in this series do not mention David, we must ask, why is he mentioned here?

Let's put this another way. David composed most of the book of Psalms. While many chapters were written by other authors, those authors are almost always named in the opening phrases of the psalms. These phrases are called *superscriptures*. Open a bible and look through the psalms and you will notice these superscriptures right at the beginning of most chapters in the book. Most psalms include the name of the author, but many do not. When David composed the fifteen chapters titled *A Song of Ascents*, he chose to include his name in the superscripture in only four. Therefore, wherever David included his name in one of these chapters, we must assume that the explicit mention of David by name is important to content and meaning of the psalm. So, why did David include his name here at the start of Psalm 122?

David never saw the Temple

The subject of this psalm is the Temple and Jerusalem. As the opening verse states:

I rejoiced with those who said to me, "Let us go to the house of the Lord."

The psalm goes on to describe the grandeur and importance of Jerusalem.

It is interesting to note that David himself was never in the Temple in Jerusalem. The Temple was built by his son, King Solomon, after David died. This was not merely an unfortunate circumstance of David's life. Rather, the fact that David did not live to see the Temple built was an explicit decree by God.

David said to Solomon: "My son, I had it in my heart to build a house for the Name of the Lord my God. But this word of the Lord came to me: 'You have shed much blood and have fought many wars. You are not to build a house for My Name, because you have shed much blood on the earth in My sight. But you will have a son who will be a man of peace and rest, and I will give him rest from all his enemies on every side. His name will be Solomon, and I will grant Israel peace and quiet during his reign. He is the one who will build a house for My Name. He will be My son, and I will be his father. And I will establish the throne of his kingdom over Israel forever.' – 1 Chronicles 22:7-10

David was a warrior who had killed many men. He yearned to build a temple to God. Yet, God told David that he could not be the one to build the Temple. The Temple would only be built under the reign of his son, after David was gone. David would never visit *the house of the Lord* built in Jerusalem. So what did David mean when he wrote: "I rejoiced with those who said to me, 'Let us go to the house of the Lord.'"

The Lesson of David's Joy

Despite God's decree, David still rejoiced over the thought of a Temple that he would never merit to visit. He rejoiced over a future that he would not live to experience. This joy is a lesson for all people of faith.

To illustrate the point: Imagine if God told you that the Messiah will come shortly after your own life has ended. Would you still rejoice over the good news of the Messiah's imminent arrival? Would it be bittersweet? David rejoiced in the thought of the Temple in Jerusalem even though the Temple would be built only after David was gone from the world.

All who have faith in the God of Israel know that the end of history is good. God will redeem the world. Knowledge of God will one day fill the earth. Evil and falsehood will be defeated. The biblical promises of the glorious future for the world are certain. And yet, each and every one of us knows that we may not be fortunate enough to live to see the Kingdom of God on this earth. We yearn for it, while knowing that this lengthy historical process may very well reach its glorious conclusion after we are gone from this world. Are we still able to rejoice in the promises of the future? Are we joyous and grateful as we envision the great redemption of humanity that may occur after we are gone, even though we will not live to see it?

This is not a small challenge for our lives of faith. It forces us to confront a fundamental question regarding our devotion to God's purposes. We know that the long march of history will end with *knowledge of God covering the earth like water covers the sea* (Habakuk 2:14). We know that we make our contributions to this future when we live our lives according to the expressed will of God. But what really motivates us? Are we in it for ourselves, or to serve God?

When we rejoice over a future that we will not live to see we make a powerful statement. It's not about me. It's about God and His kingdom. It is only fitting that we learn this lesson from King David, the anointed of Israel. David knew that he would not see the Temple, and yet the thought of the Temple brought him joy.

We show our devotion to God when we rejoice over the future, even as we acknowledge that we may not live to see it. The kingdom of God is a certainty. We must rejoice in this knowledge regardless of how far in the future it may be.

Psalm 122:6 – Praying for the wholeness of Jerusalem

Pray for the peace of Jerusalem; those that love you will be tranquil.

Jerusalem: City of Peace

The Hebrew word for "peace", *Shalom*, is often misunderstood. *Shalom* does not mean "peace" in the sense of compromise or a lack of hostilities. This contemporary meaning of "peace" is the farthest thing from *Shalom*. *Shalom* comes from the Hebrew root *shalem*, meaning "complete" or "whole". "Peace" is wholeness. Peace means that everything is complete and as it ought to be.

The word "Jerusalem" includes this Hebrew root as well. According to Jewish tradition, Jerusalem is made up of a combination of two words.

Yeru (Jeru)	will be seen
shalem (salem)	wholeness, peace

The first half of the word Jerusalem is a future tense conjugation of the verb *to see*. In other words, the name Jerusalem means *Peace will be seen*. Jerusalem is itself a promise of a future of wholeness and peace. Those who love Jerusalem have faith in her future.

Jerusalem is, of course, the city of God. It is the city that houses the Temple Mount, home of the House of Prayer for All Nations (Is. 56:7). A beautiful and rebuilt Jerusalem is synonymous with the redemption of Israel and the Biblical promises of the end times.

The Difficult History of Jerusalem

Today, Jerusalem is being rebuilt as a beautiful modern city. The population of Jerusalem is greater than at any time in history. Millions of Bible-believing pilgrims visit Jerusalem every year to connect with God at the site of the Temple. It is easy for anyone who visits to fall in love with Jerusalem. But it was not always this way.

The peace of Jerusalem has been an elusive reality over the course of history. Jerusalem has been attacked 52 times. It has been conquered 44 times, besieged 23 times, and completely destroyed twice. In the last century, Jerusalem spent 19 years divided between two countries with a hostile border cutting the city in half. All the great empires that have swept the world have wanted to control Jerusalem. Rather than being a city that represents peace, it has been a center of conflict and human cruelty for centuries. If any city needs prayers for peace, it is Jerusalem.

From the 13th Century to Today

In the year 1267, a great rabbi from Spain named Moses Nachmanides fulfilled his life-long dream and arrived in Jerusalem after a long and arduous journey. He was the greatest scholar in the Jewish community of Spain and its undisputed leader. But he loved Jerusalem and longed to live out the end of his life in the Holy Land. When he arrived in Jerusalem, he wrote a letter to his son back in Spain.

"May God Bless you, my son Nachman, and may you see the good of Jerusalem. May you see the children of your children, and may your table be like the table of Abraham our father.

In the Holy city of Jerusalem, I write this letter to you. For - with praise and thanks to the Rock of my Salvation – I merited to arrive peacefully on the ninth day of the month of Elul and I stayed in her (Jerusalem) in peace until the day after the Day of Atonement, after which I am now planning to travel to Hebron, city of the graves of our fathers, to pray there, and to dig a burial site for myself there, with God's help.

What can I tell you regarding the land? For there is much neglect and great desolation. The general rule is as follows: that which is holier is more destroyed. Jerusalem is more destroyed than anything else. Judea is more destroyed than the Galilee. But, Jerusalem, with all her destruction, is very good. It has approximately two thousand inhabitants. Around three hundred Christians among them, refugees from the Sultan's sword. There are no Jews in her, for ever since the Tatars invaded, they fled from there and others were killed by their sword. Except for two brothers, dyers, they purchase the dyes from the magistrate. These two are joined by up to a quorum of ten for communal worship in their home on the Sabbaths.

Behold, I encouraged them, and we found a destroyed house, built with marble pillars with a beautiful dome and we took it as a synagogue. For the city is abandoned. Anyone who wants to acquire a destroyed building may do so. They volunteered to repair the house. They took the initiative and sent to Shechem to bring Torah scrolls from there that were from Jerusalem but were taken there when the Tatars invaded.

Behold, they have established a synagogue and there they will pray, for many people come to Jerusalem regularly. Men and women from Damascus and Aleppo and all the regions of the land to see the temple site and to cry over it.

He who granted me to see Jerusalem in its state of destruction will grant us to see it rebuilt and established when the Glorious Presence of God returns to it. May you, my son, and your siblings and the entire family – all of you - merit seeing the good of Jerusalem and the comfort of Zion.

Your worried and rejoicing father, Moses Nachmanides

P.S. Send my greetings to Rabbi Moses son of Solomon, your mother's brother. I hereby tell him that I went up to the Mount of Olives which is opposite the Temple Mount and adjacent to it – only the Valley of Jehosaphat separates them – and there opposite the Holy Temple I read his verses with much weeping as he prophesied. May He who caused His name to dwell in the Holy Temple increase and expand your peace with the peace of your entire honored and holy community forever and for eternity. Amen."

The journey from Spain to Jerusalem in the 13th century was extremely dangerous. Rabbi Moses Nachmanides knew that he would never see his family again. He arrived to find two Jews left in Jerusalem. No protective walls around the city. No synagogue. No Torah scroll. That's how things looked in 1267. And yet, he wrote, *"But, Jerusalem, with all her destruction, is very good."*

The synagogue that Nachmanides founded remained in use for centuries until the congregation moved to its present location, a few steps away from the original site. This congregation, still known as *The Nachmanides Synagogue*, continues to conduct daily services to this day in the Old City of Jerusalem. Nachmanides struggled to rebuild the Jewish community of Jerusalem because he knew the future. He knew that, just as Jerusalem's name implies, to love Jerusalem is to be able to see the future of peace and wholeness. As King David put it in Psalm 122, *Those who love Jerusalem will be tranquil.*

While we still must pray and work toward the complete rebuilding of Jerusalem with the Temple at its center, we must equally be grateful for what we have merited to witness in our times. Jerusalem is being rebuilt. It is becoming whole again. We must continue to see the future implied in Jerusalem's name. When we pray for the peace of Jerusalem, we pray for the Kingdom of God. We pray for the peace of the world.

Psalm 119:11 – Making God's Will Second Nature

In my heart I store Your word, so as not to sin against You.

This verse describes the defense against sin that is provided by the word of God. By remembering the word of God and "storing" it in one's heart, one is protected from sin. The consciousness of God's word provides a corrective at a moment of weakness that could otherwise lead to sin.

Concealed and protected

The Hebrew word here for "I store" is *tzafanti*. The verb root is TzFN. This verb appears 32 times in the Bible. While it is translated here as "store," it does not mean "store" in the sense of collecting or gathering something. For example, this is not the verb used when describing the storing of grain or other possessions.

Based on the way this verb is used throughout the Bible we see that it has two related connotations.

1. something being concealed or hidden from view.
2. something being protected.

In other words, the meaning of this verb is not about *storage*, per se. Rather, it refers to hiding or protecting something. It is also important to note that this word is written in the past tense. A more accurate translation would be, "I *stored* Your word", rather than "I *store*".

Primary meaning: hidden

The first use of this verb is in Exodus 2, just after the birth of Moses. Moses' mother hid him so that he would not be drowned due to the decree of Pharaoh to kill all Israelite baby boys.

So the woman conceived and bore a son. And when she saw that he was a beautiful child, <u>she hid him</u> three months. – Exodus 2:2

Similarly, when Joshua sent two spies to scout out Jericho before conquering it, they were concealed in a hiding place by Rahab so they would not be discovered.

Then the woman took the two men and hid them. So she said, "Yes, the men came to me, but I did not know where they were from. – Joshua 2:4

In both these instances, the goal is to conceal and to protect from harm. In some verses where this verb is used, the connotation is only of concealment, not protection. For example:

If they say, "Come with us. Let us lie in wait to shed blood; Let us lurk secretly for the innocent without cause; - Proverbs 1:11 (see Psalm 56:6 for another example)

To sum up, the word used in our verse for "store" implies something that is being concealed from view. Often this word is used in the Bible to describe something or someone that is being protected. This makes sense, as concealing something from view is a common and effective way of protecting it.

In light of this precise understanding of the word *tzafanti* – "I store" – in our verse, it seems that this choice of word is puzzling. Does "In my heart I store Your word" mean that the word of God is *concealed, hidden* from view? That it is *protected*? What exactly is this verse teaching us?

God's word becomes second nature

I would like to suggest that there is a powerful psychological lesson in this verse. The psalmist is not describing someone who remembers the word of God and therefore makes a conscious decision to hold back from sinning in a particular situation. In fact, this verse does not refer to *consciously* remembering anything. Rather, it describes a person who is so committed to the word of God that his awareness of God's word is subconscious. It is *concealed*.

When ideas are repeated regularly and drilled into us, they become what we call "second nature." The dictionary defines "second nature" as "an acquired, deeply ingrained habit or skill" (Merriam-Webster). When we react instinctively in a way that is the result of trained values and habits, rather than our natural base instincts, we have acquired a "second nature." We are not consciously aware of the decision to behave the way we do because it has become instinct. In effect, the ideas or values that lead to this behavior are hidden from view. We are unaware of them in the moment. They are *concealed*.

I mentioned that the verb *tzafanti* is written in the past tense. The psalmist is saying, "The work of educating and conditioning myself to the word of God was already done. This conditioning prepared me for the challenge of facing the enticements of sin."

To sum up: *In my heart I have stored Your word* – I have conditioned myself through education and reinforcing the values that I have learned from Your word so that they have become hidden; they are second nature to me. My instincts have been transformed by Your word. This subconscious, second nature awareness of Your word protects me from sin.

Regular study and reinforcement of the word of God transforms our second nature instincts. In this way, we align ourselves subconsciously with God's will and His values. This is the greatest protection from sin.

Proverbs 3:5 – Developing True Trust in God

Trust in the Lord with all your heart, and on your own under-standing do not lean.

What does it mean to truly trust in the Lord? At the end of the day, we must make decisions and choices. Whether we like it or not, our own understanding will dictate what we choose to do in any given situation. How do we actualize the lesson of this verse? What is it calling on us to do?

Trust "in" or Trust "to"

The beginning of this verse calls on us to "trust in the Lord." As always, the precise Hebrew contains a nuance that is not apparent from the English translations.

The Hebrew for "Trust in the Lord" in our verse is made up of three words:

B'tach	Trust
el	in (to)
ADONAI	the Lord

To anyone familiar with Hebrew grammar and syntax, the anomaly in this verse is clear. The second word of the verse does not mean "in". The word *el* means "to" or "toward". The verb "trust" appears 120 times in the Bible. In almost all cases, this verb is followed by the prefix *be* meaning "in" or the word *al* meaning "upon". In only 10 verses, this verb is followed by the word *el*, as it is here. In other words, the literal translation here is, *Trust to the Lord*.

To sum up this point: In almost all cases in the Bible when the verb "trust" appears it appears either as "trust in" or "trust upon", i.e. "place your trust upon." In only ten instances "trust" is followed by *el* – "to", i.e. "trust to…" What is the significance of this uncommon usage?

What does "Trust to" mean?

Nine of the ten times that "trust" is followed by *el* – "to", the context is trust in God. In eight of these nine, i.e. all verses with the exception of our verse, the context is prayer in the face of imminent danger. This is an important point. Not all verses that mention trust in God are share this context. For example, here is a conventional "trust in God" verse, which does not use our unusual "trust to" form.

Vindicate me, Lord, for I have led a blameless life; I have trusted in the Lord and have not faltered. – Psalm 26:1

David attributes his avoidance of sin to his trust in the Lord. He is not referring to trusting in God's protection at a dangerous moment when facing enemies. Rather, trust in the Lord here refers to obedience to God.

Now, here are a few examples of "trust *to*" God in the Bible.

My adversaries pursue me all day long; in their pride many are attacking me. When I am afraid, I put my trust – el - to You. – Psalm 56:2-3

I hate those who cling to worthless idols; as for me, I trust - el – to the Lord.... You have not given me into the hands of the enemy. – Psalm 31:6,8

From these and other verses that use the word *el* – "to" – with the verb "trust," it is clear that "trust" here is not an emotional sense of security and reliance upon God. Rather to trust *"to"* God means to direct one's energy toward trusting in God through prayer in time of crisis.

Although this may sound awkward in English, it actually makes sense. The Bible uses "trust to" in situations where the enemy is imminent. There is legitimate reason to be afraid. This is a natural instinctive feeling at a time of acute danger. Even a person of strong faith in God will have a difficult time feeling completely secure and protected. Trust in God at such times requires effort. This is what our verse is describing. Trust *to* the Lord is different from trust *in* the Lord. Trust *in* the Lord is that common feeling of security that faith brings under normal circumstances. To trust *to* the Lord means directing one's energy to use faith to overcome the feeling of precariousness and danger from an enemy that is about to attack.

To sum up: When I trust *in* the Lord, I am describing how I feel under normal circumstances. When I trust *to* the Lord, I am describing the effort to move away from fear and *towards* God at a moment of crisis when my natural instinct is to feel distant from Him.

Moving Towards Trust in the Lord

Trust in [EL – to] the Lord with all your heart, and on your own understanding do not lean.

While our verse does not describe any explicit enemy about to attack, it does describe a situation where we might feel distant from God. When we put too much trust in our own understanding, we allow God to slip into the background. When this happens, we are vulnerable to attack by the enemy. At such times, we are called to put in the effort to regain that sense of trust. This is the message of our verse.

When we lean too much on our own wisdom and understanding rather than humbly submitting to the word of God, we are weakened. This verse calls on us to "trust to the Lord", to work to move towards trust in God to save us from our own arrogant trust in our own understanding.

Proverbs 3:6 – What it means to Know God

In all your ways know Him, and He will straighten your paths

The most striking word in this verse is "know". The verse does not say "In all your ways *remember* Him." It does not say, "In all your ways *think* of Him." If the lesson of this verse was simply that being aware of God keeps one on the straight path, the verb used would not have been "know."

It is also worth noting that the verse does not say, *"At all times* know Him." or "Know Him *all of your days."* If the point of the verse is that we should think about God at all times, why does it tie knowledge of Him to *behavior* – "all your ways" - rather than *time*?

"Knowing" in the Bible

The Hebrew verb *da* – "know" – used here, means much more than the mere knowledge of an idea. For example, this verb is used in the Bible as a euphemism for intimate sexual relations.

Now Adam knew Eve his wife, and she conceived and bore Cain, and said, "I have acquired a man from the Lord." – Genesis 4:1

Now the young woman was very beautiful to behold, a virgin; no man had known her. – Genesis 24:16

The reason for this euphemism is that the Hebrew verb *DA* – "know" – implies integration of a concept into the self, rather than mere intellectual awareness. In other words, just as a man and woman are bonded together in intimacy, an idea that is truly *known* is integrated and bonded to the personality of the person who *knows* it. The idea that is *known* becomes a part of the self of the one who *knows* it.

Knowing God

With this more precise understanding of the Biblical meaning of the Hebrew word *da* – "know", we can better understand what the Bible means when it speaks of *knowledge of God.*

Jeremiah 22 records a prophecy of rebuke to the Jehoiakim, king of Judah. Jeremiah calls out Jehoiakim for his unethical leadership and abuse of power. Jeremiah opens his rebuke with a call to the king to rule ethically.

Hear the word of the Lord, O king of Judah, you who sit on the throne of David, you and your servants and your people who enter these gates! Thus says the Lord: "Execute judgment and righteousness, and deliver the plundered out of the hand of the oppressor. Do no wrong and do no violence to the stranger, the fatherless, or the widow, nor shed innocent blood in this place. – Jeremiah 22:2-3

Jeremiah goes on to warn Jehoiakim that his kingdom will be destroyed if he does not mend his ways. Then, he invokes a contrast with the righteous reign of his father King Josiah.

Your father ate and drank and upheld justice and righteousness, did he not? And then it went well for him. He judged the case of the poor and needy. And then it went well for him. <u>Isn't this what it means to know Me?</u> – Jeremiah 22:15-16

Isn't this what it means to know Me. Here is God Himself (through Jeremiah) explicitly stating that to *know* Him is to behave according to the principles of justice and righteousness. This same idea is expressed in another passage in Jeremiah.

Let the one who boasts, boast in this: <u>that he understands and knows me,</u> for I am the Lord who acts with gracious love, justice, and righteousness in the land. I delight in these things," declares the Lord. – Jeremiah 9:24

To sum up, *knowledge of God* is not intellectual awareness of God. It is not faith in the common understanding of the word. It is not even a personal feeling of God's presence in our lives. Knowledge of God, biblically speaking, is a consciousness of God that is so deep-seated and integrated into our selves that it expresses itself in ethical, altruistic, and righteous behavior.

Look again at the passage from Jeremiah 22. God does not say that knowledge of God leads to ethical behavior. He says that knowledge of God <u>is</u> ethical behavior. In other words, if someone claims to know God but their behavior is not righteous, we may say that they have faith in God. We may say that they are aware of God. But we can not say that such a person *knows God.*

Now we can fully understand our verse.

In all your ways know Him, and He will straighten your paths.

To know God is to be intimately bonded with the idea of God. Like the marriage of a man and a woman, this knowledge transforms one's identity and dictates behavior.

Deuteronomy 6:4 – The Oneness We Cannot See

Hear O Israel, the Lord is our God, the Lord is one

This verse is the most fundamental statement of monotheistic faith in the entire Bible. Jewish practice is to recite it, and the five verse that immediately follow it, twice a day every day. According to Jewish tradition, it is customary to cover one's eyes when reciting this verse. We can understand this custom by exploring the deeper meaning of the verse.

Why the repetition?

There are no extra words in the Bible. Every word adds something important. This should be obvious. The Bible is very carefully written. It is the word of God. Any word that is not necessary would not be there at all. Therefore, it is valuable to identify words that appear to be superfluous and investigate what it is that they add.

If the point of this verse is to state the oneness of God, it could have been written as follows. *Here O Israel, the Lord, our God, is one.* Why does the verse repeat the name of the Lord a second time? The simple answer is that this verse has a lot more to teach us than the simple fact that there is only one God.

What "the Lord" actually means

In Hebrew, the name of God that is translated as "the Lord" is the four-letter name of God YHVH that according to Jewish tradition is never pronounced as it is written. In English, this name is often transliterated as Jehovah. English translations always render it as "the Lord" due to the Jewish tradition of not uttering this name. Instead, Jews replace this name with the word *Adonai*, which means "Lord," or "my Lord," as a euphemism for YHVH which is never actually pronounced. Because this practice was already the custom when Jesus and his disciples lived, they, as Jews, used the word "Lord" in place of God's sacred name.

The name YHVH is made up of a blend of three words:

Yihyeh - "will be"

Hoveh – "Present", "exists"

Hayah – "was"

A more thorough explanation of the etymology of this name can be found in the note on the names of God at the end my first book, *Cup of Salvation*. For our purposes we will keep things simple. God's name YHVH refers to the fact that God is the cause of all existence; past, present, and future.

What "our God" actually means

The Hebrew word for "*our God*" is *Eloheinu*. This is the first-person plural possessive of the name *Elohim*, universally translated as "God". The name *Elohim* or *Eloheinu* is notable because it is technically a plural word. In fact, the plain meaning of the word is "powers."

Elohim is the only name of God that appears in Genesis 1, the six days of the creation of the world. Unlike YHVH, this name is pronounced as it is written.

Three important points to help us understand this name better:

1. *Elohim* is also the Biblical Hebrew word for "judges" or "courts". One example is Exodus 22:9 "the cause of both parties shall come before the *judges*."

2. *Elohim* is also used when Scripture speaks of false gods, e.g. in the 10 commandments, "You shall have no other *gods* before Me." YHVH is never used this way.

3. *Elohim* is technically a plural word, although when referring to God, the verbs that accompany it are always in the singular. It is treated as a singular subject.

Essentially, *Elohim* means "powers". Therefore, it is the name of God in the creation story. All forces of nature are part of God. He is *All-powerful*.

When this name *Elohim* – "God" is used, it describes God as He who controls nature; God as we perceive Him in the world around us. *Elohim* is also used to describe God as He displays His ultimate and infinite power or enacts judgement.

YHVH and Elohim

Here is another way to look at the two names YHVH and *Elohim*. YHVH means that God is the sole cause of everything that has ever existed and everything that will exist in the future. In YHVH we acknowledge that all space, time, and matter are all caused by God. In Him, they are all one.

Elohim, on the other hand, describes God as we see Him in the world. We don't experience reality as a unity. We see good and evil, sickness and health, war and peace. We see different things, people, and times. Our human experience of the world is an experience of diversity. This is the meaning of *Elohim*. God is master of all the many different forces and powers in the world.

To sum up, YHVH describes God as He truly is. *Elohim* describes God as we experience Him.

God is One: But we can't see it

Now we can understand the custom of covering the eyes when reciting this verse. We are declaring that all creation, everything around us, is a complete unity within God. However, this unity is not what we see with our human eyes when we look out at the world. We cover our eyes because our limited human perception does not experience the unity of all creation that we are declaring with our mouths. By covering our eyes, we acknowledge that God's unity is beyond our perception and understanding.

The point of the verse is not to simply state that there is one God. For this, the verse could have said, Hear O Israel, the Lord our God is one. The name YHVH – the Lord – is repeated to make the point.

The meaning of our verse is this:

Hear O Israel, YHVH is our God [Eloheinu]. All of the disparate forces and beings in creation are all part of the unified will of the creator. But lest one misunderstand that we are saying that God is a plural, that He is simply the sum of many disparate powers, **the Lord is one**; i.e. there are no conflicting forces in God's creation. Even though we live in a world which appears to include conflicting and disparate forces, the truth is that all these disparate powers are part of the singular will of God. In Him, everything is one.

No matter how multifaceted and even contradictory and confusing we may find the reality of our world, we believe with perfect faith that God is the sole source of everything. All is one in Him.

Deuteronomy 6:5 – All Your Very

You shall love the Lord your God with all your heart, and with all your soul, and with all your might.

To any reader of Hebrew there is one word in this verse that stands out as unusual. The final word of the verse translated here as "your might", is *me'odecha*. The *echa* at end of the word is a suffix meaning "your". The word for "might" is me'od. *Me'od* is a common word in the Bible appearing 299 times. But our verse is one of only two verses where it means "might." Here is the only other one.

> *Now before him there was no king like him, who turned to the Lord with all his heart, with all his soul, and with all his might, according to all the Law of Moses; nor after him did there arise like him.* – 2 Kings 23:25

Here King Josiah was praised for his commitment to God, with this verse clearly making reference to our verse in Deuteronomy 6.

With all your "very"?

In *every single one of* the remaining 297 verses where the word *me'od* appears it has only one meaning. *Me'od* is the Hebrew word for "very". This makes its use in our verse even more puzzling. There are numerous words for "strength" or "might" in the Bible. The most common are *ko'ach* (125 times) and *gevurah* (61 times). Again, *me'od* is not even a noun. It is simply the word for "very." Every single time the word "very" appears in the Bible, this is the word that is used.

The first time we see the word *me'od* is in the final verse of Genesis 1, the conclusion of the six days of creation.

> *God saw all that he had made, and it was <u>very</u> good. And there was evening, and there was morning—the sixth day.*
> – Genesis 1:31

In other words, the literal translation of Deuteronomy 6:5 should be,

You shall love the Lord your God with all your heart, and
with all your soul, and with all your very.

Of course, this makes no sense. The word "very" cannot be used this way, neither in Hebrew nor in English. On the other hand, the Bible chose to use this word in this way in a verse that describes the obligation to love God. Had the verse meant only to instruct us that we must love the Lord *with all our might*, a more conventional word for "might" would have been chosen. Clearly the Bible had some other message in mind.

Unusual words contain powerful messages

As I have pointed out elsewhere in this book, whenever the Bible chooses a word that is anomalous or out of place, we must ask ourselves what the Bible is trying to tell us, beyond the simple meaning of the verse. The word *me'odecha* – "your <u>very</u>" - is a perfect example of this phenomenon.

I would like to suggest that this odd word choice contains an important lesson for our relationship to God, and specifically, our love of Him.

Love Him with what is very you

Each of us has unique personality traits. We have abilities that stand out above all others in our natural talent set. In other words, each and every human being has some emotion, trait, or talent in which they can be described as "very." Whatever aspect of who I am that most describes me or exemplifies who I am could be described as my "very."

This verse is telling us that our love of God must be expressed with our "very." Some people are very intelligent. Others are very giving. One person may be very good at organizing people. Another may be very good at standing up against a hostile crowd. Each of us must find his or her "very" and devote it to God. That is the meaning of this cryptic phrase. Love the Lord with all your *me'od*.

Ask yourself, "which trait, strength, or interest is the most me?" What is my <u>very</u>? God gave us our strengths and character traits. He gave us our very. We truly give of ourselves when we devote that part of ourselves back to Him.

Deuteronomy 6:6 – Every Day is Today

These matters that I command you today shall be upon your heart
Today?

Once again, as in many verses in this book we must investigate a word that appears to have no added value to the plain meaning. What would have been missing from the verse had it instead read as follows?

These matters that I command you shall be upon your heart.

What is added by the word "today"? One might suggest that it is necessary to identify exactly which matters are under discussion. The problem with this answer is that the verse already includes the word "these." In other words, we know that the "matters" that are being commanded that must be "upon your heart" are those matters that are being spoken of in this passage. Again, what is added by the word "today"?

An ancient Rabbinic explanation

The Jewish sages from the time of the Second Temple, over 2000 years ago, studied the Bible very carefully. They investigated the meaning of every single word, searching for any lessons that may lie beneath the simple reading. Here is their comment on this verse:

That I command you today: They shall not be in your eyes like an ancient decree that a person is not likely to respect. Rather, they shall be like a new decree that everyone eagerly fulfills. – Sifre, Deuteronomy 6:6

The rabbis noticed that the word "today" in our verse was superfluous. They explained that the message of this word is that we must look upon the word of God every single day as though it was just commanded to us. This is a very important lesson. It has great relevance for our times.

Many people look at the Bible as archaic and out of date. They read the commandments and say, "That may have made sense 3000 years ago when Moses taught them, but not today." It is to this sentiment that our verse is responding. The commandments in the Bible are never "old." They are always relevant and applicable to the times in which we live.

God gave the law, not only to a group of Israelites over 3000 years ago, but to each and every one of us. Every day.

Keep the passion alive

There is another nuance in this teaching from the sages. Notice that the verse does not refer to performance of the commandments. It instructs us to place the commandments *upon our hearts*. Performance of the commandments is a different matter.

It can be difficult to remain passionate about things that we have done all our lives and do on a regular basis. It is easier to get excited about something that is new and unusual. Following the commandments of God throughout our lives can become repetitive. As humans, we can lose that sense of excitement when we follow God's commandments repeatedly. The word "today" in this verse teaches us that we must actively work to keep the passion and "newness" of God's commandments alive within our hearts. We must be excited by them and not allow ourselves to complacently slip into rote lip service type behavior. Every day they must be new again.

We must put in the effort to maintain our passion for doing the will of God. We must never look at His commandments as out of date or irrelevant to our time and our lives. Every day we must renew our commitment to Him and to His word.

Deuteronomy 6:7 – Arming Our Children

And you shall teach them to your children, and you shall speak of them while you are sitting in your house, and while you are walking on the way, and while you are lying down, and while you are rising.

Alert: Too many translations!

Whenever we find a word that is translated differently by various Bible translations, there is a good chance that the Hebrew word in question is worthy of study. This makes sense. If a word is straightforward and easy to translate in context, all Bible translations will be similar. A variety of translations tells us that we must stop and dig deeper.

The first word of our verse is a perfect example of a word that is translated in numerous ways. Here is some of what I found:

> *You shall repeat them*
>
> *You shall teach them diligently*
>
> *You shall impress them*
>
> *You shall rehearse them*
>
> *Recite them*
>
> *You shall inculcate them*

What does the word really mean?

The Hebrew word here is *veshinantam*. We have translated this word as "And you shall teach them." It should not be surprising to find a single Hebrew word translated into five English words. Hebrew uses many prefixes and suffixes which become entire words in English. Here is a breakdown of the word:

ve	And
shinan	teach
ta	you
m	them

The verb root here is ShNN. This verb appears only nine times in the entire Bible. The problem with our verse is that this is the only time that this verb means "teach," "recite," "repeat" or anything we find in the translations of our verse. Everywhere else this verb appears it means "to sharpen."

Here are a few examples:

Hide me from the counsel of the wicked, from the tumult of evildoers, who <u>*sharpen*</u> *[shanenu] their tongues like a sword, aiming their arrows with venomous words.* – Psalm 64:3-4(2:3)

Whose arrows are <u>*sharpened*</u>*, [shenunim] and all their bows bent;* - Isaiah 5:28

⸻ *Not the word for "teach"*

There is no ambiguity regarding the meaning of the root ShNN. It means "to sharpen." If the intent of our verse is only to say, "you shall teach them," the Bible would have used the verb for "teach." As it does in a similar verse in Deuteronomy.

<u>*You shall teach them*</u> *to your children to speak of them while you are sitting in your house, while you are walking on the way, while you are lying, and while you are arising.* – Deuteronomy 11:19

Here the verb root is LMD. This is the Hebrew root meaning teach or learn. It appears over 80 times in the Bible and has this meaning in all of them. To sum up this point: LMD is the verb for "teach." Why didn't the Bible use this word in Deuteronomy 6? Why did it choose a word that means "sharpen" instead?

⸻ *SHNN = Sharpen a weapon*

I mentioned that the root ShNN – sharpen – appears in the Bible eight times in addition to our verse. In seven of these eight verses, what is being sharpened is a weapon, either a sword, an arrow, or the sharpness of the tongue of a snake, an obvious metaphor based on the sharpening of an actual weapon. The last of the eight uses of the root SHNN to refer to a person pierced by a sword or knife (Psalm 73:21).

To sum up: our verse here in Deuteronomy 6 instructs us to teach God's word to our children. Instead of using the Hebrew word for "teach" or "instruct," the Bible uses the word for "sharpen." The Bible specifically chose a word that implies the sharpening of a weapon. In fact, an etymologically accurate translation of this verse could be:

And you shall <u>sharpen them like a weapon</u> to your children, and you shall speak of them while you are sitting in your house, and while you are walking on the way, and while you are lying down, and while you are rising.

Arm your children with faith

This peculiar choice of word must draw our attention to a deeper lesson that lies beneath the surface.

I would like to suggest that the Bible is not only telling us not only that we must educate our children towards faith in God, but what the goal and purpose of that education ought to be. Our goal in educating our children is not only to give them information, but to arm them. They must be able to go out into the world with sharp weapons that can be used to defend their faith and attack falsehood and evil wherever they encounter it.

This passage began with the words "Hear O Israel, the Lord is our God, the Lord is one." Now the Bible is telling us that these words must be sharpened. They must become a weapon that can be skillfully employed as needed by our children as they face the inevitable challenges to their faith. Practically speaking, this verse instructs us to give our children the tools they need to respond.

Challenges to faith may be encountered either in the home or in the outside world. Our children must be armed to meet these challenges and defeat them. They must be sharpened.

Deuteronomy 6:8 – Improving our Vision

You shall bind them as a sign on your arm, they shall be for ornaments between your eyes.

The practice of phylacteries

Practically speaking, this verse commands the donning of phylacteries. This daily practice is still done by all Jewish males to this very day. The phylacteries are boxes made of hardened leather that contain small parchment scrolls inscribed with the words of the four passages in the Bible that mention the commandment to wear them, including this passage, Deuteronomy 6:4-9.

What this means is that every day, a Jewish man begins his day by binding the word of God proclaiming his faith upon his hand and head. Morning prayers are then said while wearing the phylacteries, unless it is a sabbath or festival day. The reason for this is that these are not days of work. We are not engaging in labors of the hand. We are not making efforts to change the world around us on these days. The phylacteries symbolize that our faith and devotion to God guides us as we engage in our daily work in the world.

You shall vs They shall

There is a nuance in this verse that is evident in the English as well as the Hebrew but can easily go unnoticed. The instruction to bind the phylacteries to the arm in the first half of the verse is phrased as a command, "You shall bind them..." But there is no second person command in the second half of the verse. The verse does not say, "you shall place them as ornaments between your eyes." The placement of the phylacteries on the head is not worded as a second-person commandment or instruction. The subject of the statement is the ornaments. The verse seems to be saying that the phylacteries will become "ornaments between your eyes" on their own.

To sum up, the binding of the phylacteries on the arm is stated as a commandment. The subject of the statement is "You."

You shall bind them as a sign on your arm

The binding of the phylacteries on the head is not worded as a commandment. The subject of the statement is "they;" i.e., the phylacteries.

they shall be for ornaments between your eyes

What can we learn from this discrepancy between the two parts of this verse?

How we act vs. How we see

I believe that this linguistic nuance teaches us a psychological lesson about how we live out our faith. When it comes to modifying our behavior, we change ourselves by discipline. We make commitments to change. We habituate ourselves to patterns of behavior through choice and conviction. In time, these changes become second nature. But the decision to act according to the dictates of the word of God is a conscious one that we make.

How we think and see the world, on the other hand, is more difficult to consciously control. One can't simply decide to think differently and immediately inoculate oneself against thoughts and attitudes that are inconsistent with God's truth. Changing how we "see" is a process that takes time and is often the long-term result of choices that we implemented to change our behavior. *As a result* of acting and living differently, we begin to see the world differently as well.

Perhaps this is the lesson of our verse. In addition to the practical commandment to wear phylacteries, the grammar and conjugation of the verse teaches us a lesson about how we become filled with greater consciousness of God.

The arm represents action. The eyes represent how we think understand the world. **You shall bind them as a sign on your arm,** - discipline and modify your behavior. Make decisions to behave in a manner that is consistent with faith in the one God. As a result, **they shall be for ornaments between your eyes.** In other words, if we accomplish the first half of the verse, the second half of the verse will be the result.

If we make conscious choices to govern our behavior by faith in God, the result is that we will begin to see the world through eyes that reflect that faith.

Deuteronomy 6:9 – Private and Public Faith

You shall write them on the doorposts of your house and on your gates.

This commandment mandates the writing of this paragraph, Deuteronomy 6:4-9, as well as Deuteronomy 11:13-21, on a parchment scroll which is then mounted on the doorpost of the home. Deuteronomy 11 is a restatement of this commandment. These two passages are "these words" that the Bible mandates to be written on the doorposts. Jews have continued to practice this Biblical commandment to this day. The common Hebrew name for the scroll that is affixed to the doorframe is *mezuzah*, the Hebrew word for "doorpost" in this verse.

The meaning of "gate" in the Bible

In modern colloquial English, the end of the verse seems somewhat redundant. What is the difference between the "doorposts of your house" and "your gates"? Couldn't the Bible have been more concise and commanded that the *mezuzah* be written on all doorposts. We would have understood that this includes doorposts of the home as well as outer gates.

The truth is that this question is based on a misunderstanding of the what the Bible means when it uses the word "gates." The Hebrew word *shaar* – gate – appears over 300 times in the Bible. It almost never refers to the gate of someone's private property. Rather, in Biblical Hebrew, the word "gate" refers to the entrance to a city, public building, or palace. In fact, there are numerous verses that use the word *shaar* as a synonym for "city." For example:

Remember the Sabbath day by keeping it holy. Six days you shall labor and do all your work, but the seventh day is a sabbath to the Lord your God. On it you shall not do any work, neither you, nor your son or daughter, nor your male or female servant, nor your animals, nor any foreigner residing in your towns. – Exodus 20:8-10

The final word of this passage from the Ten Commandments, is "in your gates." The translators correctly rendered it as "in your towns" as the word "gate" in Biblical Hebrew also means public spaces, towns, and cities. This is probably because all towns in the Ancient Near East were surrounded by protective walls with guarded gates.

To sum up, the word "gates" in the Bible refers not to gates that open onto private property but to public spaces and cities.

Private and public faith

With this in mind, we can easily see the lesson of the end of the verse. Deuteronomy 6:4-9 describes the obligation to love God and to serve Him with wholehearted dedication. Deuteronomy 11:13-21 commands obedience to God's law and the promise of reward, or punishment for disobedience. These are the words that are to be "written on the doorposts of your house and on your gates."

The house is the private domain. The gates are public. The purpose of the words on the doorposts is to continually remind us that our commitment to God must govern our lives in all contexts, private and public alike.

There are many people for whom faith is expressed only outside the home. They attend church or synagogue services at appropriate times. They send their children to religious school. They may even attend classes themselves. But for many, when the service is over and they return home, they leave God at the front door. Even for many people who worship regularly, home life is not permeated with faith. The *mezuzah* on the doorpost of the house is there to remind these people that their relationship with God continues in the home.

For others, the reverse is true. There are many people who profess faith in God and raise their families with values that are consistent with this faith. And yet, they are loath to profess this faith in the public square. They prefer faith to be a private matter. To these people, the commandment to affix a *mezuzah* on the doorpost of the gates, in the public square, sends an important message. Commitment to God is not only a private matter. Biblical faith is meant to govern society, not merely individuals.

The message is clear. Faith in God, love of Him, and commitment to His law are not meant to govern only what goes on in our homes. The covenantal commitment to God must be written on the doorposts of the "gates" as well.

We must show our love of God and commitment to His laws in both our private lives as well as in how we contribute to the greater society. This is the message of the <u>mezuzah</u>.

Proverbs 16:1-3 – Free Will to Surrender to God

To a person belongs the heart's arrangements, but from the Lord is the tongue's reply. All the ways of man are pure in his own eyes, and the Lord is the measurer of spirits. Turn your actions over to the Lord and your thoughts will be set right.

One of the fundamental principles of Biblical faith is that God has granted free will to human beings. Without free will, all our actions are meaningless. There is no basis for reward or punishment; there is neither piety nor wickedness, in the absence of free will. The belief that human beings are responsible for their choices lies at the center of our relationship with God. Without free will, our faith and our service of God are pointless and empty. God empowered us with free will so that we are able to choose Him; and choose good.

At the same time as we steadfastly believe in the doctrine of free will, we also believe in divine providence over earthly affairs. God has a plan. He has a plan for the world, and He has a plan for each and every one of us as individuals. The fact that God has a predetermined plan for us raises an important theological issue regarding the doctrine of free will.

Can free will negate prophecy?

The simplest way to understand this problem is to consider Biblical prophecy. The Bible speaks at great length about God's plan for the future of humanity. As people of Biblical faith, we have no doubt that the Kingdom of God will eventually be established. For anyone who takes the Bible seriously as the inerrant word of God, the future ingathering of Israel to the promised land and the subsequent redemption of humanity are certainties. These are not mere hopes or predictions.

But what about human free will? For example, what if every member of the nation of Israel was to decide to leave the land of Israel permanently? What if the Jews used their free will to undo the ingathering of the exiles, never to return? Is this possible? There are certainly many individual Israeli born Jews who have already made such a choice and now live outside the Holy Land. What if all Jewish citizens of Israel were to make the same free-willed choice? Simply put, do human beings have the ability to undo God's plan through the power of their God-given free will?

The same question can be asked about the effect of one person's decisions on the life of another person. Can my free will choices change the course of someone else's life regardless of what God has planned for them? If the answer is "no", does this mean that my free will is limited? If the answer is "yes," what does that say about God's providential control over the lives of people?

It is this theological quandary that the three verses in Proverbs we are studying come to address.

To a person belongs the heart's arrangements, but from the Lord is the tongue's reply.

The first verse describes the relationship between our own free will and the results of that free will on the outside world. It is true that God has granted us freedom to think and choose whatever we decide. As we explained, without this freedom, our righteousness or lack thereof would be rendered meaningless. At the same time, the results of our free will are in God's hands. In other words, whether or not our free will succeeds in a given situation is out of our hands. But our free will choices, "the hearts arrangements," are our own and we are responsible for them. And lest we think that the results of our choices are limited to actions, our verse reminds us that the utterances of our mouths constitute tangible and measurable results as well. Words have impact just as actions do.

We are judged by our choices, *not by their results.*

All the ways of man are pure in his own eyes, and the Lord is the measurer of spirits.

The second verse warns us of the danger that comes with freedom to make our own choices and judgements. Human beings have a great capacity for self-justification. We rationalize our opinions and choices so that we are comfortable. This, too, is a product of our free will. God granted us the freedom to come to our own conclusions, however twisted or corrupt they may be. We have the freedom to convince ourselves that we are always in the right. But the verse goes on to say that at a deeper level, we know when we are arrogantly declaring ourselves justified even as we are twisting morality and truth. God sees through our self-deception. When we arrogantly use our God-given free will to justify our own corruption, God sees the truth that lies beneath the surface of our conscious rationalizations. He is "the measurer of spirits."

So, what is the solution? How do we protect ourselves from the self-deception that comes with human freedom of thought and choice? How do we assure ourselves that we are being honest and true to what is right and not merely justifying our own self-serving interpretations of reality? To this problem, the third verse in the passage provides the solution.

Turn your actions over to the Lord and your thoughts will be set right.

God did more than just grant us free will. He also gave us instructions. Moreover, He commanded us to serve Him. By serving Him, we liberate ourselves from servitude to ourselves. When I serve myself, I am easily blinded by self-interest. When I serve God, I am forced to constantly ask myself, "Is this what God wants from me?" By turning outward, I disconnect from my own arrogance and selfishness, and I can see truth with Godly eyes.

Jewish tradition teaches that we are called upon to "Make His will, your will." (Chapters of the Fathers) Paradoxically, it is when I use my God-given free will to freely choose to surrender my will to God, that I am truly His servant and am truly free from self-deception. This is the higher freedom of service of God.

Zechriah 8:3 – The City of Truth

So said the Lord : I have returned to Zion, and I will dwell in the midst of Jerusalem; Jerusalem will be called the city of truth; and the mountain of the Lord of Hosts, the holy mountain.

The city of "truth"

This is the only place in the Bible where Jerusalem is called the "city of truth." The Hebrew word for "truth" is *emet*. This word does not only mean "truth" as in, the opposite of falsehood. The word *emet* also means "faithfulness" or "reliability." This is similar to the English usage, for example, when we say that someone is "true" to their word. In other words, they are *faithful* to their promises and commitments. This is especially true when the Bible refers to God as being "true". The intent is not to say that God does not lie. That is a simplistic absurdity. Of course, God tells the truth. Rather, the point is to praise God for the fulfilment of His promises and for being reliable to those who serve Him.

Here are a few examples of the use of the word EMET in reference to God in the Bible.

Draw me out of the net they laid for me; You are my stronghold. Into Your hand I commit my spirit. You have redeemed me, Lord, <u>God of truth</u>. – Psalm 31:5-6 (4-5)

<u>Truth</u> will spring up from the earth as righteousness looks down from heaven; indeed, the Lord will bestow what is good and our land will yield its produce. – Psalm 85:12-13

The Lord has sworn <u>truth</u> to David and will not recant. From the fruit of your loins, I will establish a throne for you. – Psalm 132:11

In all these examples, the word "truth" means that God can be relied on and trusted; that He keeps His promises. Zechariah was prophesying to the Jewish people who were headed into exile that God will keep His promises to the nation of Israel. Zechariah's words in this chapter were intended to reassure the exiles that the covenantal promise of the return to Zion is a certainty; that God will be *true* to His word.

I'd like to suggest another message of this reference to Jerusalem as the "city of truth." It is worth noting that the only time that Jerusalem is referred to in this way is in the context of a prophecy of the end times. Specifically, the opening verses of this prophecy are about the repopulation of Jerusalem with the ingathered exiles of the Jewish people in the future, the ingathering we are experiencing today.

One of the main tools of the enemies of the Jewish people and of the State of Israel is that they lie. More specifically, they lie about Jerusalem. There is no question that there is no city about which more lies are told than Jerusalem.

For example, on December 1, 2021, the United Nations passed a resolution in which denied that there ever was a Temple on the Temple Mount in Jerusalem. The resolution called the site only my its Muslim name. This was not the first UN resolution denying the Jewish connection to Jerusalem. In fact, the official position of the Palestinian Authority, officially Israel's "peace partner," is that there never was a Jewish Temple on the site. The absurdity of this lie need not be explored here. But this lie is only part of the larger lie that is told about Jerusalem, that it is not the historic capitol of the Jewish people.

It's actually quite amazing, with all the abundant archaeological evidence of the Jewish people and their Temple in Jerusalem, these lies are somehow voted on and passed with overwhelming majorities in the United Nations. Is there another city in the world that has more lies about its history declared on the world stage? With this in mind, we might look at Zechariah's depiction of Jerusalem as "the city of truth" ironically. But that's exactly the point.

I believe that this is what Zechariah meant when he said that, in the future, when Jerusalem is once again populated by multitudes of Jews, that Jerusalem will be called "the city of truth." The return of the Jewish people to sovereignty in Jerusalem is a statement about history. Those who deny Jerusalem as the capitol of the Jewish nation-state, deny the truth of history. Those who recognize that Jerusalem is the eternal capitol of the Jewish people assert the truth. Jerusalem has become the litmus test of truth in the world. Jerusalem truly is "the city of truth."

Jerusalem declares God's truth

This was the point of Zechariah's encouraging words to the exiles who had just experienced the destruction of their temple and homeland. Zechariah declared that despite the natural rules of history, God's word would be fulfilled. The evidence of this would be on display for all to see in the rebuilding of Jerusalem in the future.

Jerusalem will become the living expression of God's "truth", His faithfulness to His promises and His power over history.

The rebuilt city of Jerusalem is the greatest testimony to the truth of God's Biblical promises. We must step back from our own narrow view of the world and contemplate the full scope of history. From this broad perspective we see more clearly that Jerusalem has become, once again, the city of truth.

Zechariah 8:4-6 – The Miracle of Normal Life in Jerusalem

So said the Lord of Hosts: Old men and old women will again sit in the squares of Jerusalem, each man with his cane in his hand due to advanced age. The squares of the city will be filled with boys and girls playing in its squares. So said the Lord of Hosts: If it will be wondrous in the eyes of the remnant of this people in those days, will it be wondrous also in My eyes? – the utterance of the Lord of Hosts.

These verses describe a return to normal life in Jerusalem at the time of the ingathering of Israel and the rebuilding of the city.

As a personal note, I live in Israel just outside of Jerusalem. My in-laws used to live in Jerusalem. When my children were young, we would regularly take them to Jerusalem to visit their grandparents. On one of these visits, years ago, we walked together to a large park with a playground a few minutes away from my in-laws' apartment. As we sat by the playground it occurred to me that we were not only witnessing but *fulfilling* this prophecy of Zechariah. Here were the children playing. Sitting a few feet away were the aging grandparents. Zechariah's distant vision of the future was our present-day reality.

What's the great miracle here?

One question that emerges from these verses is why Zechariah refers to this as such a great miracle. Unlike most prophecies, after describing this future scene, we read:

If it will be wondrous in the eyes of the remnant of this people in those days, will it be wondrous also in My eyes?

While this is a wonderful prophecy of the restoration of Israel, there are certainly many far more supernatural and remarkable prophecies in the Bible that are not emphasized in the way that this one is.

Zechariah describes something as simple and normal as elderly men and woman sitting in the streets of Jerusalem while children play there.

This is not what anyone would describe as a supernatural or miraculous occurrence. Why does Zechariah follow this vision with a verse declaring the extreme extraordinary nature of this scene? What is so wondrous about elderly people and children living their lives in Jerusalem?

The miracle of the State of Israel

The return of the Jewish people to their ancestral homeland after almost 2000 years of exile is unprecedented in history. To call it improbable is an understatement. The history of Israel is a miracle by every definition of the word. In fact, it may be the greatest miracle the world has ever seen.

What is the definition of a miracle? Simply put, a miracle is the breaking of the rules of nature for God's purposes. When we think of miracles we tend to think of the sudden instantaneous miracles like the plagues of Egypt. But some miracles take time and perspective to see them. No other nation in history has ever gone into exile for a long time and then returned to its homeland to reconstitute itself as a nation. None. The prediction throughout the Bible that the people of Israel will return after many centuries of exile is not only improbable. It is, historically speaking, impossible. Like water running uphill, the history of the Jewish people breaks the rules of nature.

Miracles are how God reveals Himself in the world. By breaking the rules of nature for His purposes, God shows that He is the master of the world. Only the master of nature can break the rules of nature; for example, to make the Red Sea split or to make water flow from a rock. The same is true of history. History, like nature itself, has rules. Moses prophesied that one nation, chosen by God, will break all the rules of history; that their national history will be unlike any other. Then, when Jewish history unfolds just as Moses said it would, *God's mastery over history* is clear for all to see.

In 1948, the Jewish people created the State of Israel in their ancient homeland. They took possession of their land thousands of years after being exiled from it. Since then, millions of Jews have emigrated to Israel from every corner of the earth. And in the last two decades, Israel has become one of the most powerful and successful economies in the world. Let's look again at that prophecy of Moses.

Even if you have been banished to the most distant land under the heavens, from there the Lord your God will gather you and bring you back. He will bring you to the land that belonged to your ancestors, and you will take possession of it. He will make you more prosperous and numerous than your ancestors. – Deuteronomy 30:3-5

Every detail in this prophecy has been fulfilled in our days. There is no greater proof of the <u>truth</u> of Biblical prophecy and of God's control of history, than the history of the Jewish people and the State of Israel.

This is the answer to our question above. What is so miraculous and supernatural about old men and old women sitting in the rebuilt city of Jerusalem as children play? *Everything* about that scene is miraculous. This is a miracle that took 2000 years of history to create. And unlike the sudden miracles like the Ten Plagues or the splitting of the sea, this miracle is not a brief event that is gone once it has occurred. It is a miracle that continues to develop every day. It is truly *wondrous in our eyes.*

The impossibility of the return of Israel and the rebuilding of Jerusalem is the greatest miracle of history. It is cloaked in normal life. When we take a long-range historical view of God's plan, we see the State of Israel and ingathered people of Israel as truly "wondrous in our eyes."

Psalm 135:21 – Awareness of God starts from the top

Blessed be the Lord from Zion, He who dwells in Jerusalem, Halleluyah. – Psalm 135:21

What blessings does God need?

Does God need to be blessed by us? What are we actually doing when we bless God? I understand what it means to *bless* another person. It usually means either that I am bestowing gifts upon them or that I am offering a prayer for their success and well-being. When we speak of *blessing* someone, we mean that we have something to offer them that will benefit them. Colloquially, someone is *blessed* with wealth or with a particular talent.

For example, when Isaac blessed his sons, Jacob and Esau, he bestowed gifts upon them both in terms of material wealth as well as in the spiritual arena. In this context the word *blessing* indicates material wealth, spiritual gifts, or loftiness of status and power.

For example, the phrase *And He will bless your bread and your water* (Exodus 23:25) likewise refers to the granting of something beneficial by the blesser to the one being blessed.

So, what does it mean to bless God? Are we to understand that when we bless God, we are bestowing something upon Him? The implication that there is some good that we could give God makes no sense. God is complete and perfect in every way. To say that we could bestow anything upon Him implies that there is some way in which He could be improved. Furthermore, as God's creations, we cannot possibly possess anything to give God that does not come from Him to begin with. Obviously, when we talk about *blessing God,* we mean something other than the conventional use of the term.

Blessing = Abundance

The Hebrew word for blessing is *beracha*. The first time that this word - or its verb root - appears in the Torah is on the fifth day of creation.

[God] <u>blessed</u> them [the fish] saying, 'Be fruitful and multiply and fill the water in the seas.' - Genesis 1:22

God told the fish that there would be many of them. *beracha* – "blessing" – refers to *abundance*. God blessed the fish by saying, "May there be a lot of you." More broadly, *blessing* is the actualization of hidden potential for good. For example, two fish, or two people, may have the *potential* to reproduce. This is not a blessing. The *blessing* is the realization of this potential when a child is actually produced.

When we *bless* God, we are not bestowing anything on God. We are attempting to draw out the hidden potential for *more Godliness* in the world. In Judaism every blessing, whether it is over food, prior to the performance of a commandment, or as part of the prayer liturgy, begins with the words *Blessed are You, Lord*. When we say *Blessed are You, Lord...*, we are saying to God, "Let there be *more of You* revealed in this world."

Blessed <u>from</u> Zion

Notice that our verse states that God will be blessed *from* Zion, and that He *dwells in* Jerusalem. What does it mean for God to be blessed *from Zion?*

Interestingly, 7 chapters earlier in the book of Psalms there is a parallel verse where God is the one doing the blessing.

May the Lord <u>bless you from Zion</u>; and may you see the prosperity of Jerusalem all the days of your life. – Psalm 128:5

There are many names for Jerusalem in the Bible. *Zion* and *Jerusalem* are the two most common among them. In these two verses we see that the blessing is *from Zion*. The prosperity that follows is *in Jerusalem*. What is the difference between these names?

Zion vs. Jerusalem

Here is another well-known verse that uses both names.

For from Zion will come forth Torah, and the word of the Lord from Jerusalem. – Isaiah 2:3

While it is true that both Zion and Jerusalem are names for the same city, we can see from these verses that there is a subtle difference in implication when these names are used together.

In the verse we just cited from Isaiah 2, we see that Torah emerges *from Zion*, whereas *the word of the Lord* comes from Jerusalem. What is the difference between these two ways of describing God's word? Isn't Torah just another name for the word of God?

Torah refers specifically to God's law. The word Torah literally means "instruction" and is used by the Bible itself in the context of the commandments given to Israel.

Moses commanded the <u>law</u> – Torah - for us, a heritage of the congregation of Jacob. – Deuteronomy 33:4

I would like to suggest that the name *Zion* refers to the intimate relationship between God and the people of Israel as expressed by observance of the Torah, God's law for Israel. The Torah does not bind the nations of the world. It is the *heritage of the congregation of Israel*. The name, *Jerusalem*, when used in tandem with Zion, refers to the wider universal society that embraces faith in the God of Israel.

Now we can understand the verse in Isaiah. *From Zion will come forth Torah;* as a result of Israel fulfilling their covenantal obligations to God through the commandments, *the word of the Lord* – the message of faith for all of humanity will emerge *from Jerusalem.*

Blessing God - from Zion to the world

This difference between Zion and Jerusalem makes sense in our verse here in Psalms, when we consider the verses leading up to it. Here is our verse in context.

House of Israel, bless the Lord; house of Aaron, bless the Lord. House of Levi, bless the Lord; fearers of the Lord, bless the Lord. Blessed be the Lord from Zion, He who dwells in Jerusalem. Halleluyah. – Psalm 135:19-21

Blessed be the Lord means that there will be an <u>increase</u> in awareness of God. This increase in faith and knowledge of God will emerge *from Zion*, - from the spiritual leadership of Israel as well as those who are deemed "fearers of the Lord", i.e., the spiritual elite from among the nations as well. The result of that blessing, the increase in faith in and awareness of God, will be that God will *dwell in Jerusalem*. In other words, God will be more present and seen amidst the universal community of faith in the God of Israel.

The ultimate purpose of the restoration of Zion and Jerusalem is to bring about a revolution in awareness of God. This revolution will be jointly led by the spiritual elite of the nation of Israel and the Fearers of the Lord from among the nations.

Psalm 147:11 – Everything is a gift from God

The Lord wants those who fear Him, those who long for His kindness.

Psalm 147, leading up to this verse, describes how God controls nature and provides for all the needs of His creation. In that context our verse states that although God looks after the material necessities of all things, His true desire is not merely to sustain a physical animal kingdom and natural order. Rather, God's purpose in all of this is the benefit of those who fear Him.

Fear Him = Desire Blessings?

Our verse indicates that *those who fear the Lord* are *those who long for His kindness*. This is strange. At first glance, fearing God and longing for His kindness are two distinct concepts. Furthermore, the plain meaning of *fearers of the Lord*, is people who are exceedingly pious and of great spiritual depth and integrity. When we think of people who exemplify *fear of the Lord*, we do not imagine people who are longing for God's kindness.

"Those who long for His kindness" brings to mind people who are eagerly awaiting the blessings that God will bestow on them, anticipating their own benefit from their relationship with God. Why would *those who fear Him*, also be defined as *those who long for His kindness*?

Fearers of the Lord Receive His Kindness

Interestingly, this verse is one of many in Psalms that refer to those who *fear the Lord* as those who yearn for or are the recipients of God's kindness. Here are a few examples. (see also Ps. 31:20, 34:10, 111:5, 128:4)

Truly the eye of the Lord is on those who fear Him, on those who long for His kindness. – Psalm 33:18

Rather, as high as the heavens above the earth, so is His kindness great for those who fear Him. – Psalm 103:11

But the <u>kindness</u> of the Lord is forever to <u>those who fear Him</u>, His righteousness for the children's progeny. – Psalm 103:17

In fact, most of the references to *those who fear the Lord* in the Bible mention great reward and kindness that God bestows upon them. Apparently, there is a direct connection between fearing the Lord and being on the receiving end of His kindness.

While it makes sense that those who fear the Lord are *deserving* of God's kindness and blessing, it is still difficult to understand why the fearers of the Lord are those who *long for* and *await* His blessing. We can easily understand why God would grant them this reward. But is someone that is looking forward to God's kindness really expressing piety and spiritual greatness? Is hoping for blessings really a sign of *fear of the Lord?*

What is Kindness?

Psalm 33:18, quoted above, like our verse, says that the fearers of the Lord long for God's *kindness*. But in neither of these verses, nor in any other verse in the Bible, is there any mention of the fearers of the Lord longing for God's *reward, blessing,* or any other word for the good that God bestows upon human beings. In both verses the word used is "kindness." This is significant and it will help us to answer our question, and to fully understand our verse.

The Hebrew word for "kindness" used here is *chesed.* This word has a very specific meaning. *Chesed* is something that is given freely beyond what has been earned or is necessarily deserved. For example, if I work a job for an agreed upon wage and then receive a paycheck for the exact amount that I am owed for the hours that worked, this is not, technically speaking, *kindness.* If, on the other hand, my employer added an extra bonus beyond the wages owed to me, this extra amount is *kindness,* i.e., it is beyond what is earned or deserved by rights.

What is the connection between fear of the Lord and being the recipient of *chesed* – kindness?

What is a Fearer of the Lord?

To understand this, we must ask an even simpler question. What does it mean to be a *fearer of the Lord?* How does one qualify for this specific title? How is a *fearer of the Lord* different from a *lover* of the Lord or one who has *faith* in the Lord?

The answer is found in two other verses in Psalms.

Fortunate are all who fear the Lord, who walk in His ways. - Psalm 128:1

Who is the man who fears the Lord? He will teach him in the way he should choose. - Psalm 25:12

In both these verses *fear of the Lord* is associated with following *God's way*. In other words, *fear of the Lord* means *obedience to His will*. While it is true that those who *love* the Lord may also be obedient, the trait of *absolute obedience* is associated with *fear of the Lord*. To sum up: The *fearers of the Lord* are those who exemplify obedience.

Abraham: The original fearer

Proof that absolute obedience to God's will and the title *fearer of God* go hand in hand takes us all the way back to the first person who was ever described this way. When the angel prevented Abraham from killing Isaac as a sacrifice to God, the angel said,

'Do not lay a hand on the boy', he said. 'Do not do anything to him. Now I know that you are a fearer of God, because you have not withheld from me your son, your only son.' - Genesis 22:12

Bear in mind that the previous eleven chapters in Genesis leading up to this scene are almost entirely about Abraham and his relationship to God. And yet, it is only when he displayed his willingness to sacrifice his son for God that Abraham earned the title *fearer of God*.

This is because to be a *fearer of God* is to be *obedient*. There is no greater example of obedience to the will of God than Abraham's willingness to offer his son Isaac as an offering to God.

What is Obedience?

Now let us return to our verse here in Psalm 147. Those who fear the Lord are obedient to Him, not because God's will makes sense to them. They are not obedient to Him because they hope to earn some great reward for their obedience. This would not be obedience at all. Those who fear the Lord are obedient to Him because they revere God and want to serve Him to the best of their ability. They expect nothing in return. And this is the key point.

There are many people who profess faith in God and who live their lives in accordance with God's expressed will in the Bible who would not qualify as *fearers of the Lord*. This is because they serve God with an expectation of reward. Many people of faith see their relationship with God as a quid pro quo. "If I serve God, He will bless me, protect me, etc." To such people, faith becomes a tool for serving themselves. If God does not fill their wants or needs as they deem appropriate, they wonder if God is not keeping up His end of the arrangement. To these people, any blessings they receive from God are not seen as *chesed* – kindness. These people think that they deserve whatever they are receiving.

A true *fearer of the Lord* knows that he deserves nothing for his obedience to God. While He calls out to God for help and casts his needs upon the Lord in prayer, he expects nothing and takes nothing for granted. A *fearer of the Lord* does not think that he has earned anything. Therefore, when a *fearer of the Lord* looks to God for help, he anticipates only *kindness*; undeserved and unearned. He therefore sees anything and everything that he receives as a generous gift. This attitude leads directly to praise and thanksgiving to the Lord for His blessings. After all, we are much more likely to give praise and thanks for a gift that is undeserved than we are for something that we think is owed to us.

The Lord wants those who fear Him, those who long for His kindness. God wants us to serve Him for no other reason than to serve Him. He wants us to see every blessing as a gift that He has freely bestowed. This is true piety and faith.

We must not take God's gifts for granted and think that He owes us anything for our lives of faith and obedience. We must serve Him for His sake, not ours.

Psalm 147:12 – Praising and Exalting

Exalt the Lord, O Jerusalem; praise your God, O Zion.

This verse, like many others in the book of Psalms, is a seemingly repetitive poetic couplet. The first half of the verse and the second half of the verse appear to be saying the same thing in slightly different words. *Zion* is another name for *Jerusalem*. *Exalt* and *praise* are basically synonyms. Upon closer examination we will find that, while it is true that both phrases are calling upon Jerusalem, or her inhabitants, to praise and exalt God, the subtle differences in syntax reveal a deeper meaning to the verse.

Let us first point out that God is referred to as "your God" in the second phrase. This possessive description of God could have been avoided. The verse could have said,

Exalt the Lord, O Jerusalem; praise God, O Zion.

Why the possessive "your God"?

— Praise vs. Exalt

Praise implies acceptance and awareness of greatness. When I praise something or someone, this means that I am reacting to something that I have witnessed, known, or understood. This is obvious. If someone is praising God, it must mean that he believes in Him.

The Hebrew word root for *exalt* in our verse is ShBCh. This word also means *to raise in value*. To say that something has value means that it matters; that it has an effect. Simply put, *it is worth something*. In other words, *to praise* is to acknowledge greatness that I have witnessed, *to exalt* implies that this greatness has meaning for me; *that I value it beyond the experience of seeing it.*

While *praise* and *exalt* are synonyms, the connotations are different. This difference is in terms of the extent of the integration of the experience. I am arguing that *exalt* is more integrated and more personal than *praise*. To sum up this point, *praise* expresses awareness of greatness, whereas *exalt* expresses that one values that greatness more than before, i.e., it has been raised in value.

Jerusalem vs. Zion

I would like to suggest that our verse makes two subtly different points. Jerusalem represents the built and populated city. Jerusalem is the name that implies the word of God spreading to all peoples and all nations. The name Zion refers to the unique Jewish relationship to the city. This distinction is implied by numerous verses in the Bible. To cite one well-known example,

The law will go out from Zion, and the word of the Lord from Jerusalem.
– Isaiah 2:3

The law – the Torah – is God's covenant with the people of Israel. Only Israel is obligated to live under the Torah. *The word of the Lord*, on the other hand, relates to all people.

Here too, in our verse here in Psalm 147, *Zion* refers to the people of Israel. For this reason, the verse uses the possessive, *your God* with reference to Zion, implying the specific relationship of Israel to God.

The meaning of our verse

Exalt the Lord, O Jerusalem – the rebuilt and repopulated city itself declares the greatness of God and broadcasts His greatness to the world. The multitudes among the nations stream into the city to connect with the God of Israel. The fulfilment of the Biblical promises of the rebuilding of the city raises the value of the Lord in the eyes of all. Those who previously did not believe and had no relationship to Him are now believers who value God for the first time.

Praise your God, O Zion – But for the Jewish people, the children of Israel, whose relationship with him has been forever unchanged there is gratitude and *praise* for the return to their homeland. There is praise of *their* God, the God who looked after them throughout all the generations of exile. There is no raising of value in their eyes, for their faith in Him had never wavered.

The rebuilding of Jerusalem and the ingathering of Israel stand in testimony to the greatness of God. This is a message not only for those who believe in Him from tradition. Those of us who recognize the greatness of what God has done in Jerusalem must use this as tool to raise the value and status of faith in God to others who do not yet know Him.

Isaiah 41:10 – Our Strength and Support from God

Do not fear, as I am with you; do not waver, as I am your God. I have made you firm; indeed I have helped you, even supported you with My righteous right hand.

This verse is part of Isaiah's prophecies of the ingathering of Israel from their dispersion in exile. God reassures the people of Israel that He will remain with them during the ingathering and reconstruction of their nation just as He has always been with them in the exile.

Three phrases

The second half of this verse is composed of three phrases describing God's providence over His people Israel. The order of these three phrases presents a progression of ideas.

1. *I have made you firm*
2. *Indeed I have helped you*
3. *Even supported you*

A number of subtleties are evident in the Hebrew and worthy of note here. First, the Hebrew word for "indeed" in the second phrase is identical to the word for "even" in the third phrase. The word is *af*. "Even" is the more accurate translation in terms of the connotation that *af* brings. The difference between "indeed" and "even" is significant. "Even" implies a progressive relationship to the previous clause, i.e., "not only A, but even B."

With this in mind, we must read this verse as describing three aspects of God providence that progress from one to the next.

I have made you firm

The Hebrew word here is *ematzticha*. The root of this word is one of two common Biblical words for "strength" or "courage," appearing over 40 times in the Bible. Most commonly, this verb is paired with the root *chazak* – strength, for example:

Verses For Zion

Be strong – chizku - and courageous - emtzu. Do not be afraid or terrified because of them, for the Lord your God goes with you; he will never leave you nor forsake you. – Deuteronomy 31:6

Be strong – chazak - and very courageous - ematz. Be careful to obey all the law my servant Moses gave you; do not turn from it to the right or to the left, that you may be successful wherever you go. – Joshua 1:7

The subtle difference between these two Hebrew words is that *chazak* implies physical strength and force. *Ematz* , on the other hand, implies inner strength, courage, and firmness.

Indeed I have helped you

There are different kinds of help. This word for "help" – *ezer* – does not usually connote *help* in the sense of being saved from danger. Rather, it usually, it implies *sharing in a task*. For example, the first time this word appears is in the well-known scene describing the creation of the first woman. God says,

It is not good for Man to be alone. I will make for him a helper – ezer – matching him - Genesis 2:18

There are many other examples in scripture that show that the word *ezer* implies a partner sharing in a joint task. In other words, *ezer*, biblically, does not connote "help" like that of a strong young person "helping" an elderly woman with her groceries, or a doctor "helping" a patient. We might translate it as "partnering", rather than "helping." To further illustrate this point, a common use of this root appears in the Bible referring to armies of other nations joining together to "help" in fighting a battle together as equal partners.

Even supported you

The Hebrew verb here certainly does connote support, as one would support someone who would fall without it. This phrase describes God holding up His people Israel to prevent them from falling during the centuries of exile and persecution.

The progression of the three phrases in this verse is now clear. First, God is described as empowering and emboldening His people. Then, He is described as joining forces with them to assist them in their mission. Finally, He supports them and holds them up when they can not stand on their own.

Why this order?

The order of these phrases is significant. The verse could just as easily have been written in the reverse. It could have said,

I have supported you with My righteous right hand; indeed I have helped you, even made you firm.

Such a progression would have made sense. Not only does God protect His people when they are weak, He even assists them in their mission, and even gives them strength and courage to act on their own. While it might seem at first glance that the verse has identical meaning regardless of which way it is written, I would like to suggest that the order of the verse is deliberate and contains a very important message about God's relationship to Israel.

The Mission of Israel

God chose Israel so that this chosen nation would be the catalyst for the entire world to eventually recognize God's sovereignty over all the earth. This is their mission. But why does God need Israel? God could reveal Himself in overt and powerful ways, with signs and wonders like He did during the Exodus story, and instantaneously compel the entire world to acknowledge Him and believe in Him. Why doesn't He do that?

God does not step in and force Himself on humanity because He wants to give people the opportunity to choose to believe or not. He wants to empower those who have faith to spread knowledge of Him to others. God could solve all our problems in a single moment. The reason that He does not do this is to give us the agency to repair the word ourselves. This is how we serve Him. We act on His behalf; we become extensions and expressions of His will.

Ideally, we are the ones who build God's kingdom for Him. God wants us to do this so that we are His partners and so that we may earn just rewards for our efforts and suffering that we endured along the way. God grants us the opportunity to be His partners and agents for our benefit, not for His.

Priority order

Our verse is written in the order of priority, from most ideal to least. Ideally, God gives us the strength and courage that we need to fulfill our mission. Should we show ourselves to be incapable on our own, God will step in and help us. He will work alongside us and assist us. Lastly, when we are in a weakened state and even under attack by the forces that oppose us, God will then step in and come to our rescue, holding us up and supporting us until we regain the strength to stand on our own.

This lesson is very relevant to Biblical faith in our times. Many people of faith bemoan the fact that we do not experience the explicit miracles and overt divine interventions in history like those in the Bible. We long for another splitting of the Red Sea or Ten Plagues. We want God to swoop down and fix the world with signs and wonders as we stand by and cheer from the sidelines.

But this is not what God wants from us. God wants us to be His agents in this world. There is far more glory to God when we choose to recognize Him and share that faith with others. God wants us to build His kingdom, and He gives us the strength to do it.

We must rejoice and praise God for empowering His people in our times. He supported Israel at their weakest points in the centuries of exile and suffering. He assisted Israel when needed. He empowers Israel to be His light to the nations of the world.

Genesis 32:28 – The Meaning of the name "Israel"

He said: No more shall Jacob be said to be your name; rather, Israel;
for you have striven with God and with men, and you have prevailed.

The night before the encounter with his brother Esau after so many years away, an angel wrestled with Jacob. After Jacob showed his strength and resilience in overcoming the attack, the angel blessed Jacob and gave him a new name – Israel. This verse, spoken by the angel, is the first mention of the name "Israel" in the entire Bible.

"Striven"?

The angel explained the meaning of the name – "*for you have striven with God and with men, and you have prevailed.*" But what exactly does this mean? To understand the deeper meaning of the name "Israel" we must look carefully at the Hebrew.

The operative verb used in the explanation of the new name is translated here as "striven". Other translations have "contended", "struggled", "displayed power", and other related terms. The Hebrew word for "you have striven" is *sarita*. The *ta* suffix means "you have". The verb root is *sar*.

It is fascinating to note that this word appears as a verb only 3 times in the entire Bible. Here, and two more times in a passage from the prophet Hosea that describes events from the life of Jacob.

In the womb he grasped his brother's heel; as a man he <u>struggled</u> with God.
He <u>struggled</u> with the angel and overcame him; he wept and begged for his
favor. – Hosea 12:3-4

In other words, the only 3 times that this verb is used in the entire Bible, it refers to Jacob wrestling with the angel in Genesis 32.

A rare verb, a common noun

While this verb appears only 3 times in the Bible, *sar* as a noun is a very common word, appearing in over 400 verses. Its meaning is always the same. A *sar* is a prince or minister, in the governing sense. It refers to someone who has political or governing power but is not the highest authority. A general of an army in the Bible is called a *sar tzava* (army). A *sar* is subservient to the king. Here is the first example of the word in the Bible.

And when Pharaoh's <u>officials</u> [sarei] saw her, they praised her to Pharaoh, and she was taken into his palace. – Genesis 12:15

To sum up: *Sar*, as a noun is a very common word in the Bible. The verb form of this word appears only 3 times, and only in reference to Jacob. Considering that there is no other context for the use of this verb that can be used for comparison, it is puzzling that the translations render it as "struggle" or "striven." If this is the verb from of the Hebrew word for minister, official, or prince, the common translation here appears to be mistaken.

"Striven" or "Empowered"

Based on the above understanding of the root of this word, I would like to suggest a different translation of our verse. I believe it is a more accurate understanding of what is meant by Jacob's new name, Israel.

He said: No more shall Jacob be said to be your name; rather, Israel; for you have become empowered with God and with men, and you have prevailed.

It is true that Jacob "struggled" and "strived" in his battle with the angel. It is also true that Jacob prayed to God for assistance when Esau approached with an army of 400 men. That said, I do not believe that the name "Israel" refers to the fact that Jacob struggled. It is meant to refer to the effect that this struggle had on him.

Overcoming empowers us

When people face adversity and crisis situations, they often discover heretofore unknown strengths within themselves. When they use these newly discovered strengths effectively to overcome the crisis, they emerge stronger than before. This is the literal meaning of becoming "empowered." A person who has been empowered by an experience, has literally uncovered powers that they did not have before.

Jacob began his life as a quiet "dweller of tents." (Gen. 25:23). His brother Esau was the hunter and warrior. He then lived with Laban as an obedient and hard-working son-in-law, even as he was repeatedly deceived by Laban. He escaped from that situation without ever confronting Laban.

Now, with his brother Esau approaching, Jacob confronted this angel head on. He did not flee. He did not try to avoid the conflict. He prayed to God and engaged in battle. And he won. Jacob proved to himself and to God that he could fight battles and win.

Israel's mission in the world is to defeat evil and to build the kingdom of God on this earth. This mission is not only about faith and ideas. It is also, oftentimes, about actual struggle and battle in the real world facing real dangers. The statement of the angel who changed Jacob's name to Israel teaches us about the inner strength of the nation of Israel.

for you have become empowered with God and with men, and you have prevailed.

Israel is empowered spiritually – *with God* - and physically – *with men* - and prevails.

The mission of Israel and all who share the faith in the God of Israel is to be empowered by our struggles to prevail over evil. God empowers us spiritually and materially to accomplish this task.

Isaiah 11:11 – Beyond Freedom

It shall be on that day that the Lord will continue, setting his hand a second time to acquire the remnant of His people that will remain from Assyria, from Lower Egypt, from Upper Egypt, from Kush, from Elam, from Babylonia, from Hamath and from the islands of the Mediterranean.

Here Isaiah prophecies regarding the redemption and ingathering of the nation of Israel from exile, scattered among the nations of the world. There are Biblical scholars who misunderstand this prophecy as referring to the return to the land of Israel at the end of the Babylonian exile as recounted in the books of Ezrah and Nehemiah.

Not about the return from Babylon

This interpretation is demonstrably incorrect based on a number of textual indications, both in this verse, as well as in the verses that precede it.

For example, the earlier verses in this chapter describe the messianic age; a time when "the earth will be filled with knowledge of the Lord like water covers the sea." (Is. 11:8) This was certainly not the case at the time of the return from the Babylonian exile. At that time, it was only the Jewish people, a tiny nation, who had faith in the God of Israel. Christianity, which was responsible for the future spread of awareness of the God of Israel among the nations of the earth, would not begin for until more than 500 years later. Anyone suggesting that these verses in Isaiah refer to the return from the Babylonian exile must ignore the description of worldwide knowledge of God included in this prophecy.

Furthermore, this verse itself includes further evidence that it cannot be describing the return to the land in the days of Ezra. Notice that the verse refers to "the remnant that will remain" from all these lands. These are the people that God will ingather at this time. The return to the land of Israel at the end of the Babylonian exile was not of a "remnant that remained" in those lands at all. As described in detail in the opening chapters of the book of Ezra, most Jews refused to return and chose to remain in exile. The phrase "the remnant that will remain" implies that those who are left over, the remnant, will be gathered into the land of Israel; not that the majority will remain after a small number return to the land.

Lastly, it was not until the 20th century that the lands listed in this verse saw their large Jewish communities almost completely empty out and come to Israel. Egypt, Syria, Iraq, and Greece are described in this verse. All these lands, and their surrounding areas, had large Jewish communities up until the Second World War. After the war, the "remnant that remained" in these countries made their way, almost entirely, to the land of Israel.

Just in case what I have written in not convincing, let me sum it up this way. If we ask ourselves, which of the two historical time periods is a better fit with the prophecy of Isaiah, the return from Babylon 2500 years ago or the return to Israel in the last century, the answer is clear.

We stand in awe as we witness the fulfilment of so many Biblical promises in our time.

"to acquire the remnant of His people..."

Our verse states that God will "acquire the remnant of His people..." "Acquire" is not a common word to describe the ingathering of Israel. The very next verse uses the more usual verbs "gather" and "assemble."

This is a profound description of our relationship to God. It is reminiscent of a verse in Leviticus.

for the Israelites belong to me as servants. They are my servants, whom I brought out of Egypt. I am the Lord your God. – Leviticus 25:55

We often think of our relationship to God as one of honor, praise, and gratitude. We love Him, worship Him, and fear Him. With all our devotion to God, do we really feel that we are *His*? That he owns us?

Beyond freedom

I would like to suggest that Isaiah chose to use this verb here, precisely because of the context. When we think about the redemption of Israel from centuries of exile and persecution, instinctively we focus on the theme of freedom. After all, what is the Exodus from the slavery of Egypt or the redemption and return of Israel from 2000 years of suffering in exile, if not a great emancipation – from bondage to freedom.

While this is true, we must always remember that the purpose of God's redemption of His people is not for us be free to live our lives according to our own desires. Rather, God redeems us from human masters and governments that are hostile to Godly values so that we will be able to serve Him and build His kingdom.

For this reason, as Isaiah describes the great ingathering of Israel, the redemption from the bondage of exile to the freedom of return to the promised land of Israel, Isaiah reminds us what freedom is really about. Yes, God will bring us out of exile. Yes, He will restore Israel to the Holy Land. But he is "acquiring" His people. They are redeemed so that they may serve Him.

When God saves us from our sufferings and bondage to human masters, He does so not so that we may live lives of our own choosing. God saves us in order to acquire us and make us His servants.

Isaiah 11:12 – A Banner for the Nations

He will raise a banner for the nations, and He will gather the outcasts of Israel; He will assemble the scattered of Judah from the four corners of the earth.

The verse just prior to this described the ingathering of the dispersed of Israel to their homeland. This verse continues that theme. However, the opening phrase of this verse is unclear. Let's look at the two verses together.

It shall be on that day that the Lord will continue, setting his hand a second time to acquire the remnant of His people that will remain from Assyria, from Lower Egypt, from Upper Egypt, from Kush, from Elam, from Babylonia, from Hamath and from the islands of the Mediterranean. He will raise a banner for the nations, and He will gather the outcasts of Israel; He will assemble the scattered of Judah from the four corners of the earth.

"He will raise a banner"?

Every word of these two verses, both before and after the phrase, "He will raise a banner for the nations" describes only the ingathering of the exiles of Israel and Judah. What is the meaning of this phrase? Here is a phrase-by-phrase summary of the verses to illustrate the point.

1. The Lord will continue to acquire His people
2. From Assyria, Egypt, Kush, etc.
3. He will raise a banner for the nations
4. He will gather the outcasts of Israel
5. He will assemble the scattered of Judah

What does "He will raise a banner for the nations" mean? What role does this play in the ingathering of Israel? What is the purpose of this "banner"?

The Hebrew word for "banner" is *nes*. In several passages in the Bible, *nes* is translated as a "sign", while clearly not implying an actual physical banner or flag. Consider these examples. The translations of *nes* are underlined.

The earth opened its mouth and swallowed them along with Korah, whose followers died when the fire devoured the 250 men. And they served as a warning sign. – Numbers 26:10

Raise the signal *to go to Zion! Flee for safety without delay! For I am bringing disaster from the north, even terrible destruction."* – Jeremiah 4:6

From these examples we see that the meaning of *nes* is a signal or sign from which those who witness it are supposed to take instruction. This is also the meaning of *nes* when translated as "banner." The purpose of a banner is to attract the attention of the viewer to whatever the banner signifies.

What is the role of raising a banner for the nations in our verse? What does God want from them? As I mentioned earlier, all the active verbs in these verses describe God gathering the dispersed of Israel. The passage is certainly not saying that the nations are also being gathered, as the verse plainly states that God is gathering the "outcasts of *Israel*" and the "scattered of *Judah*."

Israel's universal mission

To answer this question, we must recall that the mission and purpose of Israel is not Israel itself. Beginning with God's call to Abraham to bring blessing to all the families of the earth (Gen. 12), to the designation of Israel as "a kingdom of priests", with the mission of ministering to the world, Israel's purpose is to bring knowledge of God to all humanity on the face of the earth. Israel's particularistic history is meant to serve a universalistic purpose.

God chose Israel so that He could reveal Himself to the world through them. The miraculous survival over 2000 years of exile and the rebirth of Israel as a nation in our times is a great revelation of God. Through the story of Jewish history, the whole world can see that God keeps His promises. Precisely due to the impossibility of Jewish survival as a tiny percentage of the world's population, scattered and persecuted for centuries, we are able to see the hand of God in history.

This is the meaning of the phrase "He will raise a banner (a sign) for the nations" in our verse.

God will gather in His nation from the four corners of the earth. He will bring them into the land. But most importantly, He will make sure that the nations of the world see and understand what He is doing. "He will raise a banner for the nations."

This verse is a reminder to all people of faith to pay close attention to the history of Israel. It is through Israel that God shows us all that He is in control and that He keeps His promises.

God uses the miraculous history of Israel and the fulfilment of Biblical prophecies in our times to reveal Himself to the entire world. We must pay attention to the signs that God provides for us.

Ezekiel 37:21 – Unity as a Prerequisite for Redemption

Then say to them, 'Thus says the Lord God: "Surely I will take the children of Israel from among the nations, wherever they have gone, and will gather them from every side and bring them into their own land;

This verse in Ezekiel is taken from one of the longest and most elaborate prophecies of the redemption and ingathering of Israel.

"Gather"

What makes this verse particularly interesting is the three verbs used to describe what God will do.

1. I will **take** them from among the nations
2. and will **gather** them from every side
3. and **bring** them into their own land

The Hebrew word in the second of these three phrases, translated as "will gather" is *vekibatzti*, "I will gather." The verb root KBTz is quite common, appearing over one hundred times in the Bible. This verb means to gather people or objects things together into one place. Here are a few examples:

And you shall gather all its plunder into the middle of the street, and completely burn with fire the city and all its plunder,- Deuteronomy 13:17

Gather together and hear, you sons of Jacob, And listen to Israel your father. – Genesis 49:2

Therefore, thus says the Lord God: 'Because you have all become dross, therefore behold, I will gather you into the midst of Jerusalem. – Ezekiel 22:19

Gather before Bring?

What makes this verb interesting in our verse is the order of the three phrases in the verse. Since this verb means to gather things together in one place, it is strange that this phrase appears before the third phrase, "and bring them into their own land." After all, the people of Israel, scattered in exile to all corners of the earth, were not gathered together in one place until they entered the land. On the contrary, they came back to the land from every direction. It would make more sense for the verse to describe the return to the land before using this word, which implies that they are being brought together in one place.

I'd like to suggest that there is a lesson in this order. The verses that precede ours describe the unification of the tribes of Israel into one nation again. This point is then emphasized in the verse immediately following ours. Clearly, the theme of this entire passage in Ezekiel is not only the return from exile, but more importantly, the rebuilding of the unity of the nation of Israel.

Then say to them, 'Thus says the Lord God: "Surely I will take the children of Israel from among the nations, wherever they have gone, and will gather them from every side and bring them into their own land; and I will make them one nation in the land, on the mountains of Israel; and one king shall be king over them all; they shall no longer be two nations, nor shall they ever be divided into two kingdoms again. – Ezekiel 37:21-22

A higher unity

By placing the "gathering" or unifying of Israel into one nation before the reentry to the land of Israel, the prophet is teaching us an important lesson. The unity of most nations is a function of the naturally shared concerns among people who live in the same place. People of a city or state must work together to have a safe and productive society. Without some measure of unity, there would be no law, no infrastructure, no safety. But this kind of unity is the result of people living in the same place.

The unity of the nation of Israel must be different. Their unity cannot be merely a result of the shared concerns that come with sharing a land with each other. They must be unified in faith, purpose, and identity as a prerequisite to acquiring the land. In fact, Jewish sources from the late 2nd Temple period stress the fact that there was great disunity and in-fighting within the Jewish people in the generation leading to the destruction of the temple and the beginning of the long exile. So too, the redemption from exile requires a return to unity of purpose, of mission, and of faith.

By placing the "gathering" of Israel before the entry to the land, this verse in Ezekiel teaches us that the unity of Israel must be in place in order for us to merit the promised land.

The unity of people of faith must be more than a practical function of their shared worldly needs. Unity of purpose and mission are essential if we are to build the kingdom of God.

Ezekiel 11:17 – Taking the Exile out of the Jews

Yet say: Thus said the Lord God: I will gather you from the peoples and assemble you out of the countries where you have been scattered, and I will give you the Land of Israel.

A restatement of other prophecies?

At first glance, this verse is like many others that foretell the ingathering of the nation of Israel from their exile, scattered across the world. For example, we first see this prophecy in Deuteronomy 30.

The Lord your God will bring you back from captivity, and have compassion on you, and gather you again from all the nations where the Lord your God has scattered you. If any of you are driven out to the farthest parts under heaven, from there the Lord your God will gather you, and from there He will bring you. Then the Lord your God will bring you to the land which your fathers possessed, and you shall possess it. He will prosper you and multiply you more than your fathers. – Deuteronomy 30:3-5

Or another verse from Ezekiel discussed in this book:

Then say to them, 'Thus says the Lord God: "Surely I will take the children of Israel from among the nations, wherever they have gone, and will gather them from every side and bring them into their own land; - Ezekiel 37:21

But a more careful reading of this verse reveals that there is a unique lesson here, beyond a simple restatement of the prophecy of the ingathering of Israel.

Peoples vs. Lands

Our verse states that God will do 3 things:

1. Gather you from the peoples
2. Assemble you out of the countries
3. Give you the land of Israel

The first two of these three promises appear to be identical, essentially repeating the same idea. After all, what is the difference between gathering the exiles of Israel from "the peoples," and assembling them from "the countries" where they are scattered in exile?

Let's take a closer look at these two phrases. In the first, God will gather the exiles of Israel from the "peoples," *amim* in Hebrew. *Amim* are peoples or nations. But in the second phrase, God will assemble them from the "countries." The Hebrew for "countries" is *aratzot*, which literally translates as "lands."

Jews identify with the exile

The 2000 year exile of the Jewish people, scattered across the globe, had many different aspects to it. The Jewish people were not only physically separated from the land of Israel, but they were also living for centuries in foreign cultures and societies. Over these many centuries Jews became part of the nations wherever they lived. Of course, in many places and times, the Jews were persecuted and denied full rights. But for most of this history, in most places and times, Jews lived in relative peace, fully participating as members of these nations. Even today, the millions of Jews who live in the United States, for example, very much identify as American Jews. They are culturally American, are often quite patriotic citizens, and usually feel more at home in American society than they would in Israel. The same is true for Jews from every other country in the world over the course of the past 2000 years.

The return of the Jewish people from their exile is not defined only by the physical return to the land of Israel and the forming of a government of a Jewish state there. The end of the exile is also means the end of the national identification of Jews in exile with their host countries. As a popular Jewish expression goes, "It's easier to take a Jew out of exile, than it is to take the exile out of a Jew."

Redemption of Jewish identity

Our verse describes these two different aspects of the return of the Jewish people from exile. First, there must be an awakening of Jewish national identity. There can be no ingathering of the exiles of Israel so long as Jews see themselves as fully integrated members of other nations.

Ezekiel is describing the process of the Jewish people rediscovering their national identity, seeing themselves as a Jewish nation, rather than as Americans, French, or Russian people of the Jewish faith. This is what is meant by God gathering the people of Israel "from the _peoples_." In other words, this is the emergence of the Jew from the exile identity, no longer seeing himself as part of "the peoples."

The second phrase in our verse refers to the physical exodus from the lands of the exile. This phase comes second because without the first stage, the development of Jewish national identity, Jews would not even realize that they are in exile at all. Why would they ever emigrate to Israel if they feel fully at home among the nations?

Three stages of redemption

To sum up: Our verse describes a 3-stage process in the redemption of Israel.

1.   Disconnecting from national identification with "the peoples" in which the exiled Jews live
2.   Leaving those lands behind
3.   Taking possession of the land of Israel

We live in a time when the nation of Israel has been restored. Millions of Jews have left their host nations and forged a reborn national identity in Israel. But there are still millions who choose to remain in the exile. Most have no intention of leaving. They fully identify with the nationalities of the peoples among whom they are exiled. As I mentioned above, these Jews would not even describe themselves as living in exile at all.

We pray for the awakening of all Jews to rediscover their identity as members of the nation of Israel, leading them home to the only Jewish homeland.

Amos 9:14-15 – Restoring Israel, Restoring God

I will restore the fortunes of my people and they will rebuild the desolate cities, and they will inhabit them; they will plant vineyards and drink their wine; they will till gardens and eat their fruits. I will plant them upon their land, and they will not be uprooted from their land that I gave them, said the Lord your God.

It is impossible to read these verses at our time in history without reflecting on the events that have occurred in Israel over the last century. The modern state of Israel has literally returned to desolate cities, rebuilt and inhabited them; planted wine-producing vineyards, and created a flourishing agricultural industry.

Fortunes or Captives

The opening words of this passage, *ve'shavti et shevut* - "I will restore the fortunes," are difficult to translate precisely. In fact, a look at dozens of translations of this verse reveals that there is an almost even split among translators between two options.

Option #1:   *I will restore the fortunes*

Option #2   *I will return the exiles/captives*

At issue is the meaning of the second word, *shevut*. The first word, *ve'shavti*, means "I will return" or "I will restore," which are the same word, with slightly differing meaning depending on context. We will deal with this word soon.

I believe the translation of *shevut* as "captives" or "returning exiles" is imprecise, if not incorrect. Allow me to explain. The word *shevut* appears in 26 verses in the Bible. 20 of these refer to the restoration of the nation of Israel. Now certainly the restoration of Israel involves large numbers returning from "captivity" and "exile." But consider the following use of *shevut*.

"The Lord restored the fortunes – shav et shevut - of Job when he prayed for his friends. And the Lord added to Job double of all that he had before."
– Job 42:10

This verse describes God restoring Job's possessions and family situation at the end of the book, after his great suffering. The phrase *shav et shevut* is identical to the phrase here in our verse in Amos 9. Clearly, there were neither captives nor exiles returning to Job.

In another use of *shevut*, Ezekiel, is describing the destruction and future restoration of the cities of Sodom and Samaria. The descriptions of the destruction of these cities make no mention of any exile. And yet,

I will restore their fortunes, the fortunes – [shevut] of Sodom and her daughters and the fortunes of Samaria and her daughters, and your fortunes along with them. – Ezekiel 16:53

The word "daughters" here does not refer to people. This Hebrew word *banot*, also refers to suburbs or secondary towns that surround a larger city. The subject is the future restoration of the destroyed cities of Samaria and Sodom in the redemptive era. While it is true that the inhabitants of Samaria were sent into exile along with the rest of Israel, Sodom was never sent into exile. The people of Sodom, as we know from the story in Genesis 19, were wiped out due to their wicked, sinful behavior. Ezekiel is using the restoration of Sodom as a paradigm of God's full forgiveness of Israel and humanity in the future. To translate *shevut* as "captives" or "exiles" here would make the Sodom imagery incoherent.

The Hebrew word for "captive" is *shavui*; "captivity" is *shevi*. On the other hand, the verb root ShOV means "return" or "restore." This is the basis for the disagreement about the meaning of *shevut*. Without getting too far into the weeds of Hebrew grammar, the word *shevut*, as a form of the root ShOV would translate best as, "the state of being fully restored."

To sum this up, the opening phrase of our verses in Amos 9, *ve'shavti et shevut ami*, are most accurately translated as "I will fully restore my people to their original state."

God's promise here, and elsewhere in the Bible, is not only to redeem Israel from exile, but to fully restore them. Why does this matter? Think about it. Full restoration means that there is no lasting damage, no permanent blemish in that which has been restored. The pain and suffering of the exile are completely erased. That is what God promises in these verses.

— *Who is being restored?*

This brings us to the second issue with the opening phrase of our verses, the first word in the verse, *Veshavti* – I will restore / return.

I mentioned earlier that the word *shevut* appears 26 times in the Bible. Every single time *shevut* appears in the Bible, God is mentioned as the one who does the "restoring/returning." The words "I will restore/return" or "He will restore/return" always accompany the word *shevut*. However, the Hebrew word that means "I will restore/return" is not always the same. And the difference is quite significant in the original Hebrew, while completely undetectable in the English. Allow me to explain.

In Hebrew grammar, there is a causative form of verb conjugation that does not exist in English. Take the following two sentences:

I will return home this evening.

I will return the book that I borrowed.

The word "return" has two different meanings. In the first sentence, the person who is speaking *is returning*. In the second sentence, the book is *being returned by* the person who is speaking. The second sentence uses the word "return" as a causative verb. The person speaking is *causing* the book to be returned. "Return" is something being done to the book. But in the first sentence the person speaking is, themselves, returning.

In Hebrew these are not the same word even though they share a root. There are innumerable examples of this phenomenon in Hebrew to English translation.

But here's where things get interesting. In 17 of the 26 instances of *shevut* in the Bible including here in Amos, the verb used to describe what God will do is "restore/return" in the non-causative form. In the other 9 appearances of *shevut*, the verb is, in fact, causative. Consider these two verses:

I will restore the fortunes of Judah and the fortunes of Israel, and I will build them as at first. – Jeremiah 33:7

For behold days are coming – the utterance of the Lord – and I will restore the fortunes of My people Israel and Judah, says the Lord, and I will restore them to the land that I gave to their fathers, and they will take possession of it. – Jeremiah 30:3

The word for "I will restore" in Jeremiah 33 is *ve'hashivoti*. This is the causative conjugation, meaning that the fortunes of Judah and of Israel are being restored by God. He is restoring them. This makes sense.

But in Jeremiah 30:7, the first "I will restore" is *ve'shavti* – the non-causative. The second "I will restore" in this verse is then back to the causative, *ve'hashivoti*. The key here is to understand the two Hebrew words that are both translated as "I will restore."

Ve'shavti   I will restore (myself)   "direct" conjugation

Ve'hashivoti   I will restore (something else)   causative conjugation

Are you confused? Let's sum this up. Across the 26 instances of "fortunes" being "restored" by God in the Bible, there are two words that are translated as "I will restore." The direct conjugation is used for 17 of these. In the other 9 the causative conjugation is used.

Now, let's be clear. *In all 26 instances*, we should expect the causative conjugation. After all, in all these verses God is restoring something to its original full state. The non-causative conjugation, implying that God is restoring Himself, appears incorrect. God Himself is not returning or being restored.

But perhaps this is exactly the point.

Only God fully restores

I mentioned that in every one of the 26 times that *shevut* appears, God is restoring something to its full, complete state. Think about that. In not a single verse in the entire Bible is there an example of a human being restoring something to its original full state. There is a powerful message here. God, and only God, is able to fully restore something that has been lost or broken. *Shevut* – the state of being fully restored, can only be accomplished by God.

The second point is that the direct, non-causative conjugation seems to imply that God Himself is being returned or restored as He restores others. There is an important theological idea here. When God restores something – Job's life, the nation of Israel, the other nations mentioned in some of these verses, etc – God Himself is "restored" as well.

God is perfect. He is perfection. All imperfections and brokenness in the world are the result of human iniquity and error. And yet, the flaws in the world that we yearn to fix are, so to speak, flaws in God's world. God Himself, as it were, appears flawed or imperfect when the world itself is flawed and imperfect. When the broken parts of the world are restored, God, so to speak, is restored as well.

Let me put this another way. Many people lose faith because they look at the world and see all that is broken. They see the wicked succeeding, Israel in exile, disease and suffering, and a host of other problems and say, "Where is God?" They don't see God because of the imperfections. The more perfected the world becomes, the more visible God is to us. The restoration of all that is lost or broken does not only restore those nations or people, it restores God as well.

Only God has the ability to fully restore Israel and world. And as He restores us, we see Him more clearly. His restoration of our world restores our awareness of Him.

Genesis 17:7-8 – The Eternally Renewed Covenant

I will establish My covenant between me and you and your descendants after you throughout their generations for an eternal covenant to be your God and for your descendants after you. I will give to you and to your descendants after you the land of your residence, the entire land of Canaan, for an eternal portion.

This text, part of the covenant of circumcision, is the fourth time in Genesis that God promised the land to Abraham and his descendants. Here are the first three:

The Lord appeared to Abram and said: To your descendants I will give this land. He built an altar there to the Lord who had appeared to him. – Genesis 12:7

The Lord said to Abram after Lot parted from him: Raise now your eyes and look from the place where you are, northward, southward, eastward, and westward; for all the land that you see I will give to you and to your descendants forever. – Genesis 13:14-15

On that day, the Lord established a covenant with Abram saying: To your descendants I have given this land, from the river of Egypt until the great river, the Euphrates River. – Genesis 16:18

"After you"

In each of these three prior instances of God's promise to Abram, God promised the land to Abram's descendants. But then here in Genesis 17, God's promise to Abraham includes an additional word each time his descendants are mentioned. Here are our verses again:

I will establish My covenant between me and you and your descendants after you throughout their generations for an eternal covenant to be your God and for your descendants after you. I will give to you and to your descendants after you the land of your residence, the entire land of Canaan, for an eternal portion. – Genesis 17:7-8

In Hebrew, the word *acharecha* – "after you" – appears each time Abraham's descendants are mentioned here in the covenant of Genesis 17. And it doesn't stop with these two verses. Here are the next 2 verses that follow:

God said to Abraham: And you, you shall observe My covenant; you and your descendants after you throughout their generations. This is My covenant that you shall observe, between Me and you and between your descendants after you: circumcise every male among you. – Genesis 17:9-10

Five times across these four verses, God refers to Abraham's descendants. And all five include the word *acharecha* – "after you" – an additional word that never appears in any of the other times that God promised the land to Abraham and his descendants.

Furthermore, the word *acharecha* – "after you" – does not appear to serve any purpose. Just try reading these verses without the words "after you." What is added by this word? Descendants are always "after you."

"Between"

There is another nuance in the Hebrew syntax of the first of our verses that is not evident from the English translations.

In Biblical Hebrew, when there is a covenant between two parties, the word for "between" is repeated for each party to the covenant. Here's another example from the book of Genesis:

I will remember My covenant that his between Me and you and every living soul of all flesh, and the water shall not become a flood anymore to destroy all flesh. – Genesis 9:15

The words "between Me and you and every living soul of all flesh," if translated word for word from Hebrew would read: "<u>between</u> me and <u>between</u> you, and <u>between</u> every living soul of all flesh." In this covenant, God was promising not only to humans, through Noah, but also to the animal kingdom, that He would never bring another flood.

Here's how our verse would look if we included every "between" where it appears in the Hebrew.

I will establish My covenant between Me and between you and between your descendants after you throughout their generations for an eternal covenant to be your God and for your descendants after you.

Why does this matter?

To whom did God promise the land of Israel? The most straightforward answer is that God promised to the land to Abram. That promise would then be inherited by all the generations of Abraham's descendants after him. In other words, the land of Israel belongs to the nation of Israel because we are the descendants of Abraham and have thus inherited his rights to the land. Our right of ownership of the land is an extension of the promise made to Abraham. It is a right of ownership based solely on ancestry and familial inheritance. This is the plain meaning of the first time God promised the land to Abram.

On that day, the Lord established a covenant <u>with Abram</u> saying: To your descendants I have given this land, from the river of Egypt until the great river, the Euphrates River. – Genesis 16:18

Notice that here, the covenantal promise is only with Abram. It is worth noting that in this land promise God says that he has already <u>given</u> the land to Abram's descendants. In other words, God gave the land to Abram, and as a result of that promise, the land already belongs to Abram's descendants.

But here in Genesis 17, God makes a covenant "between Me and you and your descendants after you." The covenant is not only with Abraham. The land promise to Abraham's descendants forever is not only an extension of the promise to Abraham. The ownership claim of the Jewish people to the land is not merely the ancestral claim of inheritance. Here the covenant of land is not only between God and Abraham. The covenant is also, independently, between God and Abraham's descendants.

Let's now look again at the verses of this covenant:

I will establish My covenant between me and you and your descendants after you throughout their generations for an eternal covenant to be your God and for your descendants after you. I will give to you and to your descendants after you the land of your residence, the entire land of Canaan, for an eternal portion. God said to Abraham: And you, you shall observe My covenant; you and your descendants after you throughout their generations. This is My covenant that you shall observe, between Me and you and between your descendants after you: circumcise every male among you. – Genesis 17:7-10

Here, God made a covenant with Abraham. But He also made a covenant with Abraham's descendants. The condition of this covenant is that all males must be circumcised. By carrying out their side of the covenant with God, i.e. circumcision, the descendants of Abraham *themselves* merit the land.

According to this covenant, the nation of Israel's claim to the land of Israel is not based on ancestry and inheritance. *It is based on their own obedience to God.*

Now we can understand why the word *acharecha* – "after you" – was repeatedly inserted into this covenant. God was saying to Abraham, that even though this covenant is binding on him and his descendants, the future claim to the land will not be merely an inherited extension of the covenant made between God and Abraham. Each and every Jew, for generations to come, "after you" will enter into this covenant directly with God.

While our spiritual legacy is passed on to us from earlier generations, each and every one of us is responsible to create our own covenant with God, our own independent relationship that justifies His providence in our lives.

Ezekiel 37:11 – Back from the Dead

He said to me: Son of man, these bones are the entire house of Israel. Behold, they say: Our bones have dried up, and our hope has been lost; we have been excised.

In one of the most memorable and powerful prophecies of the revival of the nation of Israel, God shows Ezekiel a vision of dried bones. Not only are these bones dead, but they are also *dried*. In other words, they lack all moisture and vitality. All hope for renewal is lost.

Because we are fortunate enough to live in a time when the nation of Israel has been reborn, it is easy to lose perspective regarding the length and extent of the exile to which the Jewish people were subjected. The chances of the Jewish people returning to our homeland and becoming "more numerous and more prosperous than our ancestors," (Deut. 30:4) were miniscule to the point of absurdity.

Luther's sarcastic remark

I am reminded of a fascinating quote from Martin Luther, who initiated and led the Protestant Reformation, the mass movement of Christians away from the Catholic church in the early 16th century. After Luther had translated the Bible into German and Christians began to read it for themselves, many Christians began to take on practices from the Biblical law of Moses. These Christians were reading the entire Bible. Prior to Luther's translation, most Christians had not read the Bible. They were largely unaware of the stories and legal portions of the Hebrew Bible, portions that had been deliberately ignored and distorted by the church leadership.

With their newfound freedom from the doctrines of the Catholic church, these Christians read about the covenant of Israel and the laws of the five books of Moses and wanted to practice them. Luther fought hard against this movement, pushing these Christian "Judaizers" to abandon the practice of the law.

In his attempt to discourage this mimicking of Jewish practice among

Christians, Luther wrote extensively about the idea that God's covenant with the Jews was no longer in effect. God had abandoned the Jews. They would never be reconstituted as a nation in their homeland. Therefore, there is no reason to pay any mind to the covenant of the law. In one remarkable quote, Luther wrote:

"Let them go to the Land and to Jerusalem, build the Temple, raise up the priesthood, principality and Moses with his Law so that they again become Jews and possess the Land. If that happened they should soon see us on their heels and also become Jews." - (Heiko Augustinus Oberman, Wurzeln des Antisemitismus. Christenangst und Judenplage im Zeitalter von Humanismus und Reformation (Berlin: Severin und Siedler, 2. Auflage 1981), footnote 137)

We need not speculate about whether Luther truly intended to become Jewish, had the Jewish people returned to their land in his time. And that is exactly the point. From Luther's perspective in the early 16th century, the return of the Jews to the land of Israel and their rebirth as a nation was absurd to the point of being impossible.

Luther made sense at the time

Before we shake our heads with disdain at Luther for thinking this way, we should bear in mind that Martin Luther was a person of intense Biblical faith. This was not some atheist hyper-rationalist. We should humbly admit that anyone alive in the 16th century would have looked at the state of the Jewish people and arrived at the same conclusion. After all, the Jews had been scattered to the ends of earth, powerless and impoverished, for over 1500 years at that point. There was no reason to believe that the Christian doctrine that asserted that God no longer considered the Jews to be His chosen people was incorrect.

For all intents and purposes, the hope of the revival of the Jewish people as a nation in their land was dead. It was obvious that it was never going to happen.

Dry bones = impossible to revive

This is the meaning of the prophecy of Ezekiel.

It is worth noting that the "dry bones" prophecy in this chapter of Ezekiel begins with God bringing Ezekiel to a valley that was filled with bones. Notice that God did not tell Ezekiel to dig up bones from a grave. They were lying out in the open in the valley.

In other words, the "death" of the hopes of the nation of Israel was not some hidden matter. It was plain for all to see. Anyone alive for most of the past 2000 years would have asserted, just as Martin Luther did, that the revival of the nation of Israel was simply impossible and never going to happen.

With this in mind, the fact that the Jews never lost faith, but stubbornly clung to the promises of God, believing all the time that eventually He would lead them back to their homeland, is astounding. If we take a moment to think about it, the faith of the Jews that they would one day be revived as a nation is perhaps the greatest miracle of all.

The "impossibility" of the rebirth of the nation of Israel after so many centuries of exile and dispersion causes us to marvel at the faith of the Jews. Their confidence in the promises of God is a message to us all. Are there still promises of God in the Bible that we think are impossible and will never be fulfilled?

Deuteronomy 28:1 – Heeding God's Voice

It shall be if you shall heed the voice of the Lord your God to take care to perform all His commandments that I am commanding you today, the Lord your God will place you uppermost above all the nations of the earth.

No Extra Words

This verse introduces the promise of blessings of reward to the nation of Israel should they be obedient to God's covenant of law.

We have mentioned many times that the Bible contains no extra words. Every phrase, every word, matters. A good rule of thumb for reading the Bible carefully is this: If you could omit a word or phrase from the text without losing any of the apparent meaning of the verse, the words that seem to be extra must be carefully studied. This makes sense. If every word in the Bible is necessary, it follows that those words or phrases that seem at first glance to be unnecessary must be studied. It is precisely the fact that a word appears to add nothing significant to the text that must make us question why it was included.

Heed the voice?

This verse is a prime example of this phenomenon. The intent of the verse is simple enough to understand. If we are obedient in performing all the commandments, God will bless us with great status among the nations. The problem with this understanding of the verse is that it leaves us with words that appear unnecessary. The verse could just as easily have been written as follows:

It shall be if you shall take care to perform all the commandments the Lord your God has commanded you, He will place you uppermost above all the nations of the earth.

Same idea, right? In this paraphrase of our verse, I omitted two phrases. Here's the actual verse:

It shall be if you shall heed the voice of the Lord your God to take care to perform all His commandments that I am commanding you today, the Lord your God will place you uppermost above all the nations of the earth.

What does it mean to "heed the voice of the Lord your God,"? How is this any different from the obedience demonstrated by taking care to perform all God's commandments? Furthermore, what is added to the message of this verse by the words, "that I am commanding you today"? Does this verse refer only to commandments given on that specific day?

Fulfilling the Spirit of the Law

Based on these questions, I would like to suggest that this verse describes an attitude towards obedience to God's law, in addition to the fulfillment of the commandments themselves.

To listen to God's voice means something much more than mere performance of the commandments. Imagine an instruction given to you by a person of authority. It could be a parent, a boss, or a military officer. Besides the content of the instruction or command, there is also the "voice" of the command. The tone of voice with which the command is spoken tells us a great deal about the intent of the command. When we listen to the *voice*, we get a sense of the urgency and meaning of the command. The better we understand the commander, the more we are able to improvise and carry out the full intent of the command, even if the circumstances change and we need to innovate. In short, the "voice" of the command reveals the intent of the commander beyond the mere content of the commandment.

It's not enough for us to simply obey God's command. This verse teaches us that we must go beyond mere fulfilment of the details of the command in question. We must fulfil God's commandments while also listening to his "voice." What did God intend for us to accomplish with these commands? What is the purpose of the command? How can I fulfil God's will in the best possible way so that my actions have the maximum effect? Are there things that I should be doing that add to God's goals for the world that may not have been explicitly stated as part of the commandments?

This is what it means to listen to God's voice when fulfilling His commandments.

Perhaps this is also what is meant by the words "that I am commanding you today." As we stated, the vast majority of the commandments were not commanded on that day. I'd like to suggest that this phrase too, describes the attitude that we are meant to bring to our obedience.

Imagine that God commanded you to do a specific act today. Imagine your excitement and the sense of urgency you would feel. The Bible is telling us that if we are truly listening to the "voice" of God, we will feel a sense of importance and urgency, as though we were commanded today, in every way that we serve Him.

When the Bible says we must heed the "voice" of God, we are told that we must probe the meaning of the commandments and endeavor to fulfil the spirit and letter of God's law in the best possible way.

Deuteronomy 28:1-2 – The Admiration of the Nations

It shall be if you shall heed the voice of the Lord your God to take care to perform all His commandments that I am commanding you today, the Lord your God will place you uppermost over all the nations of the earth. All these blessings will come upon you, and reach you, if you shall heed the voice of the Lord your God.

In the previous teaching we explored the meaning of the words "if you shall heed the voice of the Lord your God." This phrase appears twice in these two verses. Now we will examine the meaning of the repetition of this phrase in verse 2.

Does Israel seek the admiration of the Nations?

These verses introduce a series of blessings that God will bestow on the people of Israel. At first glance, the verses are stating that as a reward for our obedience to the commandments of the Torah, God will elevate our status above all other nations. The question that comes to mind is, "Do we want this?" Do the Jewish people harbor some desire to be rulers of the earth, dominating all other nations? Do we seek the admiration of others? In other words, these verses appear to be promising some kind of Israelite-supremacy. Is this the goal of God's covenant? Is this the proper motivation for obedience to God's commandments?

This verse brings to mind another verse in Deuteronomy that seems to present a similar message.

You shall observe and you shall perform, as this [fulfilment of the Torah] is your wisdom and your understanding in the eyes of the peoples; when they hear all these statutes they will say: 'It is a particularly wise and understanding people, this great nation.' – Deuteronomy 4:6

Are we to understand that the motivation for obedience to God's law is the desire to be admired and praised by the nations of the world? Are these verses, both in Deuteronomy 4 and here in chapter 28, appeals to a national arrogance and a desire for Judeo-supremacy over other nations?

A Kingdom of Priests

Let's recall the purpose of the nation of Israel. When God first called on Abraham, He told him that his mission was to bring blessing to "all the families of the earth." (Gen. 12:3, 18:18) Later, when the children of Israel stood at Mount Sinai, God introduced the covenant with Israel as follows:

Now if you will heed my voice, and observe My covenant, you shall be distinguished for me from among all the peoples, as all the earth is mine. You shall be for Me a kingdom of priests and a holy nation. – Exodus 19:5-6

Like our verses in Deuteronomy, here too we see God promising the children of Israel that they will have the highest status among all the nations of the earth. But in Exodus 19, at the moment of the inception of the covenant with Israel, God tells the children of Israel what their role will be in relation to the nations of the world.

You shall be for Me a kingdom of priests and a holy nation.

What is a kingdom of priests?

The Hebrew word for priest, *kohen*, does not refer only to the family of Aaron, the priests of the Tabernacle and Temple. *Kohen* is a generic term for all priests, regardless of religion. For example, Jethro, Moses' father-in-law is called "priest of Midian" (Ex. 18:1). The priests who served pagan gods are likewise referred to as *kohen*. (e.g. see 1 Sam. 5:5, 1 Kings 12:32, 13:2) Put simply, a *kohen* is someone who serves a deity by facilitating the worship of others. This is the simplest definition of the word "priest."

So what exactly is a "kingdom of priests"? Does it mean that everyone in the nation of Israel is meant to serve as clergy? How can a society made up entirely of priests function properly? Clearly this is not the intent of the phrase.

If the role of a *kohen* is to help the flock serve and connect with God, then we must understand a "kingdom of priests" the same way. In other words, the purpose and mission of the nation of Israel is to facilitate the faith, worship, and service to God of the world. Just as a single priest helps individual people in their faith and worship, so too the priestly nation, the kingdom of priests, has a collective, national mission to promote faith and worship of God to the other nations of the world.

Admiration = Influence

It is essential to the fulfilment of this mission that the nation of Israel have influence. Nobody is going to be led to faith by a nation that does not inspire admiration. It is essential to the mission of Israel that they be seen and admired by the nations of the world. But here's the thing, it is equally essential to the mission of Israel that they are admired and respected *for the right reasons*. It is not enough for the nation of Israel to be admired for being economically or militarily successful. To fulfil the mission that God placed before Israel at Sinai, Israel must serve a *priestly* role. In other words, Israel must be admired in such a way that the nations of the world are drawn to faith and service of the God of Israel.

Now let's reread the verses in Deuteronomy 28 that we are studying:

It shall be if you shall heed the voice of the Lord your God to take care to perform all His commandments that I am commanding you today, the Lord your God will place you uppermost over all the nations of the earth. All these blessings will come upon you, and reach you, if you shall heed the voice of the Lord your God. – Deuteronomy 28:1-2

Notice the seemingly needless repetition at the end of these two verses. The passage begins by saying "if you shall heed the voice of the Lord your God," certain blessings will happen. But then the same words are repeated at the end of the second verse. For the sake of illustration, imagine if a friend who needed help packing up and moving apartments said to you, "If you help me pack and move apartments I will buy you dinner, if you help me pack and move apartments." The repetition of the condition for the reward of dinner is obvious and needless.

A good rule for studying the Bible carefully is that anytime there is repetition that does not appear to add any new idea, we must pay close attention. The Bible does not include bold face, italics, or underlines. The way the Bible stresses a point is through seemingly needless repetition or a restatement of information that is already known. When the Bible does this, the words that seem to be needlessly repeated are actually being stressed through the repetition.

The fact that the words "if you shall heed the voice of the Lord your God," are repeated here tells us that they are the main point of the passage.

What Moses was telling the nation of Israel was this. If you are careful to be obedient to God and build the Israelite society according to His commandments, the result is that you will admired as the greatest of nations. Most importantly, the object of that admiration will be the fact that you have built a nation, a society, that is governed by the will of God. That will be the source of your elevated status among the nations of the world. From such a position, you will be able to fulfil your mission, stated all the way back at Mount Sinai, to be a "kingdom of priests and a holy nation."

When we live according to God's word, the ultimate result is that others see us and come to admire the Godly life. Engendering admiration and respect is a key tool to influence others and draw them closer to God.

Jeremiah 30:3 – Behold the Future is Now

For behold, days are coming – the utterance of the Lord – and I will restore the returnees of My people Israel and Judah, says the Lord, and I will restore them to the land that I gave to their fathers, and they will take possession of it.

Jeremiah lived in the tragic days of the destruction of the First Temple in Jerusalem, leading to the exile in Babylon. That exile lasted only 70 years. Due to the timing of Jeremiah's life, many scholars interpret his prophecies of the return from exile as referring to the return from the Babylonian exile. In other words, according to these scholars, Jeremiah's prophecies of the exile and restoration of Israel do not foretell the lengthy exile after the destruction of the Second temple and the restoration of Israel as an independent nation in our time. But a careful reading of the details of this verse shows this standard interpretation of Jeremiah's prophecy to be mistaken.

Israel and Judah return

The first indication that this prophecy does not refer to the return from the Babylonian exile is the reference to "the returnees of My people Israel and Judah."

If the verse had simply referred to the restoration of "Israel," without mentioning Judah at all, we would understand the word "Israel" as a reference to the Jewish people generally. In other words, had the verse spoken only of "Israel," we could easily understand that Jeremiah was foretelling the return of Jews to the land, regardless of what tribe they are from. After all, Israel is the name of the entire nation.

Since the verse refers to "Israel and Judah," we know that the name Israel is not to be understood according to its more expansive meaning – i.e. referring to the Jewish people generally – but rather according to the narrower meaning of "Israel," namely, the northern tribes who had separated from Judah during the reign of Rehoboam. Otherwise, it would make no sense to refer to "Judah and Israel."

Why does this matter?

After the 70 year Babylonian exile, the only Jews who returned to the land were from the southern kingdom, the kingdom of *Judah*. They were from the tribes of Benjamin and Judah, in addition to some members of the tribe of Levi who lived in those areas. Put simply, the return of "Israel and Judah" did not happen at that time. Jews were not gathered from all the places of their exile. This prophecy was not fulfilled.

A second indication that Jeremiah's prophecy was not referring to the return to the land after the Babylonian exile is the closing words of the verse, "and they will take possession of it." This phrase is not about the physical return of members of the nation of Israel to their land. Rather, what is described here is Jewish sovereignty over the land as well. What else could "and they will take possession of it" mean?

The return of the Jewish people to the land of Israel after the Babylonian exile was with the permission of Cyrus, king of Persia. Persia ruled the land of Israel at the time. In fact, for almost the entire period of the Second Temple, the land of Israel was ruled by foreign powers. The nation of Israel, or at least portions of it, did certainly return to the land, by they did not "take possession of it."

Let's sum up these points. When the Jewish people returned from the Babylonian exile in the days of Ezra and began building the Second Temple:

1. Only Jews from the kingdom of Judah returned
2. While the Jewish people returned to the land, they did not have sovereignty over the land

Based on these two factors, it makes no sense to say that Jeremiah's prophecy was fulfilled by the return to the land after the Babylonian exile.

"Behold" means it's happening

All this leads to a powerful point about this verse. The verse begins with the words, "Behold days are coming." Throughout the Bible, the word "Behold" implies something that is readily visible or immediate. What's more, the verse does not say "days will come" in the future tense, but "are coming" in the present tense. The implication of the words is that the full restoration of Israel to the land is either underway or is in the near future.

There is an important lesson here. As we explained, Jeremiah is fore-telling the redemption and restoration of Israel that will not come to pass for thousands of years in the future. And yet, he describes this historical development as though it is already happening in the immediate present. Jeremiah is poetically conveying the proper attitude that we are meant to have regarding God's plan for the future redemption. Even though it will come to pass far in the future, the fact that God has promised it makes it an absolute certainty. Because it is a certainty, we ought to see everything that happens in history as part of the story of the redemption of Israel. So even if the Jews are headed into exile, and even if that exile lasts two thousand years, all these ups and downs are simply chapters in the ongoing story of the restoration of Israel. The process of redemption is underway.

Even before the full redemption of Israel and the world is complete, we must always view the promises of God as certain and present in our own reality. We must be confident enough in God's word that we can look to the future and say, "Behold!"

Deuteronomy 26:7-9 – The Land of Milk and Honey

Then we cried out to the Lord God of our fathers, and the Lord heard our voice and looked on our affliction and our labor and our oppression. And the Lord brought us out of Egypt with a mighty hand and with an outstretched arm, with great terror and with signs and wonders. He has brought us to this place and has given us this land, "a land flowing with milk and honey";

These verses are taken from the text that was recited by someone bringing first fruits to the Temple in Jerusalem each year. There are several lessons we can derive from the precise wording of this statement.

— *And the Lord heard our voice*

Throughout the Bible generally, and the Exodus story in particular, we find God listening to "the voice" of His people. It is important to note that in many contexts in the Bible the Hebrew word for "voice," *kol*, does not refer to the words that are spoken. Rather, *kol* more narrowly refers to the actual sound of the voice. For example,

Then you returned and wept before the Lord, but the Lord would not listen to your voice nor give ear to you. – Deuteronomy 1:45

The end of this verse appears repetitive. What is the difference between saying that God "would not listen to your voice" and saying that He would not "give ear to you"? The answer is that "voice" – *kol* – refers more to the way something is said, rather than the content of the words. This verse from Deuteronomy 1 is saying that when the children of Israel sinned by weeping in despair after the negative report of the spies regarding the land of Israel, God did not listen to the pain and despair in the sound of their cries in addition to not paying attention to the actual content of their complaint.

What's more, the word *kol* translated as voice, is actually the word for "sound." For example,

Then it came to pass on the third day, in the morning, that there were thunderings and lightnings, and a thick cloud on the mountain; and the

sound of the trumpet was very loud, so that all the people who were in the camp trembled. – Exodus 19:16

The Hebrew for "sound of the trumpet" is *kol shofar*. To sum up the point: the primary meaning of the word *kol* is "sound" or "voice," not the content of the words that are spoken.

What's the point of all this?

Let's reread the verses we are studying here.

and the Lord <u>heard</u> our voice and <u>looked</u> on our affliction and our labor and our oppression. And the Lord <u>brought us out</u> of Egypt with a mighty hand and with an outstretched arm, with great terror and with signs and wonders.

First God "heard our voice." This led God to "look" and the rest of the Exodus story proceeded from there. In other words, the initial step in the redemption process was God hearing "our voice," our *kol*.

In other words, the exact words that were said by the children of Israel when they cried out to God is an irrelevant point. God heard "our voice." He listened to the pain, the suffering, and the anguish that was expressed in that cry to Him.

There is an important message for us whenever we are going through a period of hardship. When we are in need, we must call out to God. Oftentimes, people hesitate to pray in the most heartfelt way because they feel that they don't possess the right words. They fear that they just don't know how to pray to God. But God loves us. He's our father. We must never hesitate to cry out to Him because we lack confidence in the content of our prayers. God hears our *kol*. No matter the exact choice of words, God hears our pain. And as we see in our verses, when God hears our honestly expressed heartfelt pain, this leads Him to "see" and redeem us.

Milk and Honey

I would like to address another phrase in the verses we are studying. The land of Israel is called a land flowing with milk and honey. Elsewhere, we see the bounty of the land of Israel described by listing certain indigenous fruits and produce.

For the Lord your God is bringing you into a good land, a land of brooks of water, of fountains and springs, that flow out of valleys and hills; a land of wheat and barley, of vines and fig trees and pomegranates, a land of olive oil and honey; - Deuteronomy 8:7-8

So why does our verse mention only "milk and honey"? This question is especially relevant considering that this passage is part of what was recited upon presenting the first fruits to the Temple. Milk is not a fruit. I would have expected the description of the land of Israel here to focus more on the bounty of the land that is relevant to the first fruits.

I'd like to suggest that the choice of milk and honey here teaches a powerful message about the entire passage preceding it. Here is the full text recited by one who brought first fruits.

And you shall proclaim and say before the Lord your God: 'My father was a lost Aramean, and he went down to Egypt and dwelt there, few in number; and there he became a nation, great, mighty, and populous. But the Egyptians mistreated us, afflicted us, and placed hard labor upon us. We cried out to the Lord God of our fathers, and the Lord heard our voice and looked on our affliction and our labor and our oppression. The Lord took us out of Egypt with a mighty hand and with an outstretched arm, with great terror and with signs and wonders. He has brought us to this place and has given us this land, a land flowing with milk and honey. And now, behold, I have brought the first fruits of the land which you, Lord, have given me.' – Deuteronomy 26:5-10

We see that a person presenting first fruits at the Temple recounted the earliest history of the children of Israel, going all the way back to the patriarchs. The declaration then connects the story of the patriarchs with the current bounty of the land being enjoyed by the one bringing his fruits.

The point of milk is to nurture the young. Milk is produced by mothers for that purpose. Milk represents growth and building the future. Honey, on the other hand, is a preservative. In fact, in the ancient world, the primary use of honey was as a preservative. This is due to the fact that honey does not spoil. Honey can be stored for centuries and it will remain sweet.

Milk and honey represent building towards the future and preserving the past. The nation of Israel was redeemed from exile and given the land of Israel as a place to build the future.

This dual theme of the land of Israel is truer in our times than it has ever been. The land of Israel is obviously rich in history. Anyone who visits Israel is constantly in direct contact with the history of Biblical faith going all the way back to Abraham. But the land of Israel is also the focal point for the future. No other nation has developed and flourished as rapidly as Israel over the last few decades. More importantly, the future of God's kingdom here on Earth will be based in Jerusalem and the land of Israel.

Israel is the land of milk and honey because no land is more connected to the future of the world than Israel, and no land preserves the past of the world as Israel does.

Genesis 13:14-17 – Forever means Forever

The Lord said to Abram after Lot parted from him, "Raise now your eyes, and look from the place where you are, northward, southward, eastward, and westward. For all the land that you see I will give to you and your descendants forever. I will render your descendants like the dust of the earth, if a man could count the dust of the earth, so your descendants shall be counted. Arise, walk in the land to its length and to its breadth, as to you I will give it"

— God's response to the split with Lot

These words were spoken by God to Abram in the wake of his split with his nephew Lot. The reason for God relaying this exact message at this time is straightforward. Because Lot was Abram's nephew and had joined Abram and Sarah in their journey to the promised land, Abram may have thought that Lot was entitled to a portion of the land God had promised. Furthermore, a few verses earlier, at the time of the break between Lot and Abram, we read,

[Abram said] "Isn't the whole land before you? Please part from me. If you go to the left, I will go to the right; and if you go to the right, I will go to the left"…. Lot chose for himself all the plain of the Jordan. – Genesis 13:9,11

From the simple meaning of this passage, it appears that Abram was willing to cede a portion of the land God had promised him to his nephew Lot. Abram may have believed that as a result, Lot and his own descendants would have a legitimate claim to a portion of the promised land. So here in our verse, God stepped in and told Abram in no uncertain terms that this is not the case. "After Lot parted from him," God reiterated to Abram that the entire land is to be the eternal possession of Abram's offspring alone.

— Three questions

A careful reading of our verses raises a number of questions.

First, why did God say "Raise your eyes and look <u>from the place where</u>

you are"? What exactly is the intent of this phrase? What does it add to God's message to Abram? Where else would Abram be looking from, if not from the place where he was?

Second, God first told Abram to "look" and that "all the land that you see" will be given to Abram and his descendants forever. God then told Abram to "walk in the land to its length and breadth, as to you I will give it." Is Abram's possession of the land dependent upon walking the length and breadth? If not, what is the point of this instruction from God?

Lastly, when God told Abram to look at the land He said, "For all the land that you see I will give to you and your descendants forever." Then, when God told Abram to walk the length and breadth of the land He said, "as to you I will give it." No mention of Abram's descendants. And no mention of "forever." Why?

Does "forever" mean "always"?

To begin answering these questions, let's first raise another issue with what God said to Abram here. God told Abram that He will give the land to Abram and his descendants "forever." Now, it is an obvious historical fact that there were many centuries during which the descendants of Abram were not in possession of the land. For most of Jewish history since Abraham, the land of Israel was not under the control and ownership of the people of Israel. At other times, such as the time we currently live in, the Jewish people do indeed have ownership and sovereignty over the land.

I'd like to suggest that when God said that He gave the land to Abram and his descendants "forever," He did not mean that they would always be in literal full possession and control of the land. Rather, God meant that the Jewish people have an eternal rightful claim of ownership to the land. He meant that the descendants of Abram would retain their identification with the land of Israel as their homeland forever.

The eternal covenant of land

During the centuries of exile, when the Jewish people were not in active control and possession of the land, the covenant of the land remained, even though it was not actualized on the ground. The Jewish people continued to express their connection to the land through daily prayer. They continued to view themselves as being in exile, remembering always that their true homeland was the land of Israel. Every year, sitting at the Passover meal, telling the story of exile and redemption, Jews would continue to say, "Next year in Jerusalem." The connection of the Jewish people to the land of Israel was never lost. The land of Israel remained their land, even when in practice it wasn't "theirs."

In addition to this unbroken, eternal connection to the land of Israel, there would also be periods in history when the Jews would be in full possession of the land. Our verses describe both aspects of the relationship of the people of Israel to the land of Israel.

First God told Abram to ""Raise your eyes and look *from the place where you are*." God's message to Abram was a message for all of Abram's descendants, the Jewish people forever. God was saying, "Regardless of your location, from wherever you may be scattered across the globe. 'Raise your eyes!' Look beyond the current situation and see with higher, more spiritual eyes, that the land is yours forever."

This eternal connection of the Jewish people to the land of Israel, wherever they may be, "from the place where you are," does not depend on actual sovereignty, physically occupying the land. It requires only that we "raise" our eyes and see.

But of course, this connection to the land of Israel is not the end goal. The fullest expression of the covenant of land is when the people of Israel "Arise" and "walk in the land to its length and to its breadth." Only by physically conquering and taking possession of the land, only by governing the land with full Jewish sovereignty is the promise of the land fulfilled completely.

For this second promise, God did not mention Abram's "descendants forever." This ownership of the land, must be actualized by each and every generation on its own. Only then is the covenant of land fully realized.

God's promise of the land to Abram and his descendants is eternal. The Jewish people have never ceased to identify the Land of Israel as their homeland. Even in exile, they looked to the land and proclaimed this eternal bond.

Deuteronomy 1:21 – The Past Assures the Future

See that the Lord your God has placed the land before you; ascend, take possession, as the Lord, God of your fathers, spoke to you; do not fear, and do not be frightened.

Behold or See

The first word of this verse is *re'eh* – "see." Many translations, including the classic King James, translate this word here as "behold." This is inaccurate. The Hebrew word that is always translated as "behold" is *hineh*. *Re'eh* is simply the second-person conjugation of the verb "to see."

Despite what I just wrote, those who translate *re'eh* as "behold" have a point. After all, what really is the difference between "see" and "behold," in a context such as this? It is certainly quite common for declarative statements such as this to be introduced with the word "behold."

But the difference here is significant and will help us understand several nuances in this verse.

While "behold" is commonly used for declarations of fact, it can also literally mean "see." The word *re'eh,* on the other hand, more literally means "see," as in, see with one's eyes. This verb root describes the literal sense of sight.

Why does this matter?

Moses is retelling the story of the sin of the spies 40 years after the event took place. He is speaking to the children and grandchildren of the generation that left Egypt in the Exodus. In this retelling, the request of the children of Israel to send spies was a response to what Moses told them in this verse.

But this statement of Moses does not appear in the original narrative in the book of Numbers. For some reason, Moses chose to include this in the retelling of the story to the children and grandchildren 40 years later.

In other words, what Moses says here is intended for the new generation who are listening to him retell that story.

Whenever a story is retold, we must pay attention to what is being emphasized for the new audience. My point is that Moses choice of words here is meant for the children of Israel who will enter the land to conquer it now, 40 years after the original event took place.

The entire point of this verse is to express the confidence that they were supposed to have in their ability to conquer the land of Israel. By introducing this statement with the word "see," Moses was telling the children of Israel that their ability to conquer the land of Israel need not be a matter of hope or faith. Rather, they should see it as an empirical reality, as a fact before their eyes.

— *Why "God of your fathers"*

Notice that Moses refers to God as "the Lord, <u>God of your fathers</u>," rather than "the Lord your God," which is used throughout these sections of the book of Deuteronomy. The simple explanation is that God promised the land to Abraham, Isaac, and Jacob, the patriarchs in Genesis. And considering that Moses is telling the current generation that he said this to their parents and grandparents 40 years earlier, this is certainly the plain meaning of the verse.

But I believe that Moses' choice to call God, "God of your fathers" was also meant to speak directly to his audience. Allow me to explain.

The generation that left Egypt experienced the greatest overt miracles in history. The Ten Plagues, the splitting of the Red Sea, the revelation at Sinai; the power of God was known to them as an empirical fact. It was not a matter of faith. They knew God's power from what they experienced with their five senses.

I believe that Moses' intent with this verse was to remind his audience that their "fathers," i.e. the generation of the Exodus, had experienced God this way. Based on this, Moses was appealing to his audience to have full confidence in their ability to conquer the land as though victory is already an established fact. After all, do they need any stronger proof of God's providence and power than what their parents and grandparents experienced only 40 years earlier?

God's promises are certain

The use of the word "see" emphasizes this point. Moses was saying to them, "This is not merely a matter of faith and trust. Based on what you *know*, based on what God did for your parents, you can be absolutely certain that the land is yours for the taking."

There is an important lesson for all of us, especially living in these times. We have all witnessed the miracle of the modern state of Israel. The return of the Jewish people and the restoration of our nation in the promised land as foretold in the Bible is not a matter of faith. It's a matter of fact. We don't believe that prophecy is being fulfilled in our days. We know it!

We must look to the past, to what God has already done throughout history, to remember that God's promises for the future are as certain as facts that are right before our eyes. We can see it!

Deuteronomy 11:31-32 – The Purpose of Jewish Sovereignty

For you are crossing the Jordan to come to take possession of the land that the Lord you God is giving you, and you shall take possession of it, and you shall reside in it. You shall take care to perform all the statutes and the ordinances that I put before you today.

One of the main themes of this book, and the direct subject of many of the verses in this book, is the promise of God to give the land of Israel to the people of Israel. This verse is one of many that reiterates God's gift of the land. But it does more than that.

Not only a gift, a command

In addition to stating that God has given the land to the nation of Israel, this verse also includes a direct command to the people of Israel, "and you shall take possession of it, and you shall reside in it." More precisely, these are two commandments.

1. You shall take possession of it
2. You shall reside in it

The importance of these commandments to Jewish identity and faith cannot be overstated. Simply put, according to Biblical law, as stated right here in this verse, the Jewish people are commanded by God to take possession of the land of Israel and to live in it. The land of Israel is not only a gift from God to the nation of Israel so that we have a land to call our own. Jewish sovereignty over the land of Israel is a requirement of Divine law.

Two distinct commands

I mentioned that there are two commandments here. If we think about Jewish history, we can easily see the implications of this. There have been many time-periods, from Roman times to the Ottoman Empire to the era of the British Mandate in the 20th century, when Jews were allowed to live in the land of Israel but were not sovereign. Had the verse commanded us only to live in the land of Israel, we might think that Jewish residence there is the goal, regardless of who rules the land. The first commandment "you shall take possession of it," teaches us that the Jewish people are commanded to establish sovereignty over the land.

On the other hand, had the verse stated only the first command, "you shall take possession of it," we might be led to believe that living there is not obligatory, so long as there is Jewish sovereignty over the land. And in fact, as we know all too well, there are many Jews who are content to live outside of Israel, even during our times when Jews do have possession of the land of Israel. The second commandment, "you shall reside in it," comes to teach us that it is the obligation of every member of the nation of Israel to make every effort to live in the land of Israel.

The purpose of sovereignty

This verse, commanding Jewish sovereignty and residence in the land of Israel, is followed by a verse that does not appear to be directly related.

You shall take care to perform all the statutes and the ordinances that I put before you today.

This is certainly an important message. However, it's a message that is stated many times throughout the Torah in general and the book of Deuteronomy in particular. Why is it stated right here? What is the connection to the previous verse? Furthermore, why does it refer to the "all the statutes and the ordinances that I put before you today." What particular statutes and ordinances is Moses referring to? If he means to include all the commandments of the Torah, why include the words, "that I put before you today"? Obviously, only a small number of the 613 commandments in the Torah were stated on that day.

We can answer both these questions by reading the verses that immediately follow.

These are the statutes and ordinances that you shall take care to perform in the land that the Lord, God of your fathers, has given you to take possession of it, all the days that you live on the earth. You shall eradicate all the places where the nations from whom you are taking possession served their gods; on the high mountains, and on the hills, and under every flourishing tree. You shall smash their altars, and you shall shatter their monuments, and their sacred trees you shall burn in fire, and the idols of their gods you shall cut down, and you shall eradicate their name from that place. – Deuteronomy 12:1-3

I encourage you to open a Bible and continue reading the rest of Deuteronomy 12. It goes on to command the establishment of a temple to God, to worship Him there with sacrifices and other offerings.

Now we can see the connection between our two verses. The first verse commands us to take possession of and dwell in the land that God has given us. The second verse tells us that we must be careful to fulfill the commandments of God outlined in the verses that follow. The connection between these verses is now clear. The purpose of our sovereignty and nationhood in the land of Israel is to establish a society that rejects false gods and serves only the God of Israel.

The Jewish people are not like any other nation. The sole basis of our identity is our covenant with God. The purpose of Israel is the establishment of a nation that exemplifies obedience to God and serves as the worldwide epicenter of faith in the God of Israel.

Isaiah 14:1 – The House of Jacob

For the Lord will have mercy on Jacob and will again choose Israel, and He will place them on their land; the stranger will accompany them, and they will be appended to the house of Jacob.

What is most striking about this verse are the three terms for the Jewish people; *Jacob, Israel,* and *the house of Jacob.* Of course, both Jacob and Israel are names for the third patriarch, and subsequently appear as names for the nation as a whole. That said, why did Isaiah use each of these terms the way that he did here in this verse?

First, let's understand the connotation of each of these names for the nation of Israel.

Jacob as a name for the Jewish people

In my discussion of Isaiah 2:3 in this book, I discussed the the meaning of Jacob's name, and what it implies when it is used as a name for the entire Jewish people. If you haven't read that yet or don't recall what I wrote, pause here and read the detailed explanation there.

Here's the key point, taken from that teaching:

The People of Israel, like their forefather and namesake are sometimes forced to live in exile as subordinates and second-class citizens – the follower, the heel - in a hostile anti-Semitic environment. Like Jacob their father, Jews have repeatedly been forced to flee after being unjustly accused and targeted. When scripture refers to the People of Israel as Jacob, it is this weakened, exile identity that is being described.

When the Jewish people as a whole are referred to as *Jacob*, the implication is their weakened, subordinate status in the exile. The name, *Israel*, on the other hand, refers to the strong, influential, and free nation of Israel.

House of Jacob

Now what about the term, *House of Jacob*? This name for the Jewish people appears in many verses in the Bible. In fact, there are two verses that describe the nation of Israel during their forty-year sojourn in the Sinai desert that use both names, Jacob and Israel, in the same verse.

The first is right after the exodus from Egypt when the nation arrives at Mount Sinai to receive the Torah.

Then Moses went up to God, and the Lord called to him from the mountain and said, 'This is what you are to say to the House of Jacob and what you are to tell the People of Israel.' - Exodus 19:3

These two names appear together a second time when Bilaam the wicked prophet was overcome by the spirit of God and, despite his original evil intent to curse Israel, he blessed them:

How beautiful are your tents, Jacob; your tabernacles, Israel! - Numbers 24:5

Tents and Tabernacles

Notice that Bilaam refers to *tents* in relation to *Jacob* and *tabernacles* in relation to *Israel*.

The juxtaposition of *Jacob* to *tents* reminds us of Genesis 25:27 where, as youngsters, Jacob is described as a *dweller of tents* in contrast to his brother Esau; a hunter and a man of the field.

Tents and houses are private places. A tabernacle, on the other hand, is very public. The entire purpose of a tabernacle is the glory of God. It is open to all to come to worship and be inspired.

◊   Tent = Private dwelling
◊   Tabernacle = Public place of worship

The public covenantal relationship with God is implied by the tabernacle. Anyone who has faith in God and devotes their life to serving Him understands that the focus of that service is to bring knowledge of God to the entire earth. *Israel* is a name that implies this grand mission of influence. It is derived from two words. *Sar* – meaning prince or minister, and *El* – God. Israel connotes the ministering, influencing role of God's people.

House of Jacob = private relationship to God

The House of Jacob describes the private relationship to God. Any devoted servant of God confronts challenges on a daily basis. It is true that the primary task in serving God is to influence, to lead, and to help others get close to Him. But there can be no influence without interaction. It is impossible to repair the world without engaging with it. And with that engagement, people of faith often find themselves in the position of being influenced by the darker parts of society, even as they try to make the world a better place.

To face this challenge, we need to be like Jacob; dwellers of tents. To stay strong in one's faith values; to have the strength to continue to influence the world for the good, we must sometimes retreat from it. We must travel inward to our homes; to our families; to our tents. This is the "house of Jacob."

◊ Israel = Public, ministering role
◊ House of Jacob = Private relationship to God; retreat from the outside influences

Back to Isaiah 14:1

Now we can understand our verse in Isaiah.

For the Lord will have mercy on Jacob and will again choose Israel, and He will place them on their land; the stranger will accompany them, and they will be appended to the house of Jacob.

First, the Lord will have mercy on "Jacob," on the Jewish people suffering in the exile. Then God will choose "Israel," meaning that God will choose to return the Jewish people to their status as a powerful nation in their land, charged with the mission to influence and minister to the world. Finally, the verse refers to the fact that even as Israel fulfils its outward facing purpose to the world as Israel, they retain their private spiritual life, the House of Jacob.

This verse describes those among the nations who join together with the Jewish people to assist them in their lofty mission. It is these gentiles, these "strangers," who "accompany them," participating in the spiritual life of the Jewish people. These gentiles join the nation of Israel in their mission to the world, and by proximity and involvement with the Jewish people, they are privy to the more private spiritual life and teachings of the House of Jacob.

The mission to influence the world requires engagement with it. This engagement can sometimes challenge us. We must fortify our private life of faith as we reach out to others.

Ezekiel 34:13 – The Shepherd of Israel

I will take them out of from the peoples and I will gather them from the lands, and I will bring them to their soil, and I will herd them on the mountains of Israel, in the streams and in all the dwellings of the land.

This verse is part of an extended prophecy of Ezekiel in which God likens Himself to a shepherd, and the Jewish people to His sheep.

Shepherd = Leadership

The metaphor of a shepherd for leadership is one of the most common in the Bible. For example, when Moses was nearing the end of his life and turned to God to ask him to choose the next leader of Israel, he used the metaphor of a shepherd.

Let the Lord, the God of the spirits of all flesh, set a man over the congregation, who may go out before them and go in before them, who may lead them out and bring them in, that the congregation of the Lord may not be like sheep which have no shepherd. – Numbers 27:16-17

But beyond being a metaphor for leadership, we also see that God chose actual shepherds for many of the primary roles of leadership over Israel. For example, Moses and King David, the two most prominent paradigms of leadership in the entire Bible, both started out as shepherds. And of course, in what is likely the best-known passage in the entire Bible, God is compared to a shepherd.

A psalm of David: The Lord is my Shepherd, I shall not lack. – Psalm 23:1

Shepherds were menial laborers

We should note that in the ancient world, as well as today, the role of a shepherd was considered a position for a low-level laborer. It was not a job that was viewed with any respect. It was often the role of servants or members of the family who had no real skills. The job of a shepherd is to graze the flock and to protect it from danger. Comparing someone to a shepherd is not necessarily a compliment.

For example, Ezekiel 34, the source of our verses, opens with a rebuke by God of the corrupt leaders of Israel, the bad shepherds, who abused the people and led to their exile.

The word of the Lord was with me, saying: Son of man, prophesy concerning the shepherds of Israel, prophesy and say to them, to the shepherds: "So said the Lord God: 'Woe! Shepherds of Israel who have been shepherding themselves, isn't it the flocks that the shepherd should shepherd? You eat the fat, and you wear the wool, you slaughter the fat ones but you do not shepherd the flocks. The weak you did not strengthen, the ill you did not heal, and the injured you did not bind; the outcast you did not return, and the lost you did not seek. You subjugated them forcefully and with travail. – Ezekiel 34: 1-4

Good vs Bad Shepherds

Shepherds have a lot of freedom. In the Middle East, where it does not rain for much of the year, a shepherd is out with the flock for long periods with no supervision, often for days at a time. The shepherd travels with the flock, sleeps where they sleep, and is always on guard for dangers. Because the shepherd is out alone with the flock, a dishonest shepherd who lost a few sheep, or even killed and ate from the flock, could plausibly deny any responsibility. He could easily claim that a dangerous wild animal or roaming thieves attacked the flock, and there is not much the owner can say to object.

The point here is that the difference between good and bad shepherds is extreme. A good shepherd has a dangerous job, will get no honor, and must protect and care for the needs of the entire flock. A bad shepherd, if he so chooses, will use the sheep for his own benefit with impunity.

Leadership is meant to serve

Political leaders, like shepherds, are supposed to serve the flock that they lead. Their purpose is to care for the people, not to abuse them for their own benefit. But just like shepherds, political leaders have ample opportunity for corruption. The examples of this are too numerous to mention here. Corrupt leadership that takes advantage of the people instead of caring for them, leads to the destruction of society. In the case of the people of Israel, as Ezekiel tells us, it leads to exile from the land.

The promise of redemption spelled out in this chapter of Ezekiel is not merely one more among the many passages in the Bible that foretell the return of the nation of Israel to the promised land. By choosing to metaphorically refer to God as a shepherd, Ezekiel draws out attention to the contrast between good and bad leadership.

The leadership of God is that of a good shepherd. He cares for us. He protects us. He brings us back home.

Isaiah 43:5-7 – The True Purpose of Creation

Fear not, as I am with you; I will bring your descendants from the East, and from the West I will gather you. I will say to the North: "Give," and to the South: "Do not withhold; bring My sons from afar and My daughters from the ends of the earth." Everything that is called by My name, and for My honor I created it, I fashioned it, truly, I made it.

These verses are happening now

I am writing these words from my home in Bet Shemesh, about 30 minutes' drive from Jerusalem. My apartment block includes Jewish families who came to Israel from the United States, Ethiopia, Morocco, and Russia. One of my neighbors across the street is from India. My daughter is married to a wonderful young man whose family is from Yemen. This is Israel at the time of the ingathering of the exiles.

Think about that. These verses in Isaiah 43 are the day-to-day reality of life in Israel. Plain and simple. No commentary necessary. In these verses, Isaiah describes my neighborhood and family. He speaks of the nation of Israel returning to our land from the East (my Indian neighbor), the West (my family and our other neighbors of American origin), the North (Russia), and the South (Yemen). And I am not unique. Not at all. My experience is the experience of all who call Israel their home. We live in Biblical times.

A non-sequitur?

But what about the third verse in this sequence?

Everything that is called by My name, and for My honor I created it, I fashioned it, truly, I made it.

What is the connection between this verse and the verses that precede it? For greater context, I'll point out that chapter 43 is entirely about the ingathering of the exiles of Israel. This verse, a general statement about God's purpose in the creation of all things, seems out of place.

Let's first understand what exactly the verse is telling us on its own.

"Name" and "Honor"

God is saying that everything He created, fashioned, and made was made for the purpose of His "honor." He refers to "everything that is called by My name." God's "name" – *shem*, in Hebrew, and "honor" – *kavod* - are often paired in the Bible. (see Malachi 2:2, Psalm 29:2, Psalm 66:2, Psalm 72:19, Psalm 79;9, Psalm 96:8, Psalm 115:1, Nehemiah 9:5,1 Chronicles 16:9)

The connection between these two words makes sense. "Name" refers to the fact that people know who God is. If someone is unknown, they don't functionally have a name. Their name is never used. "Honor," of course, is the product of *awareness* of some great deed or trait. The very definition of honor is the honor given by others who are aware. If nobody knows what you did, there is no honor.

To sum this up: a *name* means that other know who you are. *Honor* means that others know what you accomplished. Both words imply knowledge by others.

What God is saying in our verse is that everything in creation was created to serve only one purpose, to give honor and glory to God; *to make people aware of His greatness.* The Jewish sages, 2000 years ago, interpreted this verse just this way.

Whatever the Holy Blessed One created in His world, he created only for His honor, as it is said: "All who are linked to My name, whom I have created, formed and made for My honor" (Isaiah 43:7) – Mishna Avot 6:11

So why is this verse here?

The three verbs, "created," "fashioned," and "made," each refer to a different stage of creation. "Created" refers to the initial creation of matter, the emergence of physical reality into existence. In fact, it's this Hebrew word that is used in the first verse in the Bible, "In the beginning God <u>created</u> heaven and earth." (Gen. 1:1). "Fashioned," refers to the formation of all the different details of creation, minerals, plants, animals, etc.

"Made" refers to the completed creation. It is this verb that is used in the final verse of the creation story, the last verse of Genesis 1. "And God saw all that He had <u>made</u>, and behold it was very good." – (Gen. 1:31)

So, what is the meaning of this verse in context, here in Isaiah 43?

As stated above, the subject of this entire chapter is the redemption and ingathering of the Jewish people from their dispersion across the globe. After the opening verses describe this ingathering, the chapter goes on to declare that all who witness this great ingathering will recognize God and know that He is the only God.

The nation of Israel suffered greatly in exile. We may wonder, why did God do this? Why scatter us to the four corners of the earth, allow us to be persecuted for centuries, only to then redeem us and bring us back to our homeland? Why not simply leave us where we began? What is the point of this long story of exile and redemption?

This point of this verse is to remind us that there is one purpose for everything that happens on Earth. The full arc of history from beginning to end, is meant for one purpose alone; to make God's name known throughout the world and to bring honor to Him. In fact, this is the reason the world, and everything in it, was created, formed, and made.

The Jewish people were chosen to serve as the vehicle for God's honor in the world. God uses the story of the exile and ultimate redemption of Israel as a tool to show His greatness to all. And this is the purpose of creation.

Genesis 26:3-5 – Isaac's Mission to Reclaim the Land

Reside in this land and I will be with you, and I will bless you; for I will give all these lands to you and to your descendants, and I will keep the oath that I swore to Abraham your father. And I will multiply your descendants like the stars of the heavens, and I will give to your descendants all these lands; and all the nations of the earth shall be blessed through your descendants, because Abraham heeded My voice, and kept My commission, My commandments, My statutes, and My laws.

Context is key

To understand the significance of God's words to Isaac, we must remind ourselves of the context in which they were spoken. Here are the two verses that immediately precede this passage:

There was a famine in the land, besides the first famine that was during the days of Abraham. Isaac went to Avimelekh king of the Philistines, to Gerar. The Lord appeared to him and said: Do not go down to Egypt; dwell in the land that I will tell you. – Gen. 26:1-2

Isaac had lived his entire life in the land promised by God to his father Abraham. Now there was a famine in the land. Many years earlier, before Isaac was born, there was a famine and Abraham had traveled to Egypt to seek food for survival (Gen. 12:10). Now, with famine once again hitting the land, Isaac set off in the same direction.

The land of the Philistines lies along the southern Mediterranean coast of the land of Israel. Both in ancient times and still today, the road to Egypt leads through this territory. But unlike his father Abraham, Isaac was stopped by God on the way to Egypt. Instead, as we read in the verses just quoted, God told Isaac to "dwell in the land that I will tell you."

The very next words from God to Isaac are the opening words of the passage we are studying, "Reside in this land." And as we just read, Isaac had just arrived in Philistine territory. To understand the significance of God's statement, we must recall an earlier story from the book of Genesis.

Abraham's treaty with the Philistines

In Genesis 21 (v. 22-32) we read of a covenant made between Abraham and Avimelekh, king of the Philistines. The covenant was a treaty, an agreement to respect each other's sovereignty over their respective lands, as we read in Avimelekh's proposal and Abraham's acceptance:

"Now take an oath to me here by God that you shall not betray me or my son, or my grandson; like the kindness that I have done with you, do with me and with the land in which you resided." Abraham said: "I will swear."
– Gen. 22:23-24

In other words, Avimelekh asked Abraham to respect the boundaries of his land, to recognize Philistine sovereignty there. It is important to note that the land occupied by the Philistines is entirely within the boundaries of the land promised by God to Abraham and his descendants. With this oath, Abraham was essentially agreeing to Philistine ownership over part of the promised land.

Reasserting the claim

Now we can understand the significance of God's words to Isaac here. On his way southward, Isaac had just arrived in Gerar, in Philistine territory (26:1). From Isaac's perspective, this land had already been ceded by Abraham to Avimelekh in the aforementioned treaty. But God never told Abraham to make that treaty. God had never sanctioned Abraham's surrender of part of the promised land to the Philistines. Now, with Isaac in that very same territory, God told him to stop his journey to Egypt and "dwell in the land that I will tell you." And which land did God then tell Isaac to dwell in?

"Reside in <u>this land</u> and I will be with you, and I will bless you; for I will give all <u>these lands</u> to you and to your descendants, and I will keep the oath that I swore to Abraham your father."

In other words, God told Isaac that regardless of any treaties that Abraham may have made, the land of Gerar belongs to Isaac and his descendants. Abraham had no authority to give up ownership of any part of the promised land. Isaac was commanded by God to remain in Gerar in order to assert ownership over it.

This is an important lesson for us in our times as well. There are political forces at work that continually try to claim that parts of the land of

Israel do not really belong to the nation of Israel. Treaties are even made in attempts to give sovereignty to the enemies of the Jewish people. But here we see that God's promise of the land to Abraham and his descendants is final and eternal. Even Abraham himself, in an honest effort to make peace, could not undo God's covenant of land.

Is God repeating Himself?

As we read further in our passage, a glaring question emerges. Here are the first 2 of the 3 verses with which we began, Genesis 26 verses 3 & 4.

3. Reside in this land and I will be with you, and I will bless you; for I will give all these lands to you and to your descendants, and I will keep the oath that I swore to Abraham your father.
4. And I will multiply your descendants like the stars of the heavens, and I will give to your descendants all these lands; and all the nations of the earth shall be blessed through your descendants,

Why did God repeat Himself? After telling Isaac, in verse 3, "for I will give all these lands to you and to your descendants," why did God then repeat this same promise in verse 4?

To answer this question, let's first pay close attention to the subject of each of these verses. Verse 3 has God promising to "be with" Isaac, meaning that He will protect Isaac as he dwells in the land of the Philistines. Considering that what follows in chapter 26 is the story of Isaac's contentious disputes with the Philistines, this promise makes sense. God was telling Isaac, "Don't worry. You will live here in Gerar and no matter what happens, I've got your back." God's reasoning was that Isaac's mission in Gerar was to reassert his ownership over "these lands," for him and for future generations of his progeny.

The message of verse 4 could not be more different. Here, God tells Isaac about the universal mission of the chosen people, "and all the nations of the earth shall be blessed through your descendants." What is the relevance of this promise to Isaac's present task of reasserting ownership over disputed territory?

Fighting for the land and the universal mission

Isaac knew that he was about to enter into conflict with the Philistines. He knew that he would not be making any friends in the process. He was very aware that his father Abraham made a peace treaty with Avimelekh. Abraham was motivated by the desire for peace. While this an admirable goal, in the process of making peace Abraham had also given up his claim of ownership over lands that God had promised him. Isaac was probably hesitant to antagonize the Philistines. After all, what about the mission to teach the whole world about God? Isn't it important for the children of Abraham to be on friendly terms with the nations around them if they have any hope of drawing these nations closer to faith in the one true God? Isaac may have been wondering if it was really worth it.

God responded to this concern. First God told Isaac that He must dwell in Gerar to reassert his ownership. Then God essentially told Isaac any fear that the universal mission to bring the blessing of God to all humanity will be harmed by this conflict with the Philistines, was baseless. In other words, God said that even though "I will give to you and your descendants all these lands," lands that the Philistines currently claim as their own, nevertheless, the ultimate mission of Abraham to the world will be fulfilled, "all the nations of the earth shall be blessed through your descendants."

Notice that God did not tell Isaac that all the nations of the earth would be blessed "through you," as He told Abraham, (see Gen. 12:3). Isaac would be in conflict with his neighbors. In the short term this might mean that the Philistines would distance themselves from Isaac and his message of faith. This is the unfortunate short-term result of conflict with the nations. But in the long term, God told him, the universal mission would be fulfilled through his descendants.

We live in a time when there are powerful political forces that continue to deny the claims of the nation of Israel to the entire land of Israel. Sometimes this puts Israel and the Jewish people into conflict with the nations of the world. These contentious relationships can appear to run counter to the ultimate Jewish mission to be what Isaiah called, "a light unto the nations." But as God told Isaac, this concern is unfounded. Laying claim to the land of Israel will ultimately only serve to facilitate the mission of Israel. To bring blessing to all the families of the earth.

Leviticus 20:24 – The Morally Sensitive Land

I said to you: You shall inherit their land, and I will give it to you to inherit it, a land flowing with milk and honey. I am the Lord your God, who has distinguished you from the peoples.

Leviticus 24, leading up to this verse, is a list of prohibitions. More specifically, the first 21 verses of the chapter are a list of prohibitions against a range of pagan idolatrous practices and immoral sexual relationships. This list is followed by a warning to avoid these immoral behaviors, which were widely practiced by the Canaanite peoples, lest the land spit us out (v.22-23). Then comes our verse. With this context in mind, let's ask a few questions about our verse.

A few questions

First, the redundancy in the verse is clear. Why does it say, "you shall inherit the land" and then immediately "and I will give it to you to inherit it"? This second phrase seems purely repetitious. Why doesn't the verse simply say, "You shall inherit their land, a land flowing with milk and honey," without the words "and I will give it to you to inherit it"?

Second, the land of Israel is referred to as "a land flowing with milk and honey," in several verses in the Bible. But this descriptive phrase is still quite rare. What is the relevance of this praise of the land here? What does it have to do with the warning against immorality and paganism?

Finally, our verse is followed by a prohibition against certain forbidden unclean foods. That verse is then followed by this:

You shall be holy to Me, for I, the Lord, am holy; and I have distinguished you from the peoples to be Mine. – Leviticus 20:26

Now reread the verse we are studying. Why is this message, that God has distinguished Israel from the nations, included in our verse and then restated two verses later as the Bible concludes the chapter?

A spiritually sensitive land

The point of this verse is to tell us something unique about the land of Israel. Namely, that the land of Israel responds to the moral behavior of those who live on it. Moreover, it is well documented that for the centuries when the Jewish people were in exile, the land of Israel was mostly desolate and uninhabitable. Testimonies from travelers throughout the centuries attest to this fact. It is only since the Jewish people returned to the land that it has begun to bloom again.

Amazingly, this relationship of the land of Israel to the Jewish people is foretold by the prophets of the Bible. We see it in the prophetic warning of the exile as well as in the prophecies of return and redemption. The land of Israel flourishes for the nation of Israel. For example:

I will render your cities ruins, I will make your sanctuaries desolate, and I will not smell your pleasing aroma. I will make the land desolate, and your enemies who live in it shall be desolate upon it. - Leviticus 26:31-32

But you, mountains of Israel, you will produce your branches and bear your fruit for My people Israel, as they are drawing near. For behold, I am ready for you, and I will turn to you, and you will be tiled and sown. – Ezekiel 36:8-9

We do our part; God does His

With this in mind, let's read our verse carefully. As we pointed out above, the verse does not say, "You shall inherit their land, a land flowing with milk and honey." Rather it repeats the promise of inheritance.

First the verse states that the nation of Israel will inherit the land of the Canaanites. It is the job of the nation of Israel to seize the land from the Canaanite peoples, or from whoever takes it again in the future. Then, once the nation of Israel has taken the land, God will respond and will do His part by turning it once again into "a land flowing with milk and honey." That's why the verse states "And I will give it to you to inherit, a land flowing with milk and honey," after already telling us that "You shall inherit the land." In other words, first the verse commands Israel to take the land. Then God will affirm Israel's possession of the land by making it flourish under Jewish ownership.

Israel must merit the land

But there's another lesson here as well. First the verse tells us to take the land, "You shall inherit their land." As we mentioned, the Canaanites were an extremely depraved and pagan population. God clearly wanted the war to conquer the land to simultaneously be an all-out war on paganism and immorality. But lest we think that, once we conquered it, the land is ours as the result of our own military conquest, the verse reminds us that it is only ours so long as God grants it to us.

Let's review these points by looking again at the verse:

You shall inherit their land   commandment to conquer the land from the Canaanites

And I will give it to you to inherit   even after conquest, it is still only ours as a gift from God

A land flowing with milk and honey   the land us abundant only so long as it is God's gift to us

Now we can answer our final question. We asked why our verse ends with God's statement that He distinguished us from the other nations. The answer should now be clear. In this context, God was telling the people of Israel that unlike other nations whose land is either abundant or desolate regardless of their moral behavior, the nation of Israel is different. They are a people who will either keep their land or go into exile based on their avoidance of immorality and idol worship.

Once again, we see that just as the nation of Israel is governed by different rules from other nations, so too, the land of Israel is governed differently from other lands.

The land of Israel is God's special chosen land. The normal rules of nature do not apply. The land of Israel responds to the moral and ethical behavior of those who live in it.

Isaiah 66:8 – A Nation Born in One Day

Who has heard of something like this? Who has seen things like these? Will a land complete labor in one day? Is a nation born at one time? For Zion has labored and has also given birth to her children.

In this fascinating verse, Isaiah compares the rebirth of the nation of Israel after the lengthy exile to the birth of a child. Isaiah asks a series of rhetorical questions, implying that the sudden birth of a nation "in one day" is unprecedented and therefore, miraculous. But is this actually true?

What does it mean that Israel would be born "in one day"? Obviously, the nation of Israel, at the time of our return to our homeland after thousands of years, is an ancient people. The nation of Israel is far from a *new* nation, like a baby that had never before seen the light of day. What exactly does Isaiah mean?

The Jewish "people" vs. the "nation" of Israel

We must distinguish between the Jewish people as a *people* and Israel as a *nation*. The Jewish people certainly continued to exist as a distinct people throughout the millennia of exile. But a *people* and a *nation* are two different things. A *people* is an ethnic group, a tribe, even a religion. But a *nation* has a language of its own, a land of its own, its own national independence. The Jewish *people* are ancient. The *nation* of Israel is brand new.

Born in one day?

But what about Isaiah's comment about the nation of Israel being born "in one day"? Is this how it happened? Of course, there was November 29th 1947, the day when the United Nations voted to establish a Jewish state. A few months later, on May 14th, 1948, David Ben-Gurion declared the establishment of the State of Israel. Which "one day" is the day the nation was born? More to the point, the founding of the State of Israel was a process that lasted decades, beginning with the mass movement of Jewish return to the land in the 1800s.

I'd like to suggest that the word "day" here is not meant literally to mean a single 24-hour day. Rather, Isaiah refers to the rapid transition from the nationless, exile status of a people, the Jews, to full national independence, all happening in a short time. A "day" here should be interpreted as a single era of history.

But this leads to the question, is the rapid transition from *people* to *nation* really so unprecedented? Aren't there other examples in modern history of new nations gaining their independence? The answer is, actually, no. Allow me to explain.

Nations are usually native

Think of all the nations in the world today. When did they become nations? When did the French people become the French? Or the Japanese? These nations forged their identities by being native to the lands where they lived. Or take Germany, for example. Germany was not a country, or a distinct nationality until the 1870s. Before that, there were numerous tribes who lived in that region. For a host of political, economic, and security reasons, these tribes and provinces unified into Germany.

In other parts of the world such as East Asia, South America, and Africa, native ethnic groups that had been colonized while remaining in their homelands achieved independence. While these nations could be said to be new, the members of the nations had never gone into exile. They were there all along. These peoples and their homelands were never separated.

On the other end of the spectrum, for nations such as Australia, Canada, and the United States, people of a range of ethnicities and origins came to a new land. Once in their new lands, over time, they gradually forged new identities. Eventually, these new identities developed into new nationalities.

The uniqueness of the Jews

The Jewish people are the only example in history of a people that was completely landless and subservient to other rulers, disconnected from any original homeland, who rapidly, in the span of barely more than a single generation, created a new nation. The Hebrew language that had not been spoken in many centuries, became the primary language of a modern nation almost overnight. Never before was there an independent nation made up of people almost entirely made up of whom had arrived as immigrants within the previous few years.

In the final stage of labor when giving birth to a child, in the absence of modern pain medications, it is common for women to lose hope of ever giving birth. As strange as it may seem, it is even common for women to forget that they are actually giving birth to a baby.

With this in mind, Isaiah's metaphor is all the more appropriate to the modern state of Israel. Think about the state of the world only 3 short years prior to the declaration of the state in 1948. The Holocaust had put the Jewish people in their weakest most decimated position since the destruction of the Temple almost 2000 years prior. If there is anything that is the inverse of Jewish independent nationhood it is the Nazi concentration camps.

And yet, seemingly overnight, the Jewish people went from the lowest depths of the exile to full national independence. So yes, Isaiah's metaphor is exactly right. The nation of Israel's sudden birth is a miraculous wonder of history.

The birth of the State of Israel is unique in history. Never before had a people become a nation in a matter of a few short years. The suddenness of the birth of the Jewish nation-state is a fulfilment of Isaiah's words.

Ezekiel 20:40-42 – The Mountain of the Height of Israel

For on My holy mountain, the mountain of the height of Israel, the utterance of the Lord God, there all the house of Israel, in its entirety, will worship Me in the land. There I will grant them propitiation, there I will seek your separated portions and your choice gifts, along with all your holy sacrifices. I will accept you as fragrant incense when I bring you out from the nations and gather you from the countries where you have been scattered, and I will be proved holy through you in the sight of the nations. Then you will know that I am the Lord, when I bring you into the land of Israel, the land I had sworn with uplifted hand to give to your ancestors.

How does the Bible emphasize a point? There are no underlines, italics, or bold type. The main way the Bible expresses emphasis is by repeating or, in a similar way, by telling us information that we already knew. Another way the Bible emphasizes a point is by inserting a word or phrase into a sentence that appears to serve no purpose. It doesn't seem to be adding anything to the meaning of the verse. This calls our attention to what seems to be superfluous. Ironically, it is these words that usually contain the most central teachings of the passage.

My Holy Mountain

The opening phrase of our passage is,

For on my holy mountain, the high mountain of Israel,

The phrase "My holy mountain" in Hebrew is *har kodshi*. The related phrase "His holy mountain," referring to God, is *har kodsho*. Combined, these two descriptions of the Temple Mount in Jerusalem appear a total of 18 times in the Bible. On a few occasions, the word "Zion" is added to this phrase. But even without the word "Zion," it is always clear from context that the "holy mountain" in question is the Temple Mount in Jerusalem.

The same is true of our verse here in Ezekiel 20. The verses that follow describe all of Israel serving God, bringing sacrifices, offerings, and incense. There is no doubt about the identity of the mountain in question.

The High Mountain of Israel

Keeping in mind what I said about how the Bible uses extra words and phrases for the purpose of emphasis, the question that emerges from this careful reading of our verse is this. What is the meaning of the second phrase in the verse which goes on to describe the Temple Mount as "the high mountain of Israel"? This description is unique. Only in the book of Ezekiel is the Temple Mount described this way. What is the meaning of this phrase and why is it used here?

The Hebrew for this phrase is *behar merom Yisrael*. *Behar* means "on the mountain." *Merom* is "high place of" or "height of," and *Yisrael*, of course, is Israel. While many English Bibles render this phrase, "the high mountain of Israel," a more precise translation is "the mountain of the height of Israel." The word *marom*, "high place," appearing here as *merom*, "high place of," appears over 50 times in the Bible, and almost every time it refers to the heavens, the "high place" where God dwells, not a high place on Earth.

The meaning of the word *marom* or *merom* is of something lofty and exalted, not merely high up like a mountain top. Which brings us to the meaning of our passage. Let's look at these verses in their full context.

A rebuke of Israel

As for you, people of Israel, this is what the Sovereign Lord says: Go and serve your idols, every one of you! But afterward you will surely listen to me and no longer profane my holy name with your gifts and idols. For on my holy mountain, the high mountain of Israel, declares the Sovereign Lord, there in the land all the people of Israel will serve me, and there I will accept them. There I will require your offerings and your choice gifts, along with all your holy sacrifices. I will accept you as fragrant incense when I bring you out from the nations and gather you from the countries where you have been scattered, and I will be proved holy through you in the sight of the nations. Then you will know that I am the Lord, when I bring you into the land of Israel, the land I had sworn with uplifted hand to give to your ancestors. There you will

remember your conduct and all the actions by which you have defiled your-
selves, and you will loathe yourselves for all the evil you have done. You will
know that I am the Lord, when I deal with you for my name's sake and not
according to your evil ways and your corrupt practices, you people of Israel,
declares the Sovereign Lord. – Ezekiel 20:39-44

The verses just before and just after our verses remind Israel that they
turned to false gods and worshipped them alongside God. This behavior
leads directly to the downfall and exile of Israel.

With this context in mind, we can now understand the meaning of the
description of the Temple Mount as the "the mountain of the height of
Israel."

Israel is exalted when they worship God alone

This passage is not just another of many prophecies in the Bible fore-
telling the return of Israel to their land and the reinstatement of the Temple worship. The point of this passage is different. Ezekiel is telling us that
the prestige and exalted status of the nation of Israel will come about only
when we are worshipping God fully. In other words, the Temple Mount
is not only "my holy mountain," where we serve God in the Temple. It
is also "the mountain of the height of Israel." It is only by virtue of the
worship practiced on this mountain that Israel achieves its greatness and
lofty status among the nations.

The lesson here is profound. The Jewish people have returned to our
land. We have defended ourselves against unrelenting and genocidal enemies. We have built a flourishing economy. All these accomplishments
are wonderful. But none of them are the source of the true glory of Israel.
None of these worldly successes will place Israel as the most exalted of all
nations, the beacon for all the peoples of the earth. It is only when Israel
fully returns to the fullest expression of worship of God on His holy
mountain in the Temple that the nation of Israel will also be elevated and
revered among the nations of the world.

The Temple Mount is the epicenter of worship of God, not doubt.
But as a result of creating this universal epicenter of worship, through
the building of the Temple, the nation of Israel is raised to the highest
status among the nations as well.

Zephaniah 3:9 – One Shoulder

Then I will purify the lips of the peoples, that all of them may call on the name of the Lord and serve him shoulder to shoulder.

This verse appears within a prophecy of Zephaniah regarding the end times, a time when all the peoples of the earth will recognize the truth of God and serve Him as one. There are a great many verses in the Bible that foretell a time when all humanity will recognize and worship God. Throughout the words of the prophets Isaiah, Jeremiah, Ezekiel, Zechariah, and numerous others, we find a similar vision expressed; that there will come a time when all will serve the one and only God, the God of Israel.

Translation issue

What makes this verse unique is the words used in the closing phrase. The translation we cited here refers to all peoples calling on the name of the Lord and serving Him "shoulder to shoulder." But many Bible translations disagree. Here are two popular translations, the English Standard and the King James:

For at that time I will change the speech of the peoples to a pure speech, that all of them may call upon the name of the Lord and serve him <u>with one accord</u>. (ESV)

For then will I turn to the people a pure language, that they may all call upon the name of the Lord, to serve him <u>with one consent</u>. (King James Version)

The difference is striking. After all, the image of "shoulder to shoulder" is very specific. It names a specific body part. It would be very surprising if the original Hebrew did not mention the word "shoulder." On the other hand, if the verse is correctly translated by the later two versions I just cited, what justification is there for the first translation, "shoulder to shoulder"?

One Shoulder

So, what does the Hebrew actually say?

In Hebrew the final words of the verse are *shechem echad*. *Shechem* means "shoulder." *Echad* is the Hebrew word for "one." The precise translation of *shechem echad* is "one shoulder."

Those who translate *shechem echad* as "with one consent" or "with one accord" chose to explain the imagery of Zephaniah's prophecy rather than translate it. This is an important point. Throughout the Bible, there are situations where translators don't translate the words directly. Instead, if figurative language is used, they will sometimes "translate" it as though it was not figurative. That's what these translators did here. By doing this, the translators deprive their readers of the imagery of the text. Obviously Zephaniah was describing all humanity serving God in agreement and unison, with "one accord" or "consent." But Zephaniah used the imagery of the shoulder to express this.

Shoulder = Carrying a burden

Throughout the Bible, the *shechem* – shoulder – is figuratively used to describe the carrying of a load, bearing a burden. For example:

When he sees how good is his resting place and how pleasant is his land, he will bend his shoulder to the burden and submit to forced labor. – Genesis 49:15

I will crush the Assyrian in my land; on my mountains I will trample him down. His yoke will be taken from my people, and his burden removed from their shoulders. – Isaiah 14:25

Shechem is also the name of a city in Israel, known today by its Arabic name, Nablus. But the word *shechem*, meaning "shoulder," appears 22 times in the Bible. In 15 of these verses the context is the carrying of a burden. In other words, when the word "shoulder" appears in prophetic imagery, we are correct to understand it as alluding to a burden that needs to be carried.

As I said above, those translators who rendered our verse as "one accord" or "one consent" chose to interpret the words of Zephaniah rather than translating them. The Hebrew words simply do not say anything about "consent" or "accord," which are synonyms for "agreement." What

Zephaniah was clearly saying is that all peoples will "shoulder" the burden of serving God together. These translators lost the important nuance of what Zephaniah was saying. Allow me to explain.

Zephaniah was not merely saying that all peoples would worship God together or even that they would agree. By invoking the image of a *shoulder*, Zephaniah was describing something much more significant. Namely, Zephaniah prophesied that all peoples of the earth would carry the yoke of the burden of service of God.

Serving God can be difficult. There are battles to be waged and won on behalf of God's truth. In fact, the verses leading up to ours describe God's retribution upon those peoples who have angered Him. In other words, they describe the triumph over evil. In that context, describing serving God as something done with the *shoulder* implies that we are bearing a burden, carrying a load for God. By translating this phrase as "one consent" we are led to believe that Zephaniah is describing simple agreement in the worship of God, like people gathered to sing God's praises. This is not what Zephaniah was implying.

—— *One shoulder, not two*

But there is another important nuance in this verse. I mentioned above that the Hebrew in this verse is *shechem echad*, "one shoulder." Notice that Zephaniah did not say "shoulder to shoulder," as many translations render our verse. He said, "one shoulder." So even those translators who correctly translated the word *shechem* deviated from the original Hebrew.

The reasoning behind the "shoulder to shoulder" translation is easy to understand. Multiple people do not have a single shoulder. So, if the prophet describes many people serving God "as one shoulder," it makes sense to translate it "shoulder to shoulder." But this is still not an accurate translation. And while not as egregious as the translations who ignored the word "shoulder" in this verse, this translation misses an important part of Zephaniah's message as well.

Considering that Zephaniah is expressing an end-times vision, his language must be understood symbolically. In other words, this verse is not part of a Biblical story of two people carrying a load on their actual physical shoulders. If it was, and the words *shechem echad* were used, it may then be appropriate to translate the phrase this way. But our verse is part of an end-times prophecy. The imagery of Zephaniah is meant to express a theological vision. Zephaniah could have said "shoulder to shoulder," using slightly different words. But he did not. Zephaniah wrote "one shoulder." And this is significant.

Think about the difference between "shoulder to shoulder" and "one shoulder." Picture two people carrying a burden together on their shoulders. They are standing next to each other, shoulder to shoulder. Although they are sharing the load they are carrying, each is in his own body. If one of them feels pain, the other does not feel it. When they are done, they will go their separate ways. They are shoulder to shoulder, each one a separate body.

But in the imagery of Zephaniah, all the peoples of the earth are serving God as *one shoulder*. Zephaniah's vision is of a cooperation that is so profound that they feel each other's pain. Their efforts are fused. They are in a single body. And when they are done with the task, they will not part.

The unity described by Zephaniah, the unity of all people in the service of God in the end-times, goes beyond mere cooperation. What Zephaniah describes in this verse is a bonding so powerful that there is a fusing of identities which includes shared pain. He is describing fundamental and permanent unity in service of God.

We are fortunate to live in an age when Christians and Jews, and God-fearers of many nations are joining together to fight the battles of God. Let us pray that we feel each other's pain and that we never part ways again.

Deuteronomy 5:31-33 (27-29) – The Land of the Law

But as for you, stand here by Me, that I may speak to you all the commandments and the statutes and the judgments which you shall teach them, that they may observe them in the land which I give them to possess.' So you shall observe to do just as the Lord your God has commanded you; you shall not turn aside to the right or to the left. You shall walk in all the way which the Lord your God has commanded you, that you may live and that it may be well with you, and that you may prolong your days in the land which you will possess.

The book of Deuteronomy is a series of speeches that Moses delivered at the end of the forty-year journey through the desert, during the final five weeks of his life. In the early chapters of the book, Moses reminds the people of Israel of many of the key events that happened since the Exodus from Egypt.

Deuteronomy 5 is a retelling of the great revelation at Mount Sinai, where God spoke the Ten Commandments and the covenant with Israel was established. This passage is the final verses of this chapter.

Are the commandments only for the land?

At first glance, this passage is similar to many others in which Moses implores the people to keep God's commandments, reminding them of the reward they will receive for their obedience. But if we read carefully, we will notice that Moses is not just telling the people that they must keep God's law. In verse 31, the first verse of the passage, God tells Moses that he must teach the people the laws so that "they may observe them in the land which I give them to possess." Then again, in verse 32, the final verse of the chapter, this point is repeated. Here we read that as a reward for obedience to God's law, "you may live and that it may be well with you, and that you may prolong your days in the land which you will possess."

According to the plain meaning of the first verse in our passage, it seems that the commandments are intended to be observed "in the land which I give them to possess." Now, obviously, the plan was for the people of Israel to enter the land and establish themselves there as a nation. Clearly, the Jewish people never planned to go into exile. All the commandments were intended to be performed by the nation of Israel in the land of Israel.

But here's the problem. If the intention was for the nation of Israel to live only in the land of Israel forever, then isn't it obvious that any fulfillment of the commandments will happen where they are located, i.e., in the land? Why bother mentioning the land at all? God should simply have instructed Moses to teach the commandments to the people "that they may observe them." Period. We know that this observance will happen in the land. After all, that is where they will be!

On the other hand, if the intention of God was that the commandments must be fulfilled everywhere the people of Israel are located, in the land of Israel or in exile, then why is the verse worded this way? Again, the plain meaning of the verse appears to be saying that Moses is to teach the people to observe the commandments in the land, and not outside of it.

—— Context: The Ten Commandments

To emphasize this point, it is important to note that these verses appear just after a review of the Ten Commandments. None of the Ten Commandments is dependent on being in the land of Israel. Commandments that depend on the land generally fall into two categories. First, there are the agricultural laws such as the seven-year *shemittah* cycle, first fruits, and others that are clearly tied to the actual produce of the land of Israel. Then there are national laws that apply to kings, the Temple, and the governing of a society. These laws are clearly intended only for the land of Israel where Israel is a functioning nation-state. Such laws simply cannot be performed outside the land.

But the laws that precede our verses, the Ten Commandments, have nothing to do with the land. Honor your father and mother? Don't murder? Don't commit adultery? Are these laws meant only for the land of Israel?

The answer is yes and no. Allow me to explain.

The purpose of Israel as a nation

Of course, every individual member of Israel is obligated to keep God's commandments wherever he or she may be. But let's remind ourselves of the purpose of the people of Israel.

In Exodus 19, just before the revelation at Sinai, God told Moses what the covenant they were about to enter was really all about.

And now, if you will surely obey My voice and keep My covenant, then you shall be My own possession among all the peoples, for all the earth is Mine; and you shall be to Me a kingdom of priests and a holy nation. – Exodus 19:5-6

A kingdom of priests and a holy nation. A priest – *kohen* in Hebrew – is a person whose mission is to help others, the flock, draw closer to God. A kingdom of priests is an entire society, a nation, that has a priestly role. If the nation of Israel is a kingdom of priests, or a priestly kingdom, it means that the role of Israel is to help the flock draw closer to God. And who is that flock? The nations of the world.

The mission of the Jewish people is not individual. It is national. The laws of the Torah encompass all areas of life, from dietary laws to how to properly set up a court system. The highest calling of the nation of Israel is first and foremost, to be a nation. A *holy nation.*

The purpose of the entire body of laws in the Torah is the formation of a complete society, a nation-state, that lives out God's will and serves as a beacon of divine light for the nations of the world.

So, while it is true that every individual Jew is obligated to observe the commandments to the best of their ability wherever they may find themselves, this is not the true purpose of God's law. The plain meaning of our passage is correct. The purpose of all God's law is the formation of a Godly society. A kingdom of priests and a holy nation.

And that can only happen as a nation in our own land, in the land of Israel.

The purpose of the commandments is for us to serve God by creating a Godly society. Even the laws that address individual behavior are meant to contribute to this goal. Our own private obedience helps make this Biblical vision a reality.

Jeremiah 32-37-41 – The Theological Message of God's Anger

I will gather them from all the lands where I had scattered them, in my anger, my fury, and with great wrath; and I will return them to this place, and I will cause them to dwell securely. They will be my people, and I will be their God. I will give them a single heart and a single path to fear Me for all time, for their good and for their children after them. I will enact an eternal covenant with them, that I will not turn away from them, so I may benefit them; and I will place fear of Me in their hearts so they will never forsake Me. And I will rejoice over them to benefit them, and I will implant them in this land, assuredly, with all My heart and all My soul.

Why mention God's anger?

This passage is one of many in the prophets that foretell a time when God will gather in the scattered exiles of Israel and bring them back to their land, never to be exiled again. While this prophecy is one of reconciliation, depicting God's eternal love for Israel, Jeremiah still mentions God's "anger," "fury," and "great wrath." If the point of the passage is to remind Israel of the promise of restoration in the future, when God will re-enact His covenant with Israel and shower them with blessings, why mention God's state of rage and fury which led to the exile? How does a reminder of God's anger contribute to the vision of restoration that is the subject of the passage?

God's anger after the Golden Calf

To answer this question, let's go back to the very first time in the Bible that we find God enraged at the children of Israel. In Exodus, after the great revelation at Mount Sinai, Moses went up the mountain to receive the Torah from God. After 40 days and 40 nights, the people became impatient. They worried that Moses would never come back. In their panic, they fashioned a golden calf and declared, "These are your gods, o Israel, who brought you out of Egypt." (Ex. 32:4) The scene that followed included worship and offerings to the golden calf.

God's reaction was to tell Moses that He was going to wipe out the children of Israel. Here is Moses' response:

Then Moses entreated the Lord his God, and said, "O Lord, why does Your anger burn against Your people whom You have brought out from the land of Egypt with great power and with a mighty hand? Why should the Egyptians speak, saying, 'With evil intent He brought them out to kill them in the mountains and to destroy them from the face of the earth'? Turn from Your burning anger and change Your mind about doing harm to Your people. Remember Abraham, Isaac, and Israel, Your servants to whom You swore by Yourself, and said to them, 'I will multiply your descendants as the stars of the heavens, and all this land of which I have spoken I will give to your descendants, and they shall inherit it forever.'" So, the Lord changed His mind about the harm which He said He would do to His people. – Exodus 32:11-14

Moses' argued that if God did, in fact, destroy the children of Israel and begin anew, the message to the nations of the world would be that God's promises to Abraham, Isaac, and Jacob, were not eternal. The inescapable conclusion would be that God's promises are conditional on Israel's behavior.

— *What if God breaks a promise?*

Interestingly, this argument is exactly what was argued by the early Christian theologian Augustine. Augustine argued that God's covenant with Israel was no longer valid due to the Jews' failure to keep up their end of the relationship.

Moses' response to God was that God's promise to the patriarchs of Israel was that their descendants would inherit the land forever. If God were to now destroy Israel, God would reveal Himself to be a God who does not keep His promises. By accepting Moses' argument and changing His mind, God revealed a powerful truth about His relationship to Israel. Namely, that the covenantal promises to His people are eternal and unconditional. There is no way for Israel to break the covenant to the point that it is rendered null and void.

There is a powerful theological point here that often goes unnoticed. Moses did not try to downplay the grave sin of the children of Israel. He did not appeal to God's mercies. Moses argued that the truth of who God is and what His promises mean demands that He not end His relationship with Israel. By accepting Moses' argument, God revealed an important aspect of the covenant with Israel that could not have been learned any other way.

The lesson of Israel's disobedience

As ironic as this may sound, had the children of Israel always remained faithful and obedient to God, we would never know the extent of God's commitment to keep His promises to Abraham, Isaac, and Jacob. Without Israel turning its back on God and sinning in such a grave manner, we could be left with the impression that God's covenant with Israel is conditional. So long as Israel is faithful and obedient, the covenantal promises are intact. The assertion that God's promises to Israel are dependent on Israel's fidelity to God would be a logical assumption. Ironically, it is only due to the grave betrayal of God with the golden calf that we know that God's promises are eternal, unconditionally.

I'd like to suggest that this is the reason Jeremiah included mention of God's anger and wrath in this passage. Rather than merely taking an opportunity to include some words of rebuke in this prophecy of restoration, Jeremiah's mention of God's rage only adds to the message of reconciliation. In other words, even though God scattered Israel into exile "in my anger, my fury, and with great wrath," no one should make the mistake of thinking that this means the end of God's covenant with Israel.

For many centuries, the majority of Christians believed exactly this mistake, that God had ended His covenant with Israel. The nation of Israel does not deny the gravity of our betrayal of God. We sinned. And our exile and suffering are well-deserved. But we also never stopped believing and knowing that God would redeem us from exile and gather us back to our land, not for our sake, but for the sake of His covenant with Abraham, Isaac, and Jacob. And that covenant is forever.

God's promises to the Jewish people are eternal, not because they are earned or deserved, but because God's promises to the patriarchs are irrevocable. Those theologians who mistakenly thought that God had forsaken Israel fell into the mistake predicted by Moses.

Deuteronomy 1:8 – The Land of Abraham, Isaac, and Jacob

See, I have placed the land before you; go in and possess the land which the Lord swore to give to your fathers, to Abraham, to Isaac, and to Jacob, to them and their descendants after them.'

One of the principles of Biblical study that I have used throughout this book can be summed up as follows: every word matters. This may seem obvious, but it isn't. Think of how many details we overlook as we read the Bible because we don't stop and ask ourselves whether a particular word or phrase is necessary for the simple meaning of the text. But if we pay attention to every word, we will discover layers of meaning that we would never have seen had we not read carefully.

Why mention the forefathers by name?

I mention this because of a phrase in our verse that is so common that most of us would never think to explore it. After describing the promised land as "the land which the Lord swore to give to your fathers," what is added by naming the fathers, "to Abraham, to Isaac, and to Jacob"? Don't we know who the fathers were?

The Jewish sages of the first century, in the *Midrash Sifre*, a compendium of comments on the book of Deuteronomy based on the teachings of the great 1st century sage, Rabbi Akiva, addresses the issue in our verse:

"Which the Lord swore to give to your fathers." What is to be learned from naming Abraham, Isaac, and Jacob? Abraham was worthy of the land on his own. Isaac was worthy of the land on his own. And Jacob was worthy of the land on his own. – Sifre Devarim 8

The sages suggest that each of the three patriarchs is mentioned to draw our attention to their independent merit. Each of the three patriarchs alone was worthy of the promise of land. Let's explore this comment by the Jewish sages. Besides the simple message that all three of the patriarchs were great enough that each one would have merited the promise of land independently, what deeper understanding may we derive from this teaching?

Three different relationships to the land

Although Abraham, Isaac, and Jacob each received the land promise from God, their respective relationships to the land were not the same.

Abraham was not native to the promised land. As we know, God called on Abraham to uproot himself from his birthplace and relocate to the land of Canaan. Abraham was an immigrant. His connection to the land was based solely on the call of God, telling him to go there. And God's promise of the land to Abraham occurred shortly after he arrived by God's command.

Isaac, in contrast, was not only born in the land, but he also lived there his entire life. Never once did Isaac leave. But Isaac's relationship with the land goes beyond the fact that he was born there. After his father Abraham signed a treaty with Abimelech, ceding ownership of parts of the promised land to the Philistines, Isaac arrived and reasserted his ownership over these areas. In fact, God promised the land to Isaac upon Isaac's arrival in this Philistine controlled territory. After the Philistines stopped up the wells Abraham had dug, Isaac redug them and gave them their original names. Isaac was also the only one of the patriarchs who was a farmer, making him far more connected to the land than his herdsman father and son. Isaac's primary mission in life was the assertion of ownership over the land of Israel. He was born in the land. He lived in the land. He died in the land.

Although Jacob was born in the land of Israel, he lived much of his life outside of it. Jacob was the first of the patriarchs to go into exile. Interestingly, God's promise of the land to Jacob was made just as Jacob was on his way out of the land for the first time.

He had a dream, and behold, a ladder was set on the earth with its top reaching to heaven; and behold, the angels of God were ascending and descending on it. And behold, the Lord stood atop it and said, "I am the Lord, the God of your father Abraham and the God of Isaac; the land on which you lie, I will give it to you and to your descendants." – Genesis 28:12-13

Jacob returned 22 years later only to go into exile again, spending the final 17 years of his life in Egypt. On his deathbed, Jacob insisted that his body be buried in the promised land (Gen. 47:29).

I'd like to suggest that Abraham, Isaac, and Jacob, represent three different relationships to the land of Israel by the people of Israel.

Three lessons about the land

Abraham represents the call of God to go to the land. Abraham was the first to uproot himself from his birthplace and homeland and relocate to a new land, heeding the call of God. Abraham's journey to the land because of God's call is the first pilgrimage journey recorded in the Bible. We might suggest that every pilgrimage to seek the God of Israel in the land of Israel is an extension of that first journey. In the tradition of Abraham, almost all the millions of Jews who live in Israel today either uprooted themselves from the lands of their births, or are the children or grandchildren of those who did. To put it siimply, *Abraham represents pilgrimage to the land.*

Isaac represents Jewish sovereignty in the land. As I mentioned, Isaac never left the land. He was a native. He spent much of his life asserting ownership over lands that were in dispute with his neighbors. He planted. He dug wells. He made his sovereignty over the land clear to all. *Isaac represents the fact that the Jewish people are natives of the land, that it is our national home.*

As mentioned, Jacob spent much of his life in exile, including his final years. This may not seem like a good example of a relationship with the land. Ironically, the opposite is true. Allow me to explain. So long as someone lives in the land in which they were born, we might assume that their connection to the land is contingent on their living there. Perhaps if they left the land, whether by force or by choice, their commitment to their native land would fade into the past. With many immigrants, this is exactly what happens.

But Jacob never lost his commitment to the land. He kept his vow to God to return to the land. Later, even as he realized that he would die in Egypt, he insisted that he be buried in the land. Jacob's persistent commitment and identification with God's promised land is the Jewish experience for most of our history. Wherever Jews have been scattered, and no matter how long the exile lasted, Jews everywhere never gave up the hope and dream of returning to our homeland. *This commitment to the land of Israel despite thousands of years of exile is the extension of Jacob's relationship to the land.*

Each of the patriarchs set an example of a specific relationship to God's promised land. And as the verse concludes, all these relationships have simultaneously continued through "their descendants after them."

The Jewish people's relationship to the land of Israel is threefold. God told us to go there to build our nation. It is our homeland where we are sovereign. And we never lost our identification with the land, despite thousands of years in exile. This is the legacy of Abraham, Isaac, and Jacob.

Ezekiel 37:24-28 – The Certainty of Complete Restoration

My servant David will be king over them, and they will all have one shepherd; and they will walk in My ordinances and keep My statutes and observe them. They will live on the land that I gave to Jacob My servant, in which your fathers lived; and they will live on it, they, and their sons and their sons' sons, forever; and David My servant will be their prince forever. I will make a covenant of peace with them; it will be an everlasting covenant with them. And I will place them and multiply them and will set My sanctuary in their midst forever. My dwelling place also will be with them; and I will be their God, and they will be My people. And the nations will know that I am the Lord who sanctifies Israel, when My sanctuary is in their midst forever.

Throughout this book we are studying passages in the Bible that speak of the restoration of Israel after the long and arduous exile. This passage, like many others we have seen, describes the nation of Israel once again implanted in the land of Israel, never to be exiled again. It is all too easy to read these verses at the surface level. We see reference to Israel returning to obedience. We see the return to the land, the restoration of the kingship of the line of David, the rebuilding of the Temple, the return of God's presence to dwell within Israel, and finally, the passage concludes with the spread of knowledge of God to the nations.

Pointing to Leviticus

One of the principles of Biblical study that we must always keep in mind is that the Bible is self-referential. What this means is that it is common for phrases and passages in the Bible to point to other passages. By noticing these connections, we gain a more complete awareness of what the Bible is actually telling us.

Consider the following passage from Leviticus:

If you <u>walk</u> in My statutes and <u>keep</u> My commandments <u>and observe them</u>, then I shall give you rains in their season, so that the land will yield its pro-

duce and the trees of the field will bear their fruit. Indeed, your threshing will last for you until grape gathering, and grape gathering will last until sowing time. You will thus eat your food to the full and <u>live securely in your land</u>. ... So I will turn toward you and make you fruitful and <u>multiply you, and I will confirm My covenant with you</u>. 10 You will eat the old supply and clear out the old because of the new. Moreover, <u>I will make My sanctuary among you</u>, and My soul will not reject you. I will also walk among you <u>and be your God, and you shall be My people</u>. – Leviticus 26:3-5, 9-12

This passage in Leviticus opens the chapters of blessings and curses of Israel, in response to their obedience or disobedience to God. Now reread the verses from Ezekiel we are studying. It is clear that Ezekiel was using phrases and imagery from Leviticus 26.

────── *A full restoration*

By choosing to repeat these words and phrases in his prophecy, Ezekiel reminds us of the original covenantal promises in Leviticus. By doing so, Ezekiel is emphasizing the completeness of the restoration he is describing. Ezekiel describes the ultimate future restoration of Israel using the language and imagery of God's original blessings should Israel be obedient to God.

Why is this important? Ezekiel lived at the time of the exile after the destruction of the first temple. This was the first time that the people of Israel experienced destruction and exile. For most people living at that time, they most likely feared that this was the end of Israel as a nation. But even for those who held out hope of some future for Israel, they must certainly have feared that even if God would keep them alive for the future, things would most likely never be the same. It's human nature that when things are getting worse, we find it almost impossible to imagine them getting better. It's even more difficult to imagine them returning to the ideal, perfect state.

Imagine a married couple going through a tough stretch. One of them has betrayed the other. There is anger, rejection, loss of trust. Perhaps they even decide to separate for a while. For the guilty party in the relationship there may be some hope of reconciliation, but the possibility that things can be restored to their original ideal state, as though nothing ever went wrong, is almost certainly out of the question.

By using a series of words and phrases from the blessings in Leviticus, God's first blessings of Israel which assume total obedience, Ezekiel sends a powerful message. Full reconciliation is not only possible, but it is also assured.

In human relationships, complete reconciliation is usually impossible. Scars and imperfections remain. But not so with God. His restoration brings us back to the ideal, unblemished relationship as it was originally intended.

Deuteronomy 11:11 – A Land Built for Prayer

The land that you are crossing there to take possession of it is a land of mountains and valleys; according to the rains of the heavens it drinks water.

Israel vs. Egypt

This verse presents a contrast between the Promised Land, the land of Israel, on one hand, and the land of Egypt on the other. The verse prior to this one stated:

For the land that you are coming there to take possession of it is not like the land of Egypt, from which you emerged, where you would sow your seed, and water it on foot, like a vegetable garden. – Deuteronomy 11:10

Egypt is a land that gets its water from the Nile River. Each year the Nile naturally swells and provides an abundance of water to all the surrounding low farmland. It is an ever-present source of water. In other words, Egypt has abundant water at all times. The land of Israel does not.

Based on this context, we can see that what is described here is not a blessing. The Bible describes the land of Israel as a land where irrigation for agriculture is not so easy to come by. "It is a land of mountains and valleys." Even the water that comes through rainfall is not evenly distributed. Water on mountains flows to the valleys. And even the water found in underground springs and aquifers is the result of rainwater that seeps down through the ground. Was God telling Israel that the land they were entering was inferior to Egypt?

A land built for prayer

The point of this verse, and of the verses that surround it, is not to simply inform the people of Israel about the topography and sources of water that await them in the promised land. The message is a spiritual one. The land of Israel is built for faith and prayer.

It is worth noting that according to historical sources regarding ancient Egyptian religion, although Egyptians had an extensive religious system, prayer was almost entirely non-existent. The average person was not called upon to pray at any point. There were priests who carried out service to the gods on behalf of the people, but individual prayer was absent. Egyptians enjoyed constant abundance. They had no reason to pray.

— *The spiritual danger of abundance*

While wealth is obviously a blessing from God, it comes with spiritual risks.

Lest you eat and be satisfied, and you will build good houses, and settle. And your cattle and your flocks increase; and silver and gold increase for you; and everything that is yours increases, and your heart will grow haughty, and you will forget the Lord your God, who took you out of the land of Egypt, from the house of bondage. – Deut. 8:12-14

The simple truth is that when people are materially comfortable, faith suffers. The opposite should be true. Benefitting from the blessings of God ought to make us more grateful to Him, more aware of His hand on our lives. But human nature is such that we are prone to forget about God when our material needs are met. This is a challenge to all of us who live in the relative luxury of modern Western Civilization. For all our problems, we are undoubtedly the most secure and wealthy society in human history.

The land of Israel is a land that depends on rainwater for survival. This remains true to today. Israelis are a rare society where everyone is happy on rainy days. Israeli news media carefully follows the progress of rainfall during the winter months, reporting on the quantity and discussing how much more we still need. The need for rain is an ever-present concern for Israel.

In Jewish practice, special prayers for rain are added to the daily liturgy during the winter months of the year. We can not complacently sit back and rely on readily available resources. We need to hope. We need to pray.

With this perspective, we can understand that our verse does, in fact, describe a great blessing. Ironically, the blessing in our verse is the fact that the land of Israel *does not* have abundant natural water sources. Because of this, we more readily turn to God in prayer. And that's just the way He wants it.

We must always recognize that everything that we have, and take for granted, is a gift from God. We must always rely on Him.

Deuteronomy 11:12 – God's Conscious Concern for the Land

A land that the Lord your God seeks; always the eyes of the Lord your God are upon it, from the beginning of the year until year end.

"Seeks" or "Cares"

The Hebrew word for "seeks" in this verse is *doresh*. Almost all English translations render the word as "cares for." The problem with this translation is that the verb root DRSh, which appears over 150 times in the Bible, simply does not mean "cares." For example, this verb appears for the very first time in the Bible in Genesis 9.

After Noah and his family emerged from the ark after the flood, God gave them a number of commandments. Among them was the prohibition against murder.

But I will <u>demand</u> your blood of your lives, from every beast I will <u>demand</u> it. And from man, from every man for his brother, will I <u>demand</u> the life of man – Genesis 9:5

The word "demand," repeated 3 times, is various conjugations of DRSh, the verb in our verse.

But it's not so simple for us to conclude based on this single verse in Genesis that DRSh means "demand." Consider the following two examples, which make similar use of the word.

The children agitated within her. She said, 'If so, why am I like this?' and she went to <u>inquire</u> of the Lord. – Genesis 25:22

You will seek from there the Lord your God, and you will find Him, when you <u>search</u> for Him with all your with all your heart and with all your soul. – Deuteronomy 4:29

In neither of these two verses can we translate the verb DRSh as "demand" as it was translated in Genesis when God spoke to Noah. It is also difficult to apply the meanings that we have seen in the verses quoted from Genesis 25 and Deuteronomy 4 to our verse here in Deuteronomy 11.

Proactively anticipate

Based on the usages that we have seen in these few examples I would like to suggest that the verb root DRSh describes proactive anticipation. By "proactive anticipation" I mean, anticipation of an outcome that includes active steps by the one who is anticipating the outcome.

So, when God told Noah that He will hold people responsible for the deaths of other human beings, He meant that there will be an outcome, a punishment, that He will actively seek to bring about. Rebekah, pregnant with Jacob and Esau desperately wanted to know why her pregnancy was so difficult. She took steps to discover the explanation. And Deuteronomy 4:29 describes one who is making an effort to draw closer to God. The Bible is telling us that this must be an active process.

What does this mean for God?

Back to our verse. What does it mean that God always "seeks" or "cares for" – *doresh* – the land of Israel?

The previous verse told us that the land of Israel depends on rain. The verses that follow ours teach us that the amount of rainfall in the land of Israel depends entirely on the extent to which the nation of Israel dwelling in the land is obedient to God's commandments. Based on both the context just outlined and our brief exploration of the meaning of the verb DRSh, I'd like to suggest an important lesson of this verse.

In this passage in Deuteronomy, the Bible is describing a unique system for rainfall. If the nation of Israel prays, obeys the commandments, and lives in accordance with God's will, there will be abundant rain. If they violate God's will and turn to false gods, rain will not fall. Reading this, one might be led to think that, as supernatural as this cause-and-effect system is, it works in an unconscious and automated way. In other words, God set up a system whereby the direct result of our obedience or disobedience will be more or less rainfall. God set it up, so to speak, and the program runs. Obeying the commandments would be like putting money in a vending machine.

Our verse teaches us that this understanding is incorrect. While it's true that the quantity of rainfall will be determined by our obedience to God, it is not an automated and unconscious system. God will always be actively involved, always consciously evaluating and deciding how to respond to our actions. This idea is then emphasized by the second half of the verse, "the eyes of the Lord your God are upon it from the beginning of the year until year's end."

In other words, God is actively concerned and involved. He didn't simply set up a system within which we then operate. Our obedience to His will and His corresponding blessing of rain is a constant expression of an active and conscious relationship.

God's promises of reward or punishment are not simply rules that are then unconsciously activated by our actions. God is always watching, always concerned, always involved.

Ezekiel 36:24-28 – Physical and Spiritual Redemptions

For I will take you from the nations, gather you from all the lands and bring you into your own land. Then I will sprinkle clean water on you, and you will be clean; I will cleanse you from all your filth and from all your idols. Moreover, I will give you a new heart and put a new spirit within you; and I will remove the heart of stone from your flesh and give you a heart of flesh. I will put My spirit within you and cause you to walk in My statutes, and you will be careful to observe My ordinances. You will live in the land that I gave to your forefathers; so you will be My people, and I will be your God.

Bible readings in the synagogue

Each week, as part of the morning service in the synagogue, a section of the Torah, the five books of Moses, is read. Over the course of each year, the entire five books are completed. In addition to the weekly portion from the first five books of the Bible, the Torah, a second reading is done from the books of the prophets.

But rather than following an order through the books of the prophets, these portions from the prophets were chosen for a thematic connection either to the Torah portion that was read that day, or to the important days on the Jewish calendar that coincide with the following week. For example, on the Sabbath morning preceding *Yom Kippur*, the Day of Atonement, the prophetic reading is from Hosea 14, beginning with the words, "Return, O Israel, to the Lord your God." That passage in Hosea, focuses on repentance and return to God and sends the message that return to God is a necessary predicate to the atonement from sin achieved on *Yom Kippur*.

Similarly, in the weeks leading up to Passover a series of special portions from the prophets are read that are thematically connected to the upcoming festival. One of those portions includes the verses we are studying here. In fact, as the Jewish sages in the Talmud teach us, this chapter of

Ezekiel was chosen for one of the weeks leading up to Passover because of one specific verse in our passage.

Then I will sprinkle clean water on you, and you will be clean; I will cleanse you from all your filth and from all your idols.

Purification and redemption

According to the Jewish sages, the connection to Passover is that all who ate of the Passover lamb were required to be ritually pure. But there is another more profound spiritual lesson in the choice of this reading before Passover. As we approach the festival that recalls and celebrates our original redemption from Egypt, this special reading reminds us that purification and redemption go hand in hand.

Let's use our verses to explore the relationship between spiritual purification and God's plan for redemption.

Our verses lay out the plan for the redemption of Israel as follows:

1. Ingathering of the exiles to the land of Israel (v.24)
2. Purification by God from impurities (v.25)
3. A new heart (v.26)
4. God's spirit within Israel, leading to fulfilment of the commandments (v.27)
5. "You will live in the land … you will be My people, and I will be your God" (v.28)

Notice that the purification of Israel from impurities and idolatry happens after the ingathering of the exiles back to the land of Israel. And of course, the "new heart" and "new spirit" which then produce Israel's full obedience to God, happen after the ingathering of the exiles as well. In other words, the spiritual cleansing of Israel from impurities and idolatry is not a prerequisite for the ingathering of the nation from exile. The ingathering happens first.

First ingathering, then purification

Why is this important? Many people of Biblical faith look at the modern state of Israel and find themselves a bit perplexed. On one hand, the millions of Jews from all corners of the earth living in the land of Israel under Jewish sovereignty are clearly a fulfilment of Biblical prophecy. In fact, it's difficult to imagine a clearer fulfilment of Biblical prophecy than the ingathering of the exiles of Israel in our time. On the other hand, much of the Jewish population in Israel is far from obedient to God's word. Secularism is rampant in Israeli society. Since its founding, Israel's government has rarely been led by people who are committed to Torah law. To people of faith, the idea that God's promises of the redemption of His people are being fulfilled through a largely secular, liberal population is troubling.

But here's the thing. *This is exactly what the Bible says will happen.*

As our verses show, first God will end the exile and gather the scattered people of Israel back to the land. It is only after this ingathering that the process of the spiritual purification of Israel begins. We see the same thing in Deuteronomy 30, the first time the ingathering of the exiles was mentioned in the Bible.

The Lord your God will bring you back from captivity, and have compassion on you, and gather you again from all the nations where the Lord your God has scattered you. If any of you are driven out to the farthest parts under heaven, from there the Lord your God will gather you, and from there He will bring you. Then the Lord your God will bring you to the land which your fathers possessed, and you shall possess it. He will prosper you and multiply you more than your fathers. And the Lord your God will circumcise your heart and the heart of your descendants, to love the Lord your God with all your heart and with all your soul, that you may live. – Deuteronomy 30:3-6

Just as we read here in Ezekiel 36, Deuteronomy 30 lays out the same program of redemption. First the exiles are gathered into the land. Then, after the great ingathering, "the Lord your God will circumcise your heart..."

This is a critical lesson for anyone who seeks to understand God's plan for the redemption of Israel.

First, God redeems Israel physically, gathering them from the exile. Then, after this physical redemption is completed, the spiritual transformation of God's people begins.

Jeremiah 23:3-6 – Options in the Process of Redemption

"But I will gather the remnant of My flock out of all countries where I have driven them and bring them back to their folds; and they shall be fruitful and increase. I will set up shepherds over them who will feed them; and they shall fear no more, nor be dismayed, nor shall they be lacking," says the Lord. "Behold, the days are coming," says the Lord, "That I will raise for David a branch of righteousness; A king shall reign with wisdom and execute justice and righteousness in the land. In his days Judah will be saved, And Israel will dwell safely; and this is his name by which he will be called: The Lord is our righteousness."

As I have mentioned numerous times in this book, one of the principles of sound Biblical study is that the Bible is self-referential. Passages in the Bible that utilize similar words or imagery reveal deeper understandings when the related passages are read side by side. As valuable as this method of study is across the entire Bible, it is even more valuable, and accurate, when studying texts from the same book.

Similarities and differences in Jeremiah's words

Consider the following from Jeremiah 33, ten chapters after our passage.

"Behold, the days are coming," says the Lord, "that I will perform that good thing which I have promised to the house of Israel and to the house of Judah: 'In those days and at that time I will cause to grow up for David a branch of righteousness. He shall execute justice and righteousness in the land. In those days Judah will be saved, And Jerusalem will dwell safely. And this is the name by which she will be called: The Lord is our righteousness." – Jeremiah 33:14-16

By making note of the similarities between the passages, our attention is drawn to the differences between them. When we pay attention to the differences, we can uncover the specific lesson that each passage teaches us. Let's begin by listing these notable differences.

> Chapter 23
>
> I will <u>raise up</u> for David a branch of righteousness; <u>A king shall reign with wisdom</u>, and execute justice and righteousness in the land

> Chapter 33
>
> I will <u>sprout</u> for David a branch of righteousness. He shall execute justice and righteousness in the land.

When the prophecy is repeated in chapter 33, instead of saying God "will raise up" a leader from the house of David, Jeremiah uses the word "will sprout." Second, the verse in chapter 33 leaves out the phrase "a king shall reign with wisdom."

Here in chapter 23, near the end of the passage, the time period is called "his days," referring to the king from the seed of David, whereas in chapter 33, the it is called "those days." More strikingly, "Israel" is replaced by "Jerusalem."

Finally, in chapter 23, "The Lord is our righteousness" is the name that the king will be called, whereas in chapter 33, this is the name that Jerusalem will be called.

> and this is his name by which <u>he</u> will be called: The Lord is our righteousness

> And this is the name by which <u>she</u> will be called: The Lord is our righteousness.

Various options for redemption

To explain the meaning of these differences, we must first understand an important characteristic of Biblical prophecies about the future redemption.

Let's start with a simple question. If the future redemption of Israel is a certainty, why does it matter whether or not the people of Israel are faithful to God's covenant? Why does it matter whether or not the Jewish people stray from the ways of the Torah? Furthermore, why should the Jewish people take any action at all to bring about the ingathering of the exiles and the rebuilding of the kingdom of Israel? After all, God will bring the redemption regardless of Israel's disobedience or inaction.

While it is true and certain that God will bring about the redemption at some point in the future, the prophecies of the end times in the Bible are not entirely consistent with each other. According to the Jewish exegetical and theological tradition, these inconsistencies are due to the fact that the precise details of the redemptive process are flexible. To put this another way, the redemption of Israel is a certainty. The precise manner and pace of the redemption is not. This is where the behavior of the nation of Israel matters.

We determine the manner of redemption

According to the Jewish sages of the Talmud, there are, broadly speaking, two paths to redemption. One path is based on the Jewish people's merit. In this process, the righteous and faithful behavior of the Jewish people leads to a hastening of the process. This redemption based on merit is the ideal, and with it, the redemption reaches its completion smoothly and relatively peacefully.

The alternative to redemption based on the merit of the Jewish people is redemption "in its time," meaning, when God ordains that the time has come, even though the Jewish people have not merited to be redeemed. This redemptive process is more gradual and involves greater conflict along the way. According to this slower process of redemption, there are intermediary stages where the redemption is underway, accompanied by imperfections in Israel that will be rectified over time and with difficulties.

And this is the meaning of the two passages in Jeremiah we are studying.

Ideal vs. Imperfect redemption

In chapter 23, Jeremiah is describing the ideal, perfect redemption of Israel. Whereas in chapter 33, Jeremiah's prophecy is of an imperfect, more gradual process of redemption. So, in chapter 23, God will "raise up," which in Hebrew is the same word as "establish," the king from the seed of David. But in chapter 33 God will "sprout" such a leader. In other words, the process that will lead to a righteous king of Israel will begin, like a sprout, but will not yet reach its full mature form. This is why the phrase "A king shall reign with wisdom" is not included in chapter 33. Similarly, the redemptive time-period is called "his days" in chapter 23 because the righteous king is present and the active leader of the process. But in chapter 33, God is working without a righteous king of Israel, so the time-period is called "those days."

In chapter 23, "Israel" will be saved. But in chapter 33, it is only Judah and Jerusalem. "Israel" refers to the fully restored nation, whereas Judah and Jerusalem do not.

And finally, in the ideal redemption in chapter 23, God's righteousness is revealed through the righteous king of Israel from the seed of David who leads the nation through the process. "He will be called "the Lord is our righteousness" But in chapter 33, God's righteousness is revealed not through a righteous leader of Israel, but through what happens in the city of Jerusalem, i.e., "she will be called…"

There is much more to say on the topic of the options for how the process of redemption will unfold. But even from this short study we learn a powerful lesson. While God's redemptive plan for Israel and humanity is a certainty, the nature of the journey is up to us.

God's plan for history, and our lives, is determined by His will. At the same time, the pace and manner of that plan is affected by our own behavior. God gives us the freedom to determine how smooth or difficult the road to redemption will be.

Deuteronomy 30:3 – The Impossible Prophecy

The Lord your God will bring you back from captivity, and have compassion on you, and gather you again from all the nations where the Lord your God has scattered you.

We read with modern eyes

Have you ever thought about what it would have been like to hear the prophecies in the Bible at the time they were first spoken? Imagine you were there, over 3300 years ago, when Moses spoke the book of Deuteronomy, a series of speeches delivered to the children of Israel in the five weeks before he died. How would these words have sounded to you at the time?

When we read the Bible, whether we realize it or not, we read it through modern eyes. We read the biblical stories with the benefit of hindsight, knowing exactly how things turn out. And when we read prophecies of the future, we do so with knowledge of everything that has happened since the words were first spoken. Often, we understand details of the prophecies that those who were alive at the time could not have understood.

But there's also a downside to reading the Bible through our modern lens. Because of the changes that have taken place over the past 3000 years, the world we live in is not the same as the world in which the Biblical prophecies were spoken and written. As a result of how much has changed, we can easily miss the full power and intent of the words we are reading.

The context of Deuteronomy 30

Deuteronomy 30 is a perfect example of this phenomenon. To fully appreciate what this prophecy is saying, let's review the chapters leading up to it.

In Deuteronomy 28, Moses related the blessings that would be bestowed on the nation of Israel as reward for faithfully observing God's covenant, as well as the terrible punishments that would befall them should they stray from God. The final verses of the punishments describe the nation of Israel begin scattered into exile.

Then the Lord will scatter you among all peoples, from one end of the earth to the other, and there you shall serve other gods, which neither you nor your fathers have known — wood and stone. – Deuteronomy 28:64

Then, in chapter 29, Moses continues by telling the nation that when they are in exile, the land will lie desolate. Moses even describes how in the distant future people from other nations will see the destruction of the land and the exile of the Jewish people and conclude that God has done this because the Jews turned their backs on God. (Deut. 29:22-28)

Then comes Deuteronomy 30. Here, Moses tells the people that after many generations of exile, scattered to the four corners of the earth, the people of Israel will return to the land.

The Lord your God will bring you back from captivity, and have compassion on you, and gather you again from all the nations where the Lord your God has scattered you. If any of you are driven out to the farthest parts under heaven, from there the Lord your God will gather you, and from there He will bring you. Then the Lord your God will bring you to the land which your fathers possessed, and you shall possess it. He will prosper you and multiply you more than your fathers. – Deuteronomy 30:3-5

Deuteronomy 30 is happening now

As I write this, I am sitting in a café in a crowded shopping mall Bet Shemesh, a half hour drive from Jerusalem. The modern state of Israel is prosperous and populated by millions of Jews from every corner of the earth. Every detail of the verses I just quoted has been fulfilled in our time. Think about that. Here is a biblical prophecy spoken over 3300 years ago. Ever since then, everyone who read the Bible read these verses as a future prophecy. And today, we live in a time when every word of these verses is a reality. The Jewish people have returned en masse to our land. We have taken possession of it in the form of Jewish sovereignty. Israel is a prosperous nation. And there are more Jews in the land than at any other time in history.

How Deuteronomy 30 sounded back then

But what did the people who first heard this prophecy think? When Moses spoke these words, there were many nations who existed that are no longer around. Where are the Hittites? Or the Assyrians? Or the Emorites? What happened to these nations? The answer is that they were conquered by invading empires. In what historians refer to as "the age of empires," powerful nations swept across the earth, conquering smaller nations along the way. The Assyrians, the Persians, the Greeks, and the Romans all conquered numerous smaller peoples. And after conquering them, these empires would not simply try to rule over these peoples in their native lands. They would first kill most of the men of fighting age. And then they would send the rest of the population, or much of it, into exile. Having conquered many peoples, these empires would mix the populations throughout their empires, teaching them a new language and culture, absorbing them into their empires.

The point I am making is that exile was a common feature of the ancient world. But here's what never happened. None of the smaller nations that were conquered and exiled by these empires ever returned to their homeland after many generations scattered to the four winds. In the ancient world, going into exile meant the end of your national identity.

An impossible prophecy

With this context in mind, we can more fully grasp the enormity of Moses' prophecy. Moses declared that the nation of Israel would go into exile, scattered to many different corners of the earth. To anyone living at the time who heard these words, this could mean only one thing: the end of the nation of Israel. When Moses then prophesied that the nation of Israel would return from this exile in the very distant future, he was describing something impossible. Who would still be around to return after thousands of years? How would a national identity be preserved as a scattered nation in exile over so many centuries. The absurdity of Moses' prophecy would have been clear to someone hearing it at the time. And yet, this is exactly what happened.

The miracle of Israel's rebirth as a prosperous and independent nation after thousands of years of exile is on par with the greatest Biblical miracles that we read about in the Exodus story. Maybe even greater.

Leviticus 26:1-4 – Holiness in Time and Space

You shall not make false gods for yourselves, and you shall not erect an idol or pillar. And an ornamented stone you shall not place in your land to bow down upon it, for I am the Lord your God. You shall keep my Sabbaths and revere my sanctuary: I am the Lord. If you walk in my statutes and observe my commandments and do them, then I will give you your rains in their season, and the land shall yield its increase, and the trees of the field shall yield their fruit.

The Sabbath and the Sanctuary?

These verses are followed by blessings that will be bestowed on Israel if they are obedient to God, and the punishments, should they stray. The third verse quoted above is strange. It seems like a non sequitur. Why are the commandments to keep the Sabbath and to revere the sanctuary, which refers to the tabernacle and subsequent temple, placed together in a single sentence? What do they have to do with each other? Looking at the fuller context of this verse, what do keeping the Sabbath and revering the sanctuary have to do with the promise of abundance and blessing that follows in the next verses?

This is not the only place in the Five Books of Moses where we see the sanctuary and the Sabbath juxtaposed. Exodus 35, the first of five consecutive chapters entirely devoted to the construction of the Tabernacle, opens with three verses about the importance of the Sabbath. So, what is the connection between the sanctuary and the sabbath?

Sabbath: The beginning of Holiness

The Sabbath is the first thing in the Bible that is called "holy".

So God blessed the seventh day and <u>made it holy</u>, because on it God rested from all his work that he had done in creation. – Genesis 2:3

What does it mean when we say that something is "holy"? Something that is holy is set aside for a higher purpose. So, what is the higher purpose of the Sabbath? Here is the fourth of the ten commandments:

Remember the Sabbath day, to make it holy. Six days you shall labor, and do all your work, and the seventh day is a Sabbath to the Lord your God. On it you shall not do any work, you, or your son, or your daughter, your male servant, or your female servant, or your livestock, or the sojourner who is within your gates. For in six days the Lord made heaven and earth, the sea, and all that is in them, and rested on the seventh day. Therefore, the Lord blessed the Sabbath day and made it holy. – Exodus 20:8-11

We are commanded to rest from all work because God created the world in six days and rested on the seventh day. And as the final verse in this passage tells us, this is the reason that God made it holy.

Simply understood, the purpose of the Sabbath is for us to recognize that God is the creator and master of the world. By ceasing our own creative activity for one day each week, we acknowledge that it is God who is master of time, and not us. And this is the meaning of *holiness* in general. Let me explain.

A "Holy" nation

Another thing that is called *holy* is the nation of Israel. (Deut. 7:6, 14:2,21) What does this mean? God is the master of all nations. He is the Master of History. But how does He display this mastery? The answer is, God shows His mastery of History through the nation of Israel. Because the history of Israel fulfills the promises that God made thousands of years ago, everyone in the world can see God acting in the world. But here's the key, if Israel's history was similar to that of other nations, God's hand in Israel's history would not be clear.

Think about it. If there were other examples of nations, small in number, who were exiled and persecuted for thousands of years and then later returned to their homelands to become more numerous and more prosperous than their ancestors, there would be nothing miraculous about the history of Israel. Israel's rebirth as a nation after a long exile would not be evidence of God. It is only because of the unique and miraculous history of the Jewish people that God is revealed as the master of the histories of *all nations*. In other words, something that is *holy* is set apart to be treated differently so that God is revealed through that difference.

Holiness reveals God's control

The Sabbath works the same way. We work all week. We try to make a living. We can easily slip into the illusion that we control our own financial destiny. By singling out one day as a "sabbath to the Lord your God" where we don't do any work, we remind ourselves that it is God who controls our work and the fruit of our labors. To illustrate the point, we could easily imagine someone who chooses to work on the Sabbath because he feels that he can't miss the day of work and still make ends meet. Such a person clearly has no understanding of where his financial well-being truly comes from. By resting on the Sabbath day, we make it *holy*. Meaning, we set aside this day as different as a lens through which to see God's mastery over our labors.

Holiness in Time and Space

But the message of the Sabbath goes deeper. By strictly honoring the Sabbath day, we recognize God's mastery over *time*. Our time is not our own. God is in control. By separating this one day a week as time for God, we recognize that He is the master of all time.

And this is the purpose of the sanctuary. What the Sabbath is for time, the sanctuary is for space. The same way we can easily see ourselves as the masters of history, of our labors, and of our time; we can just as easily see ourselves as the masters of our spaces, our land, our homes. By dedicating a place for God, where we make pilgrimages and bring our first fruits, we recognize that God is master over space as well.

Now we can understand why this verse comes right before the blessings of prosperity. When we acknowledge that it is God who controls our time and space, that it is God who determines the success of our labors, we earn the blessings of God.

By keeping the Sabbath and revering God's sanctuary, we show God that we acknowledge that He is the true Master of our lives. We thus show God that we will never use our prosperity and independence to stray from Him.

Deuteronomy 28:7-10 – Fear of Israel and Fear of God

The Lord will cause your enemies who rise against you to be defeated before you. They shall come out against you one way and flee before you seven ways. The Lord will command the blessing on you in your barns and in all that you undertake. And he will bless you in the land that the Lord your God is giving you. The Lord will establish you as a people holy to himself, as he has sworn to you, if you keep the commandments of the Lord your God and walk in his ways. And all the peoples of the earth shall see that you are called by the name of the Lord, and they shall be afraid of you.

Question: Is it the goal of the nation of Israel to be feared by all the peoples of the earth?

The order of the redemption process

The sequence in these 4 verses present a step-by-step description of the process of the redemption of Israel.

1. Miraculous defeat of enemies who attack Israel
2. Blessing of material and economic abundance, in the land
3. Israel is established as a holy people to God, in obedience to the commandments
4. All the peoples of the earth will see God's special relationship to Israel
5. They all will fear Israel

Up until the final phrase in the passage, the sequence makes sense and reflects the story and mission of Israel. Consider the modern State of Israel. First, in 1948, the Jewish people had to win an impossible war against the armies of Lebanon, Syria, Jordan, Iraq, Egypt, Saudi Arabia, and the Arab Legion. And even after that war was won, the people of Israel still needed to fight more wars just to survive. The six-day war in 1967 and the

Yom Kippur war of 1973 were both conflicts in which the very survival of the Jewish state was in question. Israel was victorious every time.

The next stage is economic prosperity. And in fact, as we have mentioned many times in this book, Israel today has become an economic powerhouse, a land of prosperity and remarkable growth.

After the material blessings, the next stage in the redemptive process is the full return to obedience to the will of God, keeping all His commandments. This is a process that is underway but is far from complete. More and more Israelis of secular backgrounds are returning to tradition and to Torah observance.

As the verses continue to tell us, the next stage will be the recognition by all the peoples of the earth of God's special relationship to Israel, which in turn will cause all the nations to be afraid of Israel.

— *Does Israel want to be feared?*

Why is this a goal? We would have expected these verses to culminate in some description of how all the nations of the earth will serve God together, will stream to the land to worship God, will praise God for all He has done; as the prophets reiterate over and over. Why does this passage in Deuteronomy look forward to a time when the nations of the world will be afraid of the nation of Israel? What are they afraid of?

To appreciate what this verse is actually saying, a precise understanding of the Hebrew is in order. The phrase translated here, "and they shall be afraid of you," is made up of two words.

Ve'Yaru   and they shall be afraid

Memeka   of you

The prefix *ve* at the beginning of the first word means "and." *Yaru* means "they will fear." The *me* at the beginning of the second word means "or" or "from." *Eka* is the conjugal suffix meaning "you."

The word "fear" – *yirah* – appears hundreds of times in the Bible. But there are two ways that what is being feared can be described. Here are two examples we will use to understand this point.

Ve'yareita me'Elohecha   and you shall fear your God: I am the Lord – Leviticus 19:14

Le'yirah et Adonai Elohecha   to fear the Lord your God - Deuteronomy 10:12

Let's break down the Hebrew. *Ve'yareita* means "and you shall fear." *Elohecha* means "your God." Once again, the prefix *me* means "of" or "from." Now notice that in the second verse there is no *me* prefix. *Le'yirah* means "to fear," and *Adonai Elohecha* means "the Lord your God." But in the second verse instead of the subject of fear being introduced with the prefix *me*, it is introduced with the word *et*. Got that? If you aren't sure, pause and reread this paragraph while looking back at the two verses.

Fear of vs. Fear because of / from

Of the over 400 instances of the verb "to fear" in the Bible, there are many that introduce the subject that is feared with the prefix *me*, and many others that use the word *et*. *Et* is an untranslatable word that is used to point out a definite article. Now let's get to the explanation.

When fear of something or someone is *yirah* (fear) *et...*, it means that the thing itself is feared. A better word for this is "awe." So, for example, the verse in Deuteronomy 10 we just cited calls upon us to fear God. This does not mean fearing punishment *from* God, rather it means being in awe of God, of who He is.

On the other hand, when the verb "fear" is followed by *me*, it means that there is fear *as a result of* the subject, or fear of some consequence that emerges *from* the subject. So, in the verse from Leviticus, which comes at after a prohibition, the fear is fear of punishment that comes *from* God, not fear of God's essence itself. To sum up:

Yirah me   fear, resulting from the subject

Yirah et   awe of the subject itself

Based on this importance nuance in the text, I'd like to suggest that our verse is not describing the peoples of the earth being afraid of the nation of Israel. Rather, our verse is describing the peoples of the earth being fearful *as a result of* the nation of Israel. Here's the verse again, with a modification to the final words based on what I have explained.

And all the peoples of the earth shall see that you are called by the name of the Lord, <u>and they shall be afraid because of you.</u>

Considering the beginning of the verse, and the content of the verses that lead up to it, I believe that the verse is describing the peoples of the earth being in awe and fear of God as a result of what they see in the nation of Israel. The nations of the earth will witness the hand of God, and His name, upon the people of Israel and this will cause them to be in awe of God. Their fear of God will result from what they see in Israel.

Understood this way, our verse describes the mechanism by which God uses Israel to bring knowledge and awe of Him to the entire world.

The unique and miraculous story of the exile and redemption of Israel is the vehicle that God uses to instill fear of Him in all the peoples of the earth.

Zechariah 2:8 – The danger of attacking Israel

For so says the Lord of hosts - after glory He sent me to the nations which plunder you - that he who touches you touches the apple of His eye.

Because the Bible contains no punctuation marks, there are verses like this one that are difficult to read according to the plain, word-for-word syntax. A few of the issues that occupy the commentaries include: What does "after glory" refer to? After beginning with "so says the Lord of Hosts," where exactly does the quote from God begin? Or is Zechariah speaking and paraphrasing God in his own words?

Pupil, not apple

The Jewish sages saw our verse as an expression of the extent of God's love and affection for the nation of Israel. God takes attacks on Israel personally. Israel is described here as "the apple of His eye." The Hebrew word translated as "apple" is *bavat*, which means "pupil." It is important to note that even though the common expression "apple of my eye," referring to something that is beloved is based on this verse, the way this expression is commonly used does not reflect the accurate meaning based on how it is used here. This is an important point because we can easily misunderstand the nuances in this verse if we assume a meaning for "apple of His eye" that is based on our common use of the expression, rather than how it is used here in the text of Zechariah.

We see the allegory of God's "pupil" or "apple" of His eye in Psalm 17 as well. Here, David prays to God for salvation from his enemies.

Show the wonder of Your lovingkindness with Your right hand, You who saves those who trust in You from those who rise up. <u>Guard me as the apple of Your eye</u>; Hide me in the shadow of Your wings, from the wicked who so oppress me, from my enemies who surround me to kill. – Psalm 17:7-9

The context in both Psalm 17 and here in Zechariah 2 is similar. In both verses, there is an enemy. Based on this similarity we see that the pupil or "apple" of God's eye refers to a sensitive point of attack, a spot that must be carefully protected. This makes sense here in Zechariah as well.

To sum up this first point: the metaphor "apple of His eye" referring to Israel is not meant only to convey God's affection for Israel. Rather, it refers to the sensitivity with which God views attacks by Israel's enemies. God views such attacks as one would view an attack on one's own eye.

— *After glory*

With this in mind, we can now understand the deeper significance of our verse. In this chapter, Zechariah is describing God's judgement upon the nations who caused Israel to suffer during their exile. The verse states that God will deal with "the nations which plunder you," at a time referred to as "after glory." Based on immediate context, we can assume that "glory" here refers to what was stated three verses earlier, in the previous prophecy.

There was the angel who spoke to me, going out; and another angel was coming out to meet him who said to him, "Run, speak to this young man, saying: 'Jerusalem shall be inhabited as towns without walls, because of the many of people and livestock in it. For I,' says the Lord, 'will be a wall of fire all around her, and I will be the glory in her midst.' – Zechariah 3-5

In other words, after Jerusalem is rebuilt and filled with the ingathered multitudes of Israel, God will then turn His attention to retribution against the nations who persecuted Israel.

Because God uses Israel as a vehicle to display His mastery over history, those who oppose Israel actually oppose God. Our verse states that God will treat attacks on Israel as attacks on Him, on his own "eye." The punishment of the nations who attacked Israel is not meant as mere revenge. God's judgement of His enemies, the enemies of Israel, is a necessary part of the revelation of truth. When justice is served, truth is revealed.

— *Attacking Israel is self-destructive*

A number of classical commentaries and some translators point to an alternative way of understanding the phrase "he who touches you touches the apple of His eye." This alternative understanding is best expressed in a comment by the Jewish sages of the 2nd century:

"He who touches you touches the apple of his eye": Rabbi Elazar son of Rabbi Yosi the Galilean taught: "It is as though [the attacker] is putting out his own eye with his finger." Rabbi Simeon replied to him, "Not so. Rather the verse refers to the Holy One." – Midrash Sifre Zuta

According to Rabbi Elazar, the end of our verse is saying that the enemies of Israel – "he who touches you," – are similar to a person who would put out his own eye. In other words, attacking Israel is irrational and self-destructive. Rabbi Elazar reads the words "apple of his eye" as referring to the eye of the enemy himself.

Rabbi Elazar's comment is justified based on the syntax of our verse. The beginning of the verse explicitly says that God is speaking. If God is speaking and says, "he who touches you touches the apple of <u>his</u> eye," it makes sense that it is not referring to God's own eye. The "his" at the end of the verse refers to "he who touches you."

Multiple possible meanings

It is important to remember that the prophecies in the Bible are often written in a manner that allows for multiple ways of reading the words. This is not because the authors of these books were poor writers. Rather, the word of God expressed in these sacred texts contains layers of meaning. These various layers are implied by the multiple ways some verses can be understood.

In the case of our verse, the two possible readings of the verse contain two distinct lessons about the consequences that befall those who attack God's people Israel. First, based on the common reading of the verse, those who attack Israel are viewed by God as if they had attacked God Himself in the most sensitive way. At the same time, Rabbi Elazar's reading of our verse teaches another lesson, namely, that being an enemy of Israel is self-destructive. The enemies of Israel suffer from their own actions. History is filled with examples of nations that attacked the Jewish people, only to be destroyed while the Jewish people prevailed.

God reveals Himself to the world through the history of the Jewish people. Those who stand against the fulfilment of God's plan for Israel stand against what God cares about most, and they cause their own destruction.

Psalm 46:1 - Seeing God more clearly troubled times

God is for us a refuge and strength; a help with troubles, [He is] very present.

When the world is in turmoil, it is natural for people to feel afraid. Psalm 46 describes those times when instability and conflict reign. Let's take a look at our verse together with the two that follow it.

God is for us a refuge and strength, a help with troubles, very present. Therefore we will not fear, when the earth is transformed and the mountains collapse into the heart of the sea, though its waters roar and foam and the mountains quake with their surging, Selah – Psalm 46:1-3

The strength to face troubled times

But our verse does not declare only that God protects us, saving us from troubled times. This verse takes God's providence in times of crisis beyond mere protection. The verse states that God is our "refuge and strength." The Hebrew word for strength, *oz*, means much more than physical strength. *Oz* implies strength of spirit as well, what we would call *boldness* and *courage.*

This is not a small point. The entirety of Psalm 46 speaks of God's mastery over history. Times of turmoil and insecurity make us all uneasy. These are times of historical transition. Our verse teaches us that faith in God gives us the confidence, optimism, and strength of spirit to face such challenging times. As people of faith in the God of the Bible, we know that the end of the story of humanity is ultimately good. The dark times are temporary. Most importantly, we also know that we have a role to play. God is not only a refuge. He is also our *strength*, our *boldness*. Faith in God empowers us to fight the good fight when the world becomes a dark place.

God helps us

But it's not just that God protects us and gives us confidence and strength. He is also a "help." In other words, he doesn't just empower us, leaving us to do all the work. He *helps* us as well. The Hebrew word for "help," *ezra*, always implies a partnership. God emboldens and empowers us to act. Then when we do, He works alongside us, assisting us in battle.

This is an important point. It is not *we* who are helping *God*, but *God* who helps *us*. Obviously, God could solve all of humanity's problems in an instant. God could reveal Himself to the world as He did with the Ten Plagues and the splitting of the Red Sea in Egypt. He could perform signs and wonders and do all the work for us. But that is not what God wants from His kingdom. God wants us to fight evil. He wants us to steer history in the right direction. He protects. He empowers. He assists. But it is we, people of faith, who must fight and win the battles between truth and falsehood, good and evil.

Very present

Finally, the verse ends with an unusual statement about God. In Hebrew, the final words of the verse are *nimtza me'od. Nimtza* means "present" or "found." *Me'od* means "very." The most accurate translation of these two words is "very present." Many translations render this phrase "ever-present." This is slightly incorrect. "Ever" means "always." In Hebrew this would be *tamid*, not *me'od*. As stated, *me'od* means "very" not "ever." What does this mean?

To say that God is "ever-present" means, simply, that He is *always* there. While true, this is not the point of the end of our verse. Our verse describes God as "*very* present" in times of trouble. What does it mean to say that God is "very" present?

Times of crisis reveal God

I'd like to suggest that this phrase is not referring to the extent of God's protection or assistance during troubled times. The fact that God is with us, strengthening, protecting, and helping, has already been covered by the beginning of the verse.

After this opening verse, Psalm 46 goes on to describe God's mastery over history. For example:

Nations are in uproar, kingdoms fall; he lifts his voice, the earth melts. - v.6

He makes wars cease to the ends of the earth. He breaks the bow and shatters the spear; he burns the shields with fire. He says, "Be still, and know that I am God; I will be exalted among the nations, I will be exalted in the earth." – v. 9-10

When times are stable and the world proceeds normally, it is easy to forget that God is in control. God has a plan for history, but with our limited perspective, we rarely see that plan in action. Times of trouble, of war and instability reveal God. When nations rise and fall, God's plan becomes clearer and more visible. I believe that this is the intent of the end our verse. God is "very present" when the world is in crisis. Of course, God is always present. But we don't always feel His presence so clearly. But when times get tough, when nations are rising and falling and the world is in crisis, God becomes more visible. He becomes "very present."

God protects us and empowers us. He wants us to take the initiative to enter the field of battle in times of crisis. He is with us and will assist us. And as we experience historical upheaval, as we fight for truth and good, God's presence becomes even more present and perceptible.

Malachi 3:6 – God's Doesn't Change His Mind

For I am the Lord, I do not change; and you, sons of Jacob, are not consumed.

On the surface, when read in isolation, this verse states the promise that Israel is an eternal people. This idea is linked directly to the unchanging nature of God. Just as God does not change, so too, the nation of Israel will always exist. But if we look at the context of this verse and read carefully, we find a more specific point being made relating to Israel's survival.

Survival amidst the exile

Here is our verse in context:

I will approach you for judgment; I will be a swift witness against sorcerers, against adulterers, against perjurers, against those who exploit wage earners and widows and orphans, and against those who turn away a foreigner, and they do not fear Me," says the Lord of hosts. "For I am the Lord, I do not change; and you, sons of Jacob, are not consumed. From the days of your forefathers you have strayed from My ordinances and have not kept them. Return to Me, and I will return to you," says the Lord of hosts. But you said, 'In what way shall we return?' – Malachi 3:5-7

This passage is a rebuke of the people of Israel, calling on them to repent for their repeated disobedience to God. God promises to exact punishment on the wicked among His people and calls on Israel to repent and return to Him. In the course of this rebuke and call to repentance, God promises that Israel shall never be destroyed.

We see from context that the promise of eternal Jewish survival in our verse is not about the restoration and ingathering of Israel. It is not about God's blessings that are bestowed on Israel when the exile comes to an end. It is about survival during a long and dark exile.

Notice that the Jewish people are referred to as "Jacob," rather than "Israel." We have explained elsewhere that this name is used for the Jewish people when implying their lowly and persecuted state in the exile.

And the promise in this verse is not of blessing and bounty. It is that the Jewish people will not be utterly destroyed. Mere survival is the promise of this verse, nothing more.

The eternity of Israel

We mentioned that two important ideas are linked together in this verse.
1. The unchanging nature of God
2. The eternity of the Jewish people

Although this verse was written centuries before the beginning of Christianity, it is impossible to read this verse without thinking about the dominant theological position taken by most of the Christian world regarding the Jews.

When contemplating the question as to why God allowed the Jewish people to survive, Augustine famously formulated the position known as "Witness Theology." According to Augustine, as punishment for their rejection of Jesus and for their responsibility in killing him, the Jews were exiled from their land and would continue to live as a sorrowful, persecuted, and powerless people until the end of time. By enduring this pathetic existence, the Jewish people would bear witness for the world regarding the consequences of rejecting Jesus. All the promises made to Israel in the Bible no longer apply to the Jews, but to the Church.

What is remarkable about Augustine's version of Replacement Theology is that our verse here in Malachi appears to have been written for the expressed purpose of refuting it. It is almost as though Augustine missed this verse when he read through the Bible!

First, our verse states unequivocally that God does not change. While this may seem like an obvious theological point, we must consider the context in which God said this. This verse is not part of some abstract theological contemplation about the nature of God. As we showed above, the context of this statement is a discussion of the survival of Israel as they suffer in exile. It is in this context that God states clearly, "I do not change."

Why did God state that He does not change in this specific context? The answer is simple. Like Augustine, many Christian thinkers throughout the centuries saw the exile and suffering of the Jewish people as a sign that God's covenantal promises to Israel were no longer valid. Put simply, they believed that the seemingly never-ending suffering of the Jews was evidence that God had changed His mind. But God knew that the centuries of exile and persecution of the Jews would lead many people to this incorrect conclusion. Therefore, it makes sense that in the context of warning Israel of the punishments that would befall them, He would state clearly, "I do not change." In other words, "Just in case you might make the mistake of thinking that the suffering of the Jews is a sign that I have changed my mind and rejected them, this is incorrect. My promises are eternal."

We have said numerous times in this book that God reveals Himself to the world through the unique history of the nation of Israel. Through the millennia of this history there have been many ups and downs. Our verse is a warning. If you look at the exile of the Jews and think that God has rejected Israel, you are mistaken not only about the Jews but about God Himself.

Over the centuries, many have made the mistake of thinking that God changed His mind and revoked the promises made to Israel. But God does not change. And His promises to Israel are forever.

Isaiah 54:17 – Thwarting the Weapons of Technology

No weapon crafted against you shall succeed, every tongue that contends with you at law, you shall defeat. Such is the lot of the Lord's servants, and their justification through Me, says the Lord.

An Act of God vs. Human Agency

In modern legal terminology there are events that are considered an "Act of God." According to Merriam-Webster's dictionary, the definition of "Act of God" is as follows:

"An extraordinary interruption by a natural cause (such as a flood or earthquake) of the usual course of events that experience, prescience, or care cannot reasonably foresee or prevent." – Merriam-Webster dictionary

While this definition is meant for legal purposes, it also reflects the way most people think about which events are God's responsibility, rather than the result of decisions of people. We know that God granted freedom of choice to human beings. He allows us to choose good or evil behaviors. If God stood in the way of our free-will choices, there would hardly be a basis for reward and punishment. Only because we have the freedom to choose what we do are we responsible for our actions.

Because we are aware that we have the freedom to make choices, good or evil, most people tend to see only those events that are outside the purview of human agency as governed by God. As suggested by the legal definition of "Act of God," i.e., natural disasters that have no source in human decision.

Uniquely human weapons

For many people, even those who profess faith in God, the idea that God directly intervenes in human affairs is more difficult to accept. And this is precisely the point of our verse. Let's read the verse carefully, paying attention to the necessity of every word. The verse begins:

No weapon crafted against you shall succeed,

If the point of this phrase is to state that no attack against Israel shall succeed, the verse could have said:

No weapon against you shall succeed,

Why the addition of the word "crafted"?

The second phrase in the verse is:

every tongue that contends with you at law, you shall defeat.

Law and language are both unique to humans. By mentioning the weapons of "tongue" and "law", this phrase describes the use of the human intellect in the context of legal argumentation as a weapon against Israel. By referring to the crafting of weapons in the first phrase, the verse calls attention to the element of human ingenuity and technology to attack Israel. Similarly, in the second phrase, the tool of attack is language, specifically legal argumentation.

God's intervention in human affairs

The point of this verse is not merely to state that God will protect Israel from enemies. Isaiah is teaching us that God will intervene on Israel's behalf even in those areas that appear to be fully governed by human agency. First, the verse states that even if the enemies of Israel develop the most advanced weaponry based on the most reliable human technology, their efforts will fail. Then Isaiah takes this idea a step further. Even the arguments made against Israel based solely on human intellect, will not succeed. God will intervene to see to it that such arguments are not accepted and not implemented.

The relevance of this verse to our times is chilling. On one hand, Israel's enemies are hard at work developing the most advanced weapons, designed to destroy the Jewish nation. As I write these words, Iran presses forward in their efforts to attain the nuclear ability to destroy Israel, a goal they have openly stated on many occasions. On the other hand, the enemies of Israel continue their never-ending attacks on Israel, claiming that Israel's actions and existence are illegitimate and illegal. UN resolutions condemning Israel are a regular occurrence, and Israel is constantly under attack by those who make spurious legal arguments against us.

The State of Israel's situation is as dangerous as ever. But our verse has the solution. God will continue to defend Israel against all weapons and attacks, whether they are attacks with the most advanced military technology, or attacks in the courts of the United Nations and the court of popular public opinion. But this doesn't mean that we don't need to do our part.

We must serve God

The verse concludes:

Such is the lot of the Lord's servants, and their justification through Me, says the Lord.

Notice that Isaiah refers to "the Lord's servants." He doesn't say, "the Lord's children," "the Lord's people," or simply, "Israel." All these options would have been standard ways for Isaiah to refer to the nation of Israel in this context. By calling Israel, "the Lord's servants," Isaiah makes a powerful closing point.

God will override the human agency and free-will of the enemies of Israel. But the people of Israel must submit their will to God. So long as we think that we are in charge, that we control the affairs of history, we are not worthy of God's intervention in human affairs. To be a "servant" means that one's free will is totally submitted to his master's. When we act as God's servants, when we submit our will to His, we send a message to God. We say to Him, in effect, "God, it is Your will, not human will, that governs our lives." By submitting to God in this way, we justify God's intervention on our behalf.

God will intervene to thwart the plans of the enemies of His people, so long as His people submit to His will and serve Him.

Psalm 57:1-3 – Praying to God Most High

To the Chief Musician. Set to "Do Not Destroy." A Michtam of David when he fled from Saul into the cave. Be merciful to me, O God, be merciful to me! For my soul trusts in You; And in the shadow of Your wings I will take refuge, until these calamities pass. I will cry out to God Most High, to the God who seals my fate.

An unusual superscripture

The opening phrases that introduce most of the 150 chapters in the book of Psalms are called superscriptures. These phrases are usually very short, including only the type of Psalm and the author's name. Some common examples are "A Psalm of David," "A Song of Ascents," and "For the Chief Musician." Some superscriptures will indicate when the psalm was written, like this one. Others will indicate the proper timing and use of the psalm, such as Psalm 92, "A Psalm, a song for the Sabbath day."

The superscripture of Psalm 57 is highly unusual. First, it is one of only 4 psalms that include the words "set to 'Do not destroy.'" The meaning of this is unclear. One theory from Jewish tradition is that there was a custom to cry out to God in times of danger using the prayer of Moses in the wake of the sin of the Golden Calf, recorded in the retelling of the story in Deuteronomy:

Moses' prayer

I prayed to the Lord and said: 'O Lord God! <u>Do not destroy</u> Your people and Your inheritance that You have redeemed in Your greatness, that You have brought out of Egypt with a mighty hand. Remember Your servants, Abraham, Isaac, and Jacob; do not pay mind to the stubbornness of this people, and to their wickedness and their sin, lest the land from which You brought us should say, "It is because the Lord was not able to bring them to the land which He promised them, and because He hated them, He has brought them out to kill them in the desert." But they are Your people and

Your inheritance, whom You brought out by Your mighty power and by Your outstretched arm.' – Dueteronomy 26:29

According to this tradition, this prayer of Moses was invoked in times of great danger. It is suggested that the superscripture of our Psalm instructs one praying with this Psalm to either recite Moses' prayer first or to use a tune which may have been customarily used for it.

I would like to suggest that David inserted "Do not destroy" into the superscripture to invoke Moses' prayer as a way of framing his own perilous situation as a danger to God's overall plan for Israel and the world.

The substance of Moses' prayer is worth noting. Moses does not defend the behavior of Israel. Rather, he argues that destroying them would have a negative effect on God's ultimate purposes for humanity. Perhaps David was making a similar argument about his own private situation.

David and God's plan

David was being pursued by King Saul. Saul was hunting David because the prophet Samuel had declared that David would become king and that the royal line would not continue to Saul's son. David did not ask to become king. He did not try to overthrow Saul. The only reason David was being hunted was that God had decided that David should be king. Perhaps David was saying to God that inasmuch it is God's desire for David and his offspring to become the royal line, there will be negative consequences for God's plan if David is killed.

With this in mind, it is worth noting the description of God as "Most High."

The Hebrew word for Most High is *Elyon*. While this word is used to describe God many times in the Bible, this verse is the only time that this word is used in the context of a prayer, rather than as a praise. In other words, in every other instance of God described as Most High, the one saying it is praising God or simply describing that fact that He is Most High. This is the only verse in which someone is "crying out" or praying to God with this description.

David knew exactly why Saul saw him as a threat. Under normal circumstances, someone who would declare himself a successor to the throne while the king is still alive would be killed for treason. Even though David did not choose to be named as Saul's successor, he still knew that Saul was somewhat justified in hunting him, at least by the general rules of the day.

By invoking Moses' prayer and by appealing to God as "God Most High," David was making his case. David knew that the only justification for saving him from Saul was the fact that God's ultimate plan for the world depended on him becoming king of Israel. The line of David from the tribe of Judah would eventually lead to the Messiah. It was the plan of "God Most High," the loftiest plans that are outside the purview of human awareness in the here and now that David must be king.

David saw himself as critical to God's plan for the world and prayed to God with this in mind.

Each of us has a role to play in the building of God's kingdom. We live in a time of the fulfilment of Biblical prophecy. We must pray to God to give us strength and success because we are important to His ultimate purposes for the world.

2 Samuel 22:2-4 – God as a Rock

And he said: "The Lord is my rock and my fortress and my deliverer; God, my rock, in whom I will trust; my shield and the horn of my salvation; my stronghold and my refuge; my savior, You save me from violence. I will call upon the Lord, who is worthy to be praised; so shall I be saved from my enemies.

These verses are the opening of a poem sung by David as praise to God in the aftermath of his survival from the attacks of King Saul. This song of praise is repeated, almost identically, in Psalm 18.

The Lord is my rock and my fortress and my deliverer; my God, my strength, in whom I will trust; my shield and the horn of my salvation, my stronghold. I will call the Lord, who is worthy to be praised; so shall I be saved from my enemies. – Psalm 18:2-3

Repetition or progression?

In these verses we see a list of praises of God that seem somewhat repetitive. This is common in poetic passages in the Bible, especially those that praise God. Effusive praise often involves repeating the same ideas in a variety of ways. That said, a careful reading of these verses reveals that rather than merely effusively repeating, there is a subtle progression of ideas.

First, the passage includes two different words translated here as "rock." The first time "rock" appears, the Hebrew word is *sela*. This is not the same as the word *selah*, familiar to readers of Psalms as a common end to a section of a psalm. This *sela* is spelled differently. *Sela*, meaning "rock" is quite common in the Bible, appearing over 50 times. For example, when Moses drew water from the rock in the Sinai desert, the Hebrew word for "rock" is *sela*. The second time we see the word "rock" here, the Hebrew word is *tzur*. This word for "rock" appears over 70 times in the Bible.

Here in Samuel 22, both words are used as metaphors for God. So, if both words mean "rock," what is the difference between *sela* and *tzur*?

Tzur vs. Sela

In Exodus 4, on the way while traveling to Egypt, Moses' wife Zipporah circumcised their son.

Then Zipporah took a sharp stone and cut off the foreskin of her son – Exodus 4:25

The Hebrew word for "sharp stone" in this verse is *tzur*. Similarly, in the book of Joshua, as preparation for entering the land, God commanded Joshua to circumcise the men of Israel who had not been circumcised during the journey in the desert due to the danger of travel.

At that time the Lord said to Joshua, "Make knives for yourself, and circumcise the sons of Israel again the second time." - Joshua 5:2

The Hebrew for "knives" is *charvot tzurim*, literally, "swords (or blades) of stones."

From these two sources, we see that *tzur* refers to a very strong stone, strong enough to be used as a knife.

Sela, on the other hand, is commonly used to imply a hiding place. For example:

A man will be as a hiding place from the wind, and a cover from the tempest; As rivers of water in a dry place, as the shadow of a great rock in a weary land. – Isaiah 32:2

"Take the sash that you acquired, which is around your waist, and arise, go to the Euphrates, and hide it there in a hole in the rock." – Jeremiah 13:4

The high hills are for the ibex; The rocks are a refuge for the rock badgers. – Psalm 104:18

In all these verses, and many more, *sela* refers to a rock used for shelter or for a hiding place.

Protection and empowerment

With this distinction between *tzur* and *sela* in mind, we can now see a progression in our passage.

First David praises God for protecting him from harm. He refers to God as his *sela*, his "fortress," and his "deliverer." There is no mention of David's enemies in this verse. He is thanking God for saving him by sheltering him from harm and nothing more. Then in the next verse, David refs to God as his *tzur*. Here, the implication is that of strength, even of triumph in battle.

We see this progression in our verse from another interesting word as well. In the second verse, David refers to God as a "stronghold." The word in Hebrew is *misgav*. The root of this word - SGV -means "strength." A *misgav* is something that gives strength and support. The meaning here is that God empowers and gives strength to David to withstand his enemies.

To sum up, in these opening two verses of David's song, first he praises God for providing him shelter and cover from harm. Then he praises God for empowering and strengthening him to withstand the attacks of his enemies.

— Meriting God's salvation

Finally, in the third verse, David makes an important point about how he merited God's salvation.

I will call upon the Lord, who is worthy to be praised; so shall I be saved from my enemies.

The opening phrase of this verse in Hebrew is three words.

Mehulal	praiseworthy
ekra	I call
Adonai	the Lord

In other words, the verse should be translated as follows:

I call the Lord praiseworthy; so shall I be saved from my enemies.

In other words, David is saying that he is saved by God in the merit of his praising God. By recognizing and calling out the fact that God is worthy of praise, by attributing all his strength to God, David opens himself up to be protected, saved, and empowered by God. It is important to note that David does say that he called *upon* the Lord, that he prayed to God to save him. He does not say that he cried out to God in distress. He praised Him. And by praising Him, David merited salvation.

By giving praise to God and recognizing His supreme sovereignty over our lives, we open ourselves up to His protection. God shelters us from harm and also empowers us to defeat our enemies.

Psalm 5:11-12 – Loving God's Name

But let all those rejoice who put their trust in You; Let them forever sing for joy, and You will shelter them; those who love Your name will exult in You. For You bless the righteous, Lord, surrounding him with favor like a shield.

The first ten verses of Psalm 5 are a prayer by David, pleading with God to thwart the evil plans of his enemies and to defeat them. These two verses which conclude Psalm 5, are the end of this prayer. Here David envisions the rejoicing that comes to one who is protected by God as he witnesses the downfall of the wicked.

Loving God's <u>name</u>?

The final phrase of the first of these two verses states:

those who love Your name will exult in You

There are many verses in the Bible that mention love of God. Deuteronomy 6 famously commands:

You shall love the Lord your God with all your heart, with all your soul, and with all your resources.

But what is the difference between loving God and loving *His name*? Why doesn't our verse simply say, "those who love You will exult in You"?

What's in a name?

In my first book, *Cup of Salvation*, I explained the significance of praising God's *name*, apart from praising God Himself.

Think about what a name is. If you lived alone on a desert island you would have no need for a name. In fact, you wouldn't really have a name at all. I mean, you'd have a name but only in theory. It would never get used. A name is a means by which we are known and addressed by others. To have a name means that someone is interacting with me and recognizes me. More specifically, it means that my identity - what makes me who I am and what defines me is known. This is what makes a name different from an attribute.

An attribute is one aspect of who I am. For example, my kids call me Dad. Lots of people are called Dad. Dad is not a unique name to me. Moreover, it is only one aspect of my identity. Dad is not who I am to my wife or to my students. The title Dad refers to one attribute of my total self. My name is a different story. My name is who I am. My name encompasses the fullness of my persona. Pesach Wolicki is my name. Pesach Wolicki is a Dad, a husband, a Rabbi, an excellent scrambled egg maker (according to my kids), etc. Dad and Rabbi are attributes; Pesach Wolicki, on the other hand, is not an attribute; it's my name. It is the fullness of my self.

To sum up, a name means two things:

1. *It means that others see me and are interacting with me. (Think of the desert island).*

2. *It means that the fullness of who I am is perceived and not merely a single attribute.*

Now we can understand the difference between praising God and praising His Name. When I praise God I am praising the creator and ruler of heaven and earth – whether I see Him or not. When I praise God's Name I take it a step further. I am saying, in effect,

1. *God is perceptible, I see Him in the world and in my life. I am interacting with Him.*

2. *All of His attributes are One. I am praising the totality of who God is. All of the different aspects of His creation, of life, and of the complicated reality around me are One. They are all contained within Him. They are all parts of the same ultimate Will, plan, and purpose. They are all expressions of the same Living God.*

Loving the revelation of God

Let's apply this idea to the phrase, "those who love Your name." To love God means that I love God, plain and simple. God is the creator and ruler of heaven and earth. He is the essence of pure truth and good. All this is true whether or not He is revealed and perceptible. To say that I love His *name* means that I love the revealed presence of God in the world. I yearn for God to be visible and perceptible; it is my highest aspiration.

Our verse is one of only 3 verses in the Bible which refer to love of God's name. The other two are:

And foreigners who bind themselves to the Lord to minister to him, <u>to love the name of the Lord,</u> and to be his servants, all who keep the Sabbath without desecrating it and who hold fast to my covenant; these I will bring to my holy mountain and give them joy in my house of prayer. Their burnt offerings and sacrifices will be accepted on my altar; for my house will be called a house of prayer for all nations. – Isaiah 56:6-7

for God will save Zion and rebuild the cities of Judah. Then people will settle there and possess it; the children of his servants will inherit it, and <u>those who love his name</u> will dwell there. – Psalm 69:35-36

The relationship between these two passages is easy to see. The subject of both is the end-times restoration of Zion and the Temple in Jerusalem. Based on what I wrote regarding the difference between loving God and loving His name, this makes sense. The fullest revelation of God is, of course, the ultimate redemption. That is when He will be most visible in our world. In our terms, that is when *His name* will be seen most clearly.

In Psalm 5, David prays to God to defeat his wicked enemies. But David is not concerned only about being personally saved from the danger of attack by these adversaries. He is not pleading to God to defeat his enemies only as a way to remove him from danger. David looks forward to the revelation of God that will result from this victory.

There is a powerful lesson for all of us. For most people, when we pray to God to save us by defeating the wicked, our sole concern is our own well-being. But David points us to the higher aspiration in our struggles with our enemies. In their defeat, God's name, His presence in the world, is revealed.

We must become lovers of God's name. We must yearn for revelation of God in the world so that all will see Him clearly. To love God's name means that we pursue this vision instinctively and passionately.

Proverbs 18:10 – The Tower of Strength

The name of the Lord is a tower of strength; the righteous man runs into it and is safe.

"The Lord" vs. "The name of the Lord"

As we have discussed in a number of other verses in this book, we once again see the "name of the Lord," rather than simply, "the Lord." To put this another way, our verse does not say "the Lord is a tower of strength," but "the <u>name</u> of the Lord is a tower of strength." What is the difference between these two statements? In the teaching on Psalm 5:11, we discussed the significance of God's *name* where simply referring to God Himself would have been sufficient. As explained there, God's *name* refers to awareness of Him, God as He is seen and experienced in our world. So, what does this mean for our verse?

Running where?

Before we answer this question, let's first deal with another issue in the verse. The second half of the verse is:

"the righteous man runs into it and is safe"

To anyone familiar with Hebrew, the syntax of this phrase is somewhat awkward. The literal translation is:

"the righteous man runs <u>in it</u> and is safe"

This may not seem like a significant difference, but it is. Allow me to explain. The verse appears to describe the righteous man running to the "tower of strength" to be safe once inside. Seen this way, the verse describes God as a protector, saving the righteous from attack. This theme is found all over the Bible; God as one who shelters, protects, and guards. But here's the problem. The Hebrew of this phrase is:

bo	in it / with it
yarutz	will run

| *tzaddik* | the righteous |
| *ve'nisgav* | and is safe |

If the righteous person is running <u>to</u> or <u>into</u> the tower, the word *bo* is incorrect. In Hebrew, the way to say "will run to it" or "will run into it" would be:

Yarutz elav	will run to it
or	
Yarutz letocho	will run into it

The word *bo* means "in it" or "with it." If translated as "in it," *bo* would imply that the righteous man is running inside the tower, not towards it.

To sum up, we have posed two questions about our verse.

1. Why does the verse refer to God's *name*, rather than God, as a "tower of strength"?
2. What is the meaning of *yarutz bo* – "will run in/with it"?

Safe or raised high

We should note that the word translated here as "safe" is *nisgav*. *Nisgav* literally means "raised up high" or "exalted." For example,

And the Lord alone shall be <u>exalted</u> in that day. – Isaiah 2:11

Let them praise the name of the Lord, for His name alone is <u>exalted</u>; - Psalm 148:13

The translation "safe" implies that by being raised up high in a tower, the righteous are safe from the dangers below. But the more common meaning of *nisgav* means "exalted" or "raised above" in some qualitative way.

So, what does our verse mean?

Yet another translation issue

Before we answer these questions, it is important to note one other translation issue. The first 2 words of the verse are:

| *migdal* | tower |
| *oz* | strength |

Almost all English translations render this phrase, "a strong tower." Of the 55 translations on biblegateway.com, 52 had this translation. But here's the problem. The word *oz* does not mean "strong." It is not an adjective. *Oz* means "strength." This is the only meaning of the word. The straightforward translation of *migdal oz* is "a tower of strength," not "a strong tower." And the difference is significant.

So what does our verse mean?

Based on all the issues we have raised, I'd like to suggest the following meaning of our verse, incorporating what we have explained into the translation.

The name of the Lord is a tower of strength

If the verse were saying that God is a protector, it should have said: "The Lord is a strong tower." This would be similar to many Biblical verses describing God as protector. For example:

I will say of the Lord, "He is my refuge and my fortress; My God, in Him I will trust." – Psalm 91:2

Notice, God *is the fortress* and protector. Not *His name.* God's *name* does not protect us. As we explained in our comments to Psalm 5:11, God's *name* refers to our *awareness of Him* rather than to His essence. What our verse is saying is not that God protects us, but that His name empowers us. To say that "The name of the Lord is a tower of strength" means that our awareness of God's presence emboldens and strengthens us. It provides a platform and context for us to battle our enemies with confidence and courage.

Now the second half of the verse makes sense.

the righteous man runs with it and is raised up high.

The righteous man, emboldened by His awareness of the presence of God in the battle, "runs <u>with</u>" the name of God and is thus "raised up" – *nisgav* – above his enemies in victory. This recalls another verse in Psalms.

Some trust in chariots, and some in horses; but we recall <u>the name of the Lord our God</u>. They have bowed down and fallen; but we have risen and stand upright. – Psalm 20:7-8

Like our verse here in Proverbs, Psalm 20 describes the righteous who are emboldened by "the <u>name</u> of the Lord" to rise above and triumph over their enemies.

Awareness of God presence in our lives and in the circumstances in which we find ourselves emboldens and strengthens us. This knowledge of God's name gives us the power to triumph over our enemies, it raises us up high above them.

Isaiah 1:17 – Real Social Justice

Learn to do good, seek justice, rebuke the oppressor; defend the orphan, plead for the widow.

The first chapter of Isaiah is mostly an extended rebuke of the corrupt elite leadership of the people of Israel in Jerusalem. Our verse is made up of 5 statements calling for social justice. I'd like to raise a number of questions that will help us gain a deeper understanding of the precise lesson Isaiah is teaching.

A Translation problem

First, why does the opening phrase say, "Learn to do good"? Why does it not simply say "Do good"? The second question has to do with the translation of the third instruction in this list, "rebuke the oppressor." In Hebrew this phrase is made up of two words:

ashru   rebuke

chamotz   the oppressor

This phrase is difficult to translate. To illustrate the difficulty, here is a sample of a few popular translations of this phrase.

◊ correct oppression (ESV)
◊ Correct the oppressor (CSB)
◊ relieve the oppressed (KJV)
◊ Defend the oppressed (NIV)
◊ gladden the oppressed (DARBY)

Let's start with the second word, *chamotz*. This verse is the only occurrence of this word in the entire Bible. Most classic commentaries relate it to a similar word in Psalms.

My God, rescue me from the hand of the wicked, from the palm of one who acts corruptly and cruelly. – Psalm 71:4

The Hebrew for "cruelly," i.e, "one who acts cruelly," is *chometz*, similar to our word, *chamotz*. But here is the problem. In the verse from Psalm 71, it is clear from context that the *chometz* is a person who is wicked or cruel. The psalmist is asking God to save him from the hand of this person who is also described as wicked and corrupt. Despite the meaning of Psalm 71:4, the problem is that in our verse in Isaiah, the word *chamotz* could mean "oppressor," "oppressed," or "oppression," as we see in the translations I cited above. The rules of Hebrew grammar make the conjugation of this word unclear.

Another translation problem

Which brings us to the first word in our verse – *ashru*.

We translated *ashru* as "rebuke," which makes sense if we are dealing with an oppressor. The problem is that the root of *ashru* does not usually mean "rebuke." Just taking the examples from the additional translations we cited, *ashru* can also mean "correct," "relieve," "defend," or "gladden." The root of *ashru* usually means "content," "satisfied," "straight," or "correct." I will not belabor this point. Suffice it to say that the commentaries over the centuries have had difficulty with this phrase here in Isaiah 1:17.

Leaven and Vinegar

Although the word *chamotz* appears only once in the Bible, there are quite clearly from the same root; *chametz*, which means "leaven," and the word for "vinegar," *chometz*. I believe that the relationship between leaven and vinegar may allow us to better understand our verse here in Isaiah.

When the children of Israel left Egypt in the Exodus, they ate unleavened bread. In Exodus 34 we read:

So the people took their dough before it was leavened, having their kneading bowls bound up in their clothes on their shoulders. – Exodus 12:34

And they baked unleavened cakes of the dough which they had brought out of Egypt; for it was not leavened, because they were driven out of Egypt and could not wait, nor had they prepared provisions for themselves. – Exodus 12:39

We see from these verses that leavening requires waiting. One way to prevent bread from leavening is to continue to knead it. Allowing the dough to sit unattended causes it to leaven. The vinegar in the Bible (see Numbers 6:3) refers to wine vinegar. Wine that is left alone and not properly preserved, turns to vinegar. The similarity should now be clear.

Dough that is left will turn to leaven. Wine that is left will turn to vinegar.

—— *Chamotz = neglected*

Based on this, I'd like to suggest that *chamotz* refers to a particular kind of cruelty or oppression. The subjects of the last two phrases in our verse are the orphan and the widow. The verse calls upon the leadership to hear their cases, to look after them, to defend them. The orphan and the widow are among the most powerless people in society. They are easily and often forgotten. Just as wine turns to vinegar and dough leavens when they are left unattended, *chamotz* refers to people who have been forgotten and neglected by society.

The first word of the phrase *ashru*, could then be translated as "bring satisfaction," or "correct the situation." The entire verse would thus be read as follows:

Learn to do good, seek justice, <u>correct the state of the neglected</u>; defend the orphan, plead for the widow. – Isaiah 1:17

There are two advantages to translating *chamotz* as "neglected." First, as we indicated above, it brings consistency between this phrase and the two phrases that follow it, "defend the orphan, plead for the widow." The second advantage to translating it this way relates to the first question we asked at the beginning of this teaching. Why does the verse open by calling on the leadership to "learn to do good" and to "seek justice"? Why not simply state, "Be good and just"?

Those who are neglected by the powerful elites of society are not always consciously and intentionally neglected. That's exactly the problem. The lowest rung of society - the widow and the orphan – are neglected because they are not seen at all. They suffer from a lack of awareness and attention to their plight. Isaiah does not simply call on the powerful elites to take up the cause of the neglected widow and orphan. He tells them that they must transform the way they think.

He tells them to "<u>Learn</u> to do good, <u>seek</u> justice." In other words, they must *reeducate* themselves to be sensitive to the needs of the heretofore neglected of society. They must change the way they see others, and the way they understand their own role as wealthy, powerful, elites. Rather than neglecting the poor, the widow, and the orphan, they must reorient their attitude which will lead them to take up the cause of the needy, rather than neglecting them.

It's not enough for us to simply give charity or say that we will help the needy. First, we must see them. We must educate ourselves to be sensitive to those that society tends to neglect. We must make their cause our own.

Isaiah 62:1 – Zion and Jerusalem

For the sake of Zion I will not be silent, for the sake of Jerusalem I will not be still, till her righteousness emerge as brightness and her redemption like a flaming torch.

Zion vs. Jerusalem

Throughout the Bible, "Zion" and "Jerusalem" are used interchangeably as names for Jerusalem, or so it seems. Is there any difference between them? What does each of these names imply? By answering this question, we will understand our verse with greater depth and accuracy.

"Zion" first appears in the Bible in the context of King David's conquest of Mount Moriah, the eventual site of the Temple.

Yet, David conquered the fortress of Zion, that is the City of David. – 2 Samuel 5:7

The City of David, as we know from the extensive archaeological evidence today, is the neighborhood immediately adjacent to the Temple Mount. That Zion refers to this section of the city, rather than to all of Jerusalem is evident from many verses in the Bible. For example:

And I have anointed My King upon Zion, the mountain of My holiness – Psalm 2:6

Because of Mount Zion which is desolate, with foxes walking about on it. – Lamentations 5:18

Then the moon will be disgraced and the sun ashamed; For the Lord of hosts will reign on Mount Zion and in Jerusalem, and before His elders, gloriously. – Isaiah 24:23

It's evident from these verses, and many others, that Zion and Jerusalem are not mere synonyms. "The mountain of My holiness" is clearly referring to the Temple Mount, as is the verse in Lamentations. Whereas "Jerusalem" refers to the entire city, "Zion" more specifically refers to the Temple Mount and the City of David, the neighborhood inhabited by the king and his surrounding nobility.

What is our verse saying?

With this in mind, let's take a closer look at our verse:

For the sake of Zion I will not be silent, for the sake of Jerusalem I will not be still

The word for "be still" is *eshkot*. This word refers to the cessation of action, not a refraining from speaking. In other words, the first phrase of the verse is a promise to *speak* and cry out, and the second phrase is a promise to continue to *act*.

Now let's take a look at the second half of the verse.

till her righteousness emerge as brightness and her redemption like a flaming torch.

"Brightness" is just that, brightness. It is a shining light. It illuminates, and nothing more. "A flaming torch" on the other hand, is fire. It burns and consumes. It changes things. Now let's put it all together.

Zion and Jerusalem = two stages of redemption

Our verse describes two aspects of the restoration of Jerusalem. *Zion* represents the spiritual restoration. As we showed, Zion implies the Temple and the kingdom of David. *Jerusalem*, on the other hand, represents the wider city, the general population at large beyond the spiritual center. Throughout the Bible we see that the restoration of Israel and Jerusalem happens in stages. Specifically, there is a physical restoration of Israel that is followed by the spiritual restoration. For example, in the very first prophecy of foretelling the ingathering from exile we read:

The Lord your God will bring you back from captivity, and have compassion on you, and gather you again from all the nations where the Lord your God has scattered you. If any of you are driven out to the farthest parts under heaven, from there the Lord your God will gather you, and from there He will bring you. Then the Lord your God will bring you to the land which your fathers possessed, and you shall possess it. He will prosper you and multiply you more than your fathers. And the Lord your God will circumcise your heart and the heart of your descendants, to love the Lord your God with all your heart and with all your soul, that you may live. – Deuteronomy 30:3-6

First God will ingather Israel and make them numerous and prosperous in the land. Then, once this physical redemption has happened, the next stage of the process, the spiritual restoration, will take place. This idea is reiterated many times in the Bible.

Other than the physical redemption occurring prior to the spiritual rejuvenation, there is also a fundamental difference between these two processes. This may seem obvious, but physical redemption is a process that takes place through *action*. What I mean is that the physical restoration of Israel is defined by physical material events. People streaming from the exile to the land. The reinstatement of Jewish sovereignty. Fighting wars. Building a nation-state.

But what does the spiritual restoration look like? How does that unfold? As the verses in Deuteronomy we cited state, the spiritual renewal of Israel involves a changing of the heart. In other words, the later stage of the redemption process, the spiritual restoration, is primarily about how people think, what they believe. Do we recognize God? Do we see Him as King? Are we serving Him and worshipping Him. The facts on the ground relating to the material aspects of the rebuilding of the nation of Israel are not the defining elements of this stage of the redemptive process.

Back to our verse

For the sake of Zion I will not be silent, for the sake of Jerusalem I will not be still

The restoration of Zion – the spiritual aspect of the process, means that we hear what God is saying. He is not silent because He wants us to hear Him. The restoration of Jerusalem, on the other hand, means that God will not sit idly. He acts. He changes the reality on the ground.

The second half of the verse parallels the first half.

till her righteousness emerge as brightness and her redemption like a flaming torch.

"Her righteousness" refers to the spiritual renewal. This is likened to "brightness," a light that shines. It illuminates. It inspires. "Her redemption" refers to the ingathering of the exiles, the physical reconstruction of the nation of Israel and the city of Jerusalem. This is likened to "a flaming torch," a fire which burns what came before and clears the way for a new reality. Fire changes things materially.

I just showed from Deuteronomy 30 that the physical redemption precedes the spiritual. So why does our verse present the opposite? Why is Zion, "the brightness," come before "Jerusalem," the flaming torch?

While it is true that in the process of redemption the physical aspects take place before the spiritual renewal. But in terms of purpose and goal, the spiritual aspects of the redemption are primary. They are the ultimate goal. So, in this verse, where God is stating His commitment to the restoration of Israel both materially and spiritually, He first states what is most important, what is the true end goal of the entire process. That is *Zion*, the Temple and the kingdom of David restored to His "Holy Mountain."

To bring the ultimate kingdom of God to this earth, we must fix the world both materially as well as spiritually. Like God we must not be silent but must continue to share His word and His truth. At the same time we must also never cease to act, to repair all that is broken in the world.

Joshua 1:5-9 – The Courage to Lead

No man will stand before you all the days of your life. As I was with Moses, I shall be with you; I will neither leave you nor forsake you. Be strong and courageous, for you shall give this people possession of the land which I swore to their fathers to give them. Only be strong and very courageous to take care to do according to all the law which Moses My servant commanded you; do not turn from it to the right or to the left, so that you may have success wherever you go. This book of the law shall not slip from your mouth, but you shall meditate on it day and night, so that you may be careful to do according to all that is written in it; for then you will make your way prosperous, and then you will have success. Have I not commanded you? Be strong and courageous! Do not tremble or fear, for the Lord your God is with you wherever you go.

(This teaching is based on the commentary of Rabbi Don Isaac Abravanel, born in 1437 in Portugal, died in 1508 in Venice.)

The book of Joshua opens with God's words to Joshua as he began his assignment as the leader of the people of Israel. In the five verses quoted above there appear to be several redundancies.

1. Three times in this passage God tells Joshua to "be strong and courageous." The second time includes the word "very." And the third time God first says, "Have I not commanded you?" What exactly is this referring to?

2. Verse 7 states: "to take care to do according to all the law which Moses My servant commanded you; do not turn from it to the right or to the left, so that you may have success wherever you go." Verse 8 states: "so that you may be careful to do according to all that is written in it; for then you will make your way prosperous, and then you will have success."

This seems repetitive. What exactly was God telling Joshua? Why these apparent repetitions?

Be strong and courageous

Let's take a closer look at the three times God told Joshua to "be strong and courageous."

Be strong and courageous, for you shall give this people possession of the land which I swore to their fathers to give them. (v.6)

What does it mean that Joshua will "give this people possession" of the land? Joshua will lead them in battle to conquer it, but is he the one who *gave them the land*? Victory in battle is always attributed to God. This verse does not refers to the war of conquest. Rather, it refers to the difficult task of allotting portions of land to each of the tribes. This was a daunting assignment. Certainly, there would be contention between the various tribes of Israel, disputes over who would take possession of which piece of land. In this respect, Joshua was, indeed, the one who would "give this people possession of the land." God told Joshua to be strong and courageous in his dealings with the leaders of the tribes. This is the intent of the previous verse as well.

Your leadership will not be challenged

No man will stand before you all the days of your life. As I was with Moses, I shall be with you; I will neither leave you nor forsake you.

Imagine Joshua's mindset as he assumed the mantle of leadership after the death of Moses. He knew that nobody would ever be able to replace Moses in the eyes of the people. The final verses of Deuteronomy, just after Moses' death, testified to Moses' greatness.

No prophet has ever since risen in Israel like Moses, whom the Lord knew face to face, for all the signs and wonders which the Lord sent him to perform in the land of Egypt against Pharaoh, all his servants, and all his land, and for all the mighty hand and for all the great awe which Moses performed in the sight of all Israel. – Deuteronomy 34:10-12

Stepping in to replace Moses must have filled Joshua with doubt. He witnessed the numerous occasions when the people of Israel rebelled and challenged Moses' leadership in the desert. Now Joshua would need to lead this nation through many years of war and conquest. When God said to Joshua, "No man will stand before you," He was not talking about enemies of Israel from other nations. He was talking about challenges from the people of Israel themselves.

To sum up, in the opening two verses of our passage God encourages Joshua to *be strong and courageous* and to not fear the people he is leading. He would have difficult decisions to make in the years ahead. He must not be afraid to lead *the people.*

Be obedient to God

Then God told Joshua that to guarantee the success of his leadership, he would need to be personally obedient and pious in his adherence to the word of God.

Only be strong and very courageous to take care to do according to all the law which Moses My servant commanded you; do not turn from it to the right or to the left, so that you may have success wherever you go. This book of the law shall not slip from your mouth, but you shall meditate on it day and night, so that you may be careful to do according to all that is written in it; for then you will make your way prosperous, and then you will have success. (v. 7-8)

Here, God warns Joshua that he must "be strong and courageous" with regard to his obedience to God's law. He goes on to tell Joshua that the only way he will be able to remain obedient is by studying and "meditating" on the words of the Torah all the days of his life. Joshua must not allow his leadership position to lead him to think that he is on par with Moses. Moses was the greatest prophet. It is only through Moses that law came to Israel. Joshua must humbly recognize this and submit himself to the law of God given through Moses.

Which command?

Regarding the third time that God told Joshua to "be strong and courageous," we asked what is meant by God when He said, "Have I not commanded you, Be strong and courageous!"? Where is this command? Towards the end of Deuteronomy, just before the death of Moses, Joshua was appointed to succeed him in leadership. There we read,

Then He commanded Joshua the son of Nun, and said, "Be strong and courageous, for you shall bring the sons of Israel into the land which I swore to them, and I will be with you." – Deuteronomy 31:24

Here we have the "command" to Joshua to "be strong and courageous."

With this in mind, our verse makes perfect sense. In this third call for Joshua to "be strong and courageous," God referred back to the original command to Joshua in Deuteronomy. And as we see clearly, the subject of that command was the conquest of the land. This third time that God tells Joshua, "do not tremble or fear" in our passage He was telling him not to fear the Canaanite nations on the field of battle. And as He says to Joshua, this was already commanded earlier, in Deuteronomy 31.

This passage contains a very important lesson about leadership. First, a leader must not be afraid of the people he is leading. He must have the courage to state and implement his convictions. He must not be a follower, afraid to speak the truth because of how it may be received. Second, a leader must remain humble before God. He must immerse Himself in God's word so that He does not fall prey to the natural arrogance that often comes with power. He must overcome the urge to follow his own inclinations over the expressed will of God. Finally, a leader set the example of courage in the face of the enemy. This is God's leadership lesson for Joshua.

Leadership requires strength and courage. Here we learn that these traits must be directed in three ways. First, we must have the courage to state truth to those that we lead. Second, we must have the courage to constantly remind ourselves of God's truth. Third, we must have the courage to face the enemy from without.

Exodus 14:13-14 – Overcoming Fear in time of Crisis

But Moses said to the people, "Do not fear! Stand by and see the salvation of the Lord which He will do for you today; for the Egyptians whom you have seen today, you will never see them again forever. The Lord will fight for you, and you will keep silent."

The children of Israel had just departed Egypt a few days ago. They had witnessed the miraculous hand of God in ways that had never been seen before. They sat passively as God, through Moses and Aaron, had decimated the mighty Egyptian kingdom with the Ten Plagues, culminating in the devastating killing of all firstborn male Egyptians. Moreover, the seemingly impossible promise that God would take them out of the slavery of Egypt had been fulfilled.

Fear of the Egyptian army

They were camped on the banks of the Red Sea and the Egyptian army was fast approaching. What was going through their minds? The Bible tells us in the verses just before ours:

As Pharaoh drew near, the children of Israel lifted their eyes, and behold, Egypt was pursuing them, and they became very frightened; and the children of Israel cried out to the Lord. Then they said to Moses, "Is it because there were no graves in Egypt that you have taken us away to die in the wilderness? What is this that you have done to us, bringing us out of Egypt? Is this not the word that we spoke to you in Egypt, saying, 'Leave us that we may serve the Egyptians'? For serving the Egyptians would be better for us than our deaths in the wilderness." – Exodus 14:10-12

Considering the supernatural display that they had already experienced in the months leading to this point, it is surprising that they would now doubt Moses. Had they not seen enough to convince them that God would save them from this imminent danger?

Before we jump to harsh judgement of the children of Israel, let us recall that they had been slaves in Egypt for centuries. Longstanding mindsets are difficult to undo. Even after experiencing the greatest and most overt display of God's power, they reverted back to their old perceptions of how things were as soon as their old masters reappeared.

But can't we ask the same question about the Egyptians? What were they thinking? Hadn't they suffered enough from the Ten Plagues? Did they think that this time they would win? It seems that both the children of Israel and the Egyptians needed to learn the same lesson.

Of course, the entire scene was a setup. God deliberately told Moses to tell the people to travel back towards Egypt and to camp on the banks of the sea. This would fool the Egyptians into thinking that they were lost in the desert and were vulnerable to attack. (see Ex. 14:2-3) God hardened Pharaoh's heart one last time in order to set him up for the final defeat.

Trusting God based on what we have seen

The lesson of these verses are powerful and all too relevant to our own lives of faith, in our time. We are the generation that has witnessed God's mighty hand upon Israel as He fulfils His covenantal promises. We are the ones who are alive to witness the great ingathering of the Jewish people. But are we any different from the children of Israel? Are we any different from the Egyptians? Do we not also have doubts every time the enemies of Israel rise up to attack? Do we not also fear that God has abandoned us this time, even though He was with us so many times before? We must realize that just as He did on the banks of the Red Sea, God raises up our enemies to set them up for their ultimate destruction.

We must act first

Of course, God did come through for the children of Israel. He split the sea and drowned the entire Egyptian army. But not before calling on the children of Israel to act. Here is the verse immediately following the words of Moses in our verses.

Then the Lord said to Moses, "Why are you crying out to Me? Tell the sons of Israel to go forward. – Exodus 14:15

God told Moses to tell the people to "go forward." Only then would he split the sea, drown the Egyptian army, and save Israel. Again, the lesson for our own times is clear. God has a plan. He will keep His promises.

But He wants us to act. God will step in, but first we must take the initiative. When God sees that we are making the effort on our part, the door is open for Him.

We must draw on past experiences of God's salvation to remind ourselves that He is always there for us. And when the same enemy returns, we must have faith that just as He saved us before, He will save us again. But first, we must do our part.

Psalm 127:3-5 – The Call to Family Formation

Behold, children are the Lord's portion, the fruit of the womb is a reward. Like arrows in the hand of a warrior, so are the children of one's youth. Happy is the man fills his quiver with them; they shall not be ashamed when they confront their enemies at the gate.

The decline of family formation

The opening verse of this passage speaks directly to one of the more disturbing features of our current society. Over the past five decades, there has been a steady decline in family formation. I refer to a number of metrics. Less people are getting married. Those who do marry are doing so at a later and later age in life. Finally, and most concerning of all, people are having fewer and fewer children.

In the pre-industrialized world, birth control was not nearly as available as it is today, abortion was almost unheard of, and more people lived according to traditional faith values. All these factors contributed to the fact that the average family was larger than today.

Young men and women today generally cite a number of reasons they are delaying marriage and family formation. They will say they are focused on their education and want to wait until they are first financially secure. They argue that children are a significant financial burden. Another argument one hears from young adults is that they want a few years to focus on their own personal development before taking such important steps.

Trust God, build a family

Psalm 127 teaches us that these perspectives are not entirely consistent with faith in God. The opening verses of Psalm 127, leading up to the passage cited here, remind us that human plans to secure ourselves materially are worthless if God is not on board.

A Song of Ascents. Of Solomon. Unless the Lord builds the house, they la-bor in vain who build it; unless the Lord guards the city, the watchman stays awake in vain. It is vain for you to rise up early, to sit up late, to eat the bread of sorrows; for so He gives His beloved sleep. – Psalm 127:1-2

In other words, don't think that all your plans to secure yourself are what really protect you. The connection between this message and the verses that follow could not be more relevant to the current cultural prob-lem I raised. All the reasons to delay family formation are human designs to insulate oneself from the natural difficulties that come with raising a young family. But all these plans forget the most important ingredient. "Unless the Lord builds the house," unless God wants you to be finan-cially stable, it won't work.

Our passage, verses 3-5, are a reminder to young people of the correct perspective on family formation.

First, recognize that children are a gift from God. They are a reward, not a burden. Will there be times when it is difficult to take a vacation or buy expensive clothes because you chose to marry and have children at a young age? Of course. But that is a blessing. Next, the psalmist teaches us the added value of "children of one's youth." This refers to children born when the parents are still relatively young.

Younger parents have more energy to care for their children. They are closer in age to them and understand them better. Most importantly, young parents have a much greater likelihood of being a significant pres-ence in the lives of their grandchildren down the road. The advantages of having children at a young age are numerous.

Children are God's portion

There is another important message about having children that is im-plied by a single word in this passage. Verse 3 states:

Behold, children are the Lord's portion, the fruit of the womb is a reward.

The Hebrew word for "portion" is *nachala*. In almost all translations the English for *nachala* is "heritage" or "gift." "Gift" is almost certainly an inaccurate translation. The word *nachala* appears 220 times in the Bible. Its meaning is unambiguous. In almost all cases, *nachala* refers to a plot of land that is owned. This is the word that is used repeatedly in the book of Numbers and in the book of Joshua in the many verses that describe the dividing up of the promised land into "portions" to be owned in perpetuity by the various tribes and families. The reason that so many translations render *nachala* as "heritage" is because a *nachala* is a permanent possession, the kind of possession that is bequeathed to the next generation.

In almost all translations, the phrase *nachalat Adonai* is translated as "a heritage from the Lord" or "a gift from the Lord." Aside from the issue I just raised regarding the precise meaning of *nachala* – "portion" or "possession" – there is another problem with these translations. Even if we correctly translate *nachala* as "portion," *nachalat Adonai* still would not mean "portion from the Lord."

| *Nachalat* | portion of |
| *Adonai* (YHVH) | the Lord |

If the psalmist intended to say "portion from the Lord," he would have needed to add the prefix *me*, meaning "from," to "the Lord." The phrase would have been *nachala me'Adonai*.

Confused by the Hebrew? Let me keep this simple. *Nachalat Adonai*, means "portion of the Lord" or "possession of the Lord." To say that children are *nachalat Adonai* does not mean that God gave children to people as possessions for *them*. It means that children are *God's possessions*!

The message is powerful and relevant to the overall message of the psalm. People who are worried about worldly concerns and allow those concerns to stand in the way of having children must understand that children belong to God. They are His possessions. Like an ancestral plot of land that one owns, they are His legacy and assurance for the future. But they are His!

Just as a person cares for their own precious possessions, God will take care of the children He brings into the world. We must not allow our own human calculations stand in the way of God's legacy.

www.ingramcontent.com/pod-product-compliance
Lightning Source LLC
Chambersburg PA
CBHW070915120626
46546CB00001B/279